LOCAL AND COMMUNITY DRIVEN DEVELOPMENT

NEW FRONTIERS OF SOCIAL POLICY

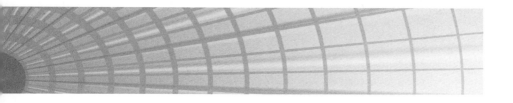

Local and Community Driven Development

Moving to Scale in Theory and Practice

Hans P. Binswanger-Mkhize
Jacomina P. de Regt
Stephen Spector
Editors

THE WORLD BANK
Washington, D.C.

1818 H Street, NW
Washington, DC 20433
Telephone: 202-473-1000
Internet: www.worldbank.org
E-mail: feedback@worldbank.org

ISBN: 978-0-8213-8194-6
eISBN: 978-0-8213-8195-3
DOI: 10.1596/978-0-8213-8194-6

Cover photo: Yonggen Li, the Water Resources Bureau of Hebei Province, China.

Cover design: Naylor Design, Inc.

Library of Congress Cataloging-in-Publication Data has been applied for.

In many developing countries, the mixed record of state effectiveness, market imperfections, and persistent structural inequities has undermined the effectiveness of social policy. To overcome these constraints, social policy needs to move beyond conventional social service approaches toward development's goals of equitable opportunity and social justice. This series has been created to promote debate among the development community, policy makers, and academia, and to broaden understanding of social policy challenges in developing country contexts.

The books in the series are linked to the World Bank's Social Development Strategy. The strategy is aimed at empowering people by transforming institutions to make them more inclusive, responsive, and accountable. This involves the transformation of subjects and beneficiaries into citizens with rights and responsibilities. Themes in this series will include equity and development, assets and livelihoods, and citizenship and rights-based social policy, as well as the social dimensions of infrastructure and climate change.

Titles in the series:

- *Assets, Livelihoods, and Social Policy*
- *Building Equality and Opportunity through Social Guarantees: New Approaches to Public Policy and the Realization of Rights*
- *Delivering Services in Multicultural Societies*
- *Inclusive States: Social Policy and Structural Inequalities*
- *Institutional Pathways to Equity: Addressing Inequality Traps*
- *Local and Community Driven Development: Moving to Scale in Theory and Practice*
- *Social Dimensions of Climate Change: Equity and Vulnerability in a Warming World*

CONTENTS

Foreword: LCDD and the World Bank   *xiii*

About the Editors   *xv*

Editors' Preface   *xvii*

Acknowledgments   *xix*

Abbreviations   *xxi*

Chapter 1.   Introduction and Executive Summary   1
              Hans P. Binswanger-Mkhize, Jacomina P. de Regt,
              and Stephen Spector

Chapter 2.   Historical Roots and Evolution of Community
              Driven Development   27
              Hans P. Binswanger-Mkhize, Swaminathan S. Anklesaria
              Aiyar, Jacomina P. de Regt, Rodrigo Serrano-Berthet,
              Louis Helling, Julie Van Domelen, David Warren,
              and Stephen Spector

Chapter 3.   Scaling Up Community Driven Development:
              Underpinnings and Program Design Implications   73
              Hans P. Binswanger-Mkhize, Swaminathan S. Anklesaria
              Aiyar, Jacomina P. de Regt, Deborah Davis, and
              Tuu-Van Nguyen

Chapter 4.   Lessons from Africa   121
              Rodrigo Serrano-Berthet, Louis Helling,
              Julie Van Domelen, Warren Van Wicklin,
              Dan Owen, Maria Poli, and Ravindra Cherukupalli

Chapter 5.   Scaling Up, Step by Step: Analysis,
             Policy Reform, Pilot Phase, and Implementation   151
             Hans P. Binswanger-Mkhize, Tuu-Van Nguyen,
             Jacomina P. de Regt, Willem Heemskerk,
             and Gerard Baltissen

Appendix A. Operational Functions and Manuals, by Level   199

Appendix B. Design Elements and Tools for Large-Scale
             LCDD Programs   201

Appendix C. The Four Core Expected Outcomes of LCDD   211

References   223

Index   231

BOXES

1.1.   Definitions and Names for Local Jurisdictions   5
1.2.   Elements of LCDD   6
1.3.   Outline of the Steps to Scaling Up   9
1.4.   Steps to Scaling Up (Expanded)   21
2.1.   India's Champions of Empowerment   30
2.2.   The Comilla Model of Rural Development   32
2.3.   From Specialized Agricultural Credit to Microfinance   34
2.4.   A Sample of India's Target Group Programs   35
2.5.   Plan Puebla, Pioneer of IRDPs   36
2.6.   Participatory Rural Appraisal   39
2.7.   Examples of Sector Programs with Community
        Participation   42
2.8.   The Integrated Approach in Mexico   49
2.9.   The Integrated Approach in Brazil   49
2.10.   The Integrated Approach in Indonesia   50
2.11.   World Bank Guidance on Key Design Principles for CDD   53
2.12.   Six Innovations in Direct Financing of Community
        Subprojects   54
2.13.   CBD/CDD: An Important Part of the Bank Strategy   61
2.14.   Trends in Project Performance   63

3.1.	Leveraging Success without Reinventing the Wheel	74
3.2.	Lessons from the Teriyaki Burger	77
3.3.	Pillars and Core Expected Outcomes of LCDD to Be Scaled Up	79
3.4.	Steps for Scaling Up: Diagnostics	88
3.5.	Indonesia: Findings and Lessons in 2003	89
3.6.	Mexico: Findings and Lessons in 2003	93
3.7.	Buy-In through Head Tax	95
3.8.	Zambia: Findings and Lessons in 2003	96
3.9.	Benin: Findings and Lessons in 2003	99
3.10.	India: Findings and Implications in 2003	106
3.11.	Uganda: Findings, Lessons, and Implications from Four Programs in 2003	110
3.12.	KDP's Research Program	116
4.1.	The Sequential Logic	128
5.1.	Steps to Scaling Up	152
5.2.	Steps to Scaling Up: Diagnostic Phase to Ensure Minimum Conditions	154
5.3.	Mexico DRD I: Building on Lessons Learned	159
5.4.	Steps to Scaling Up: Preprogram Development	163
5.5.	Steps to Scaling Up: Pilot Phase	164
5.6.	What to Do Where Local Governments Are Nonexistent or Nonfunctional	167
5.7.	Metrics	175
5.8.	Making Provisions for Fully Independent Monitoring	175
5.9.	Train the Facilitators First	178
5.10.	Standard per Diem for Volunteers	180
5.11.	An Irony of Elaborate Plans and Reports	181
5.12.	Finding Locally Available Specialists	182
5.13.	Steps to Scaling Up: Resource Flows and Accountability	185
5.14.	Priority List Menus	185
5.15.	Ethiopian Method for Gaining Legal Status	186
5.16.	Finding a Co-financing Balance	187
5.17.	Zambia and Uganda: Linking Performance, Accountability, and Incentives	189
5.18.	Steps to Scaling Up	192
5.19.	Steps to Scaling Up: Consolidation	195

FIGURES

1.1.	Linked Approaches	2
2.1.	Evolution of Social Fund Objectives and Activities, 1987 to Present	44
2.2.	Index of Sector Decentralization in 19 Countries, 1990s	47
2.3.	Linked Approaches	58
5.1.	Basic Institutional Requirements for an LCDD Program	169
5.2.	Visualizing Training Logistics between the Subdistrict Center and the Villages	178

MAP

3.1.	The LCDD Global Experience	82

TABLES

1.1.	Magnitudes of Scaling Up: An Example	7
1.2.	Timeline of Development Approaches	12
2.1.	Timeline of Development Approaches	28
2.2.	Progress of World Bank/IDA Support to CDD, 2000–08	52
2.3.	Overview of Strengths and Weaknesses of CBD/CDD Projects	56
3.1.	Examples of Scaling Up Sector-Specific Programs	83
3.2.	Examples of Scaled-Up Multisectoral Programs	85
4.1.	Classification of Country Context	123
4.2.	Assessing Strategic Fit between Country Context and Institutional Strategies	126
4.3.	Alternative Responses to Risks Associated with LCDD Implementation via Local Government	129
4.4.	Strategies of Active Operations in the Africa Region, by Country Context	132
5.1.	Examples of Key Questions to Be Pursued during the Diagnostics Phase	156
5.2.	A Shared Appreciation-Readiness Matrix (Level of Progress)	158
B.1.	Phasing and Sequencing	201
B.2.	Decentralization and Local Government Empowerment	202

B.3.	Participation and Social Inclusion	203
B.4.	Community Setup	203
B.5.	Funding Arrangements for the Community	204
B.6.	Institutional Setup and Program Management	205
B.7.	Training	206
B.8.	Facilitation	207
B.9.	Information, Education, and Communication	208
B.10.	Monitoring and Evaluation	209
B.11.	Community and Local Government Projects	210
B.12.	Government, NGO, and Donor Harmonization	210

Local and community driven development (LCDD) gives control of development decisions and resources to community groups and representative local governments. Poor communities receive funds, decide on their use, plan and execute the local projects chosen, and monitor the provision of services that result from those projects. LCDD improves not just incomes but also people's empowerment and governance capacity, the lack of which is a form of poverty as well.

LCDD operations have demonstrated effectiveness at delivering results and have received substantial support from the World Bank. Since 2000, Bank lending for LCDD has averaged around $2 billion a year. Through its support to local and community driven programs, the Bank has financed water supply and sanitation services, health care services, schools that are tailored to community needs and likely to be maintained and therefore sustainable, nutrition programs for mothers and infants, the building of rural access roads, and support services for livelihoods and microenterprise.

In addition, LCDD has proved to be an effective way to rebuild communities following political conflicts or natural disasters. By restoring trust at a local level and rebuilding social capital, it has produced valuable peace dividends in places such as Afghanistan, Bosnia and Herzegovina, Rwanda, and Timor-Leste. After the 2005 tsunami, LCDD approaches in India, Indonesia, and Sri Lanka provided a front line of response to ensure that resources were being used effectively and transparently and that the affected communities were involved in assessing their needs and designing recovery programs.

A major challenge in LCDD is the issue of scale: how to achieve national coverage rather than focus on development enclaves. Going to scale, especially to national scale, requires detailed planning, the tools for which are covered in this book.

The LCDD agenda remains relevant today because it delivers on three fronts:

- The *efficient use of public resources* by those who need them most, giving communities and local governments the authority and resources to undertake initiatives in sectors that will produce the highest impact at lower cost than centrally managed programs
- The *empowerment of communities* to plan and manage their own economic and social development
- The *possibility of better local governance* through transparent and accountable local decision making.

The World Bank will continue to play an important leadership role and to dedicate resources and promote a policy dialogue that allows promising LCDD approaches to operate at a larger scale and across sectors. Today's LCDD requires a programmatic approach that combines multiple sectors and functions. Moreover, it involves changes in the intergovernmental fiscal system as well as in governance and accountability systems.

All of this needs to be embedded in the poverty reduction strategies of countries so that scaled-up LCDD programs provide an opportunity, through poverty reduction support financing, to strengthen the institutional and fiscal systems; transfer real power, resources, and accountability to local levels; and develop implementation capacities for such programs at all levels of society.

As vice president for Sustainable Development, I am particularly pleased to see this book go to publication. The sectors that make up our vice presidency have the largest LCDD portfolio in the World Bank; this publication will be a useful resource for all of our staff working on these issues. I hope that you too will find it useful in your work as a development professional.

Katherine Sierra
Vice President, Sustainable Development
The World Bank

ABOUT THE EDITORS

Hans B. Binswanger-Mkhize has conducted research on induced innovation, agricultural mechanization, agricultural investment and supply
response, impact of technical change, risk in agriculture, production relations in agriculture, land markets and land reform, and the determinants
of agricultural and agrarian policies. At the World Bank, he has been a
manager, policy analyst, and designer of development programs, as well as
an HIV/AIDS activist. He is a fellow of the American Association for the
Advancement of Sciences and of the American Association of Agricultural
Economists, and a recipient of the Elmhirst Medal of the International
Agricultural Economics Association. He earned a doctorate in economics
from North Carolina State University, a master's degree in agricultural sciences from the Swiss Institute of Technology, and a certificate in political
sciences from the University of Paris.

Jacomina P. de Regt has been a rural sociologist at the World Bank for
more than 30 years, where she has designed development programs in
rural development, energy, health, education, and HIV/AIDS, and she has
been a manager, quality assurance adviser, and policy analyst. She has had
the privilege of working in these different sectors in Latin America and the
Caribbean and in South Asia, but for the past 20 years, she has worked
in Africa. Her work has come full circle, from bringing in the voices of
the poor in area development programs in Brazil to the coordination of
community driven development (CDD) in the Africa Region, focusing on
empowerment of the poor through CDD approaches in rural and urban
space and in crosscutting HIV/AIDS programs. She holds a master's of sci-
ence degree in development sociology, extension services, communication,
and nutrition from Wageningen University, Netherlands.

Stephen Spector was the lead editor for this report. A long-time advocate
of communications and social change, his familiarity with LCDD began

in 1975 as a producer of *RadioPlanPuebla*, a radio magazine for Mexico's Plan Puebla rural development program. He has been an editor for the World Bank since 2003 working with many different technical and social sectors and the World Bank Institute; coeditor for *The Global Development Alliance* from the U.S. Agency for International Development; and a communications analyst for the U.S. Department of Agriculture, through L-3 Communications. He has been a writer, editor, and communications specialist in the Washington area since 1979. He holds a bachelor's degree in communications from Antioch College in Ohio.

This book brings together the thoughts and experiences of many of the leading proponents and practitioners of local and community driven development, that evolved from community driven development and most clearly describes the process of empowering communities and their local governments to drive economic and social development upward and outward. This, to many, appears to be a new paradigm, although it evolved over decades, emerging from India in the 1950s. While many LCDD projects have taken root, the challenge now is to scale up such islands of success— that is, the discrete LCDD projects—into sustainable national programs that build skills in decision making, management, and governance.

This book includes a historical background, best practices, underpinnings, analysis, lessons learned, and toolkits for developing supportive national policies and implementation programs that fit the particular contexts of countries and localities. The chapters, which are adapted from previous reports that covered individual aspects of LCDD, draw on contributions from inside and outside the World Bank, with key sources and authors acknowledged here.

Chapter 1 synthesizes the book's main LCDD elements, issues, and opportunities. It serves as an executive summary, drawing from all subsequent chapters.

Chapter 2 updates *Historical Roots of Community-Driven Development and Evolution of Development Theory and Practice* (Binswanger and Aiyar 2006), with significant contributions from Jacomina P. de Regt and Rodrigo Serrano-Berthet, Louis Helling, Julie Van Domelen, David Warren, and Stephen Spector. The authors thank Rodrigo Serrano-Berthet, Louis Helling, and David Warren for contributions from their 2004 report (Helling, Serrano, and Warren 2005) and Julie Van Domelen from her 2008 report (Van Domelen 2008).

Chapter 3 is adapted from "Scaling Up Community-Driven Development: Theoretical Underpinnings and Program Implications" (Binswanger and Aiyar 2004). It also benefited from significant contributions from Jacomina P. de Regt, who helped to produce both this book and most of the reports on which it is built; Deborah Davis, who synthesized a set of comprehensive case studies used in this chapter; and Tuu-Van Nguyen, coauthor of the step-by-step guide (Binswanger and Nguyen 2005). The word *theoretical*, which appears in the title of the 2004 Binswanger and Aiyar work, has been removed here because the underpinnings that make up the LCDD framework and design principles are no longer theoretical. They have been proven through direct experience over the past 15 years and by analysis of recent program reviews and impact studies. A significant input for this chapter was the action research sponsored by the trust funds; the editors specifically thank Deborah Davis for her synthesis of that set of six comprehensive case studies.

Chapter 4 was adapted from chapters 3, 4, and 5 of *Social and Local Development Funds in the Africa Region: Evolution and Options*, prepared by a team led by Rodrigo Serrano-Berthet (World Bank/Social Development). The team included Louis Helling (consultant), Daniel Owen (World Bank/Social Development), Maria Poli (consultant), Julie Van Domelen (consultant), and Warren Van Wicklin (consultant). Ravindra Cherukupalli (consultant) prepared the assessment ratings for social and local development funds. The World Bank's Valerie Kozel (Human Development Network-Social Protection) and Bassam Ramadan (Africa Region Human Development) offered advice throughout the study. Peer reviewers Robert Chase (Social Development) and Norbert Mugwagwa (Africa Region) offered support. Feedback received from Jacomina P. de Regt, Giuseppe Zampaglione (Africa Region), and Hans P. Binswanger-Mkhize was incorporated. The report was published in August 2008 by the Human Development Sector Unit, Africa Region, Social Protection Department, Social Development Department (World Bank 2008c).

Chapter 5 is adapted from two main sources: *Community-Driven Development: Toolkit for National Stocktaking and Review* (Heemskerk and Baltissen 2005), developed by a team from the Royal Tropical Institute in the Netherlands (Willem Heemskerk, Wim van Campen, and Gerard Baltissen) and a team from the World Bank (Jacomina P. de Regt, Galia Schechter, Haddy Sey, and Hans P. Binswanger-Mkhize); and *Scaling Up Local and Community-Driven Development: A Step-by-Step Guide* (Binswanger and Nguyen 2005).

We wish to thank all who have made the LCDD effort and this book possible. For the many we name, there are countless more who have carried forward the LCDD reality country by country and community by community. We thank them on behalf of the millions more who we hope will benefit from their efforts.

The effort to bring this book together included the long-term commitment and support of many people: Kathy Sierra, vice president of Sustainable Development, who recognized the direct relationship between LCDD and efforts to strengthen and build good local governance; Steen Jorgensen, one of the foremost proponents of LCDD and director of Social Development (until 2008); and Dan Owen, World Bank–wide LCDD coordinator, who works tirelessly to disseminate LCDD lessons across the globe. The governments of Finland, the Netherlands, and Norway, through their trust funds—the Bank-Netherlands Partnership Program and the Trust Fund for Environmentally and Socially Sustainable Development—provided the resources to advance LCDD efforts around the world, keep this book alive, and bring its many elements together.

We also thank Jean-Louis Sarbib and Callisto Madavo, regional vice presidents for Africa, for their enthusiastic support early on, and later Callisto Madavo, for his critical questions and his interest in moving the LCDD agenda to scale in each country. These individuals have supported our work. Our colleagues in the Africa Region Community Driven Development (CDD) Steering Committee over the period from 2000 to 2007 were Christine Cornelius, Catherine Farvacque-Vitkovic, Laura Frigenti, Helene Grandvoinnet, Phillippe Le Houerou, Brian Levy, Letitia Obeng, Suzanne Piriou-Sall, Nadine Poupart, Galina Sotirova, Jan Weetjens, and Willem Zijp. They provided the professional support, critiques, encouragement, and resources that made this publication possible.

Numerous other people made this book possible, including those who helped to review early concept papers in September 2002 and the task managers who volunteered the programs they worked on for more in-depth fieldwork. The field researchers (all World Bank consultants) were Swaminathan S. Anklesaria Aiyar, Gerard Baltissen, Deborah Davis, Kwame M. Kwofie, Timothy Lubanga, Violetta Manoukian, Mwalimu Musheshe, Suleiman Namara, Martin Onyach-Olaa, and Bertus Wennink. We also thank the many in-country officials and task teams in the World Bank for their assistance. Several of the project managers and task managers—as well as other reviewers such as Ian Goldman (Khanya-African Institute for Community-Driven Development), Ghazala Mansuri (DEC), Keith McLean (SDV), and Vijaendra Rao (DEC)—came together to review the results of these field studies in a workshop in Washington, DC. The results were also validated in a workshop in Burkina Faso in October 2003, with 20-plus CDD project managers from across the continent. In a conference held in November 2003, African ministers of finance and of decentralization affirmed that policy makers need more advice, and this led to the development of the policy review toolkit.

The reviews of the policy stocktaking toolkit were led by Alan Gelb, who, as chief economist in the Africa Region, took a keen interest in integrating this work into the larger development vision for the continent.

A Quality Assurance Group panel, chaired by Mary McNeil (World Bank Institute), reviewed the research outputs and strongly recommended that all of the materials be published and made accessible to the public.

And we could never have managed this work over several years were it not for these World Bank consultants, Galia Schechter, who held the management of this program together; Carmelina Rebano, who kept the different grants straight; and Haddy Sey, who often stepped in when fieldwork or contact with researchers in Africa was needed.

ADP	area development program
AGETIP	Agence d'Exécution des Travaux d'Intérêt Public [Agency for Public Works Management and Employment]
AIDS	acquired immune deficiency syndrome
APL	adaptable program loan
CAMPFIRE	Communal Areas Management Program for Indigenous Resources (Zimbabwe)
CAP	Community Action Plan (Uganda)
CAS	Country Assistance Strategy
CBD	community-based development
CBO	community-based organization
CBRDP	Community-Based Rural Development Project (Burkina Faso, Ghana, Mauritania)
CDD	community driven development
CGIAR	Consultative Group on International Agricultural Research
CIF	Community Investment Fund (Zambia)
CPIA	country policy and institutional assessment
DDC	district development committee
DIF	District Investment Fund (Zambia)
DPL	development policy loan
DRD	decentralized regional development
HIV	human immunodeficiency virus
IDA	International Development Association
IEC	information, education, and communication
IEG	Independent Evaluation Group
IRDP	integrated rural development program
KDP	Kecamatan Development Project (Indonesia)
KIT	Royal Tropical Institute (Netherlands)

LCDD	local and community driven development
LCDF	local community development fund
LEEMP	Local Empowerment and Environmental Management Project (Nigeria)
LGDP	Local Government Development Program (Uganda)
LGMSDP	Local Government Management and Service Delivery Program (Uganda)
MASAF	Malawi Social Action Fund
M&E	monitoring and evaluation
MFI	microfinance institution
NAAS	National Agricultural Advisory Services (Uganda)
NGO	nongovernmental organization
NUSAF	Northern Uganda Social Action Fund
O&M	operations and maintenance
OED	Operations Evaluation Department
PIDER	Programa Integrado de Desarrollo Rural [Integrated Rural Development Program] (Mexico)
PLA	participatory learning and action
PNIR	Programme National d'Infrastructures Rurales [National Program for Rural Infrastructure] (Senegal)
PNPM	Program Nasional Pemberdayaan Masyarakat [National Program for Community Empowerment] (Indonesia)
PRA	participatory rural appraisal
PRSP	Poverty Reduction Strategy Paper
RRA	rapid rural appraisal
SWAp	sectorwide approach
TASAF	Tanzania Social Fund
UNCDF	United Nations Capital Development Fund
VCSP	Village Communities Support Program (Guinea)
ZAMSIF	Zambia Social Investment Fund

Introduction and Executive Summary

Hans P. Binswanger-Mkhize, Jacomina P. de Regt,
and Stephen Spector

Services are failing poor urban and rural people in the developing world, and poverty remains concentrated in rural areas and urban slums (World Bank 2004f, 2008d). This state of affairs prevails despite prolonged efforts by many governments to improve rural and urban services and development programs. This book focuses on how communities and local governments can be empowered to contribute to their own development and, in the process, improve infrastructure, governance, services, and economic and social development—that is, ultimately, the broad range of activities for sustainable poverty reduction.

Countries and their development partners have been trying to involve communities and local governments in their own development since the end of World War II, when the first colonies gained independence in South Asia. Pioneers in both India and Bangladesh (then a part of Pakistan) developed a clear vision of how it would be done: Local development should be planned and managed by local citizens, their communities, and their local governments within a clearly defined decentralized framework that devolves real power and resources to local governments and communities. Capacity support would be provided by technical institutions and sectors and nongovernmental institutions.

This vision set up a tension between central power and empowerment of communities and local governments. This tension has rarely been fully resolved and is still being grappled with in many countries as well as in many externally financed development projects. While the vision was often piloted successfully in individual projects, it was again and again

1

lost in the process of scaling up and, ironically, replaced by centralized, top-down bureaucratic approaches that failed. In these approaches, local citizens were treated as passive recipients, and service delivery suffered because the service providers were not accountable to their clients. This history is traced in chapter 2.

The World Bank also struggled with these issues and used a variety of development approaches, including area development programs (ADPs). These approaches also failed to translate the empowerment vision into practice and therefore failed to have a significant impact. Subsequently, different sectors and projects tried community support approaches, sectoral approaches, and local government approaches, and their practitioners often competed with one another, sometimes within the same countries, creating confusion and reducing the impact. Each of the three approaches provided many valuable lessons that are applicable today. However, evidence and a history of experience, in and outside the Bank, show that different strands can and do converge. The Local Development Conference of 2004 started to build the consensus that a synthesis, known as local and community driven development (LCDD), is needed. Under this synthesis, local development is a co-production of communities, local governments, and supportive sector institutions, with collaboration from the private sector and nongovernmental organizations (see figure 1.1). This book attempts to build greater consensus, to work from the existing knowledge and experience, to improve mutual learning, and to document outcomes. Scaling up

Figure 1.1. Linked Approaches

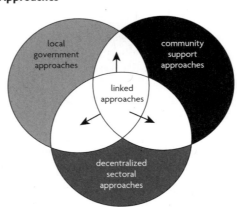

Source: Helling, Serrano, and Warren 2005.

these good experiences and outcomes requires a step-by-step approach, careful local adaptation, and clarity in what is being scaled up. The Bank will be able both to respond better when conditions and country dialogue offer the opportunity for scaling up and to make the necessary long-term commitments when the base of knowledge and experience provided in this book is exploited.

What Is Local and Community Driven Development?

The LCDD concept begins with the observation that community empowerment does not take place in a vacuum; it is affected by local government development and sectoral programs of national governments. Three alternative approaches to local development, which emphasize many of the same principles, come together in this approach: empowerment of the poor and other marginalized groups, responsiveness to beneficiary demand, autonomy of local institutions, greater downward accountability, and enhancement of local capacities. However, in the past these approaches went about things differently:

- *Sectoral approaches* are defined through functional specialization—the services they provide. They have been able to mobilize technical capacity, but they rarely have been responsive to local demand and conditions and cross-sectoral considerations.
- *Local government approaches* are organized through the institutions of territorial governance. They commonly ensure clear formal autonomy and accountability of local decision makers but are often politicized and less effective in managing service provision.
- *Direct community-support approaches* are organized around social groups that, traditionally or voluntarily, make collective decisions. Their entry point through community structure and processes sometimes complicates efforts to coordinate with public sector organizations and local government institutions.

Each approach has generated a distinct body of theory and practice. Many countries simultaneously use all three approaches. This can lead to confusion, unproductive competition, and duplication. The conclusion from the 2004 conference was that local development needs to be the outcome of co-production of all three spheres, harnessing the synergies among them rather than emphasizing their competition. The appropriate term for such a process is *local and community driven development,* which encompasses improved coordination, synergy, efficiency, and responsiveness in local development processes. LCCD becomes the foundation for the next step: scaling up. This book uses the term LCDD for all programs, even if the program itself is called community driven development or if it does not integrate the local government dimension. This is intended to promote thinking about local development as encompassing all dimensions and to reduce the stovepipe thinking of a single approach.

LCDD: A Transformative Process

Bringing about LCDD is not a project; it entails a deep transformation of political and administrative structures that aims to empower communities and local governments with powers, resources, and the authority to use these flexibly and sustainably, thus enabling them to take control of their development.

Empowerment means expanding the assets and capabilities of poor people to participate in, negotiate with, and hold accountable institutions that affect their lives. It means giving people access to voice and information, greater social inclusion and participation, greater accountability, and organizational strength. LCDD aims to harness social capital through empowerment and to increase social capital through scaling up.

In practice, this vision is imperfectly implemented in many countries and in World Bank programs. This is not surprising, since the fundamental tension between central power and local and community empowerment is a political issue that requires negotiation and compromise to resolve. Nevertheless, LCDD boasts many islands of success, although few of them have been scaled up to cover entire countries.

Scaling up is taking one or several islands of success that have addressed a national development problem and multiplying them to cover as much territory and population as possible and appropriate (see box 1.1). When we talk of scaling up LCDD, we primarily mean scaling up the entire approach to empowerment. While this approach is inherently multisectoral, it can be used to scale up a more sector-focused LCDD program—for instance, scaling up a community water supply and sanitation program, as described later for a state in India.

Definitions and Names for Local Jurisdictions

In this book we use the following definitions to designate different local jurisdictions:

- *Districts* of a country are usually fairly large subdivisions of a small country or of regions, provinces, or states in a large country. Depending on the country, they can have populations from 50,000 to several million inhabitants. Districts can have different names: municipality, canton, and province, among others. Districts are usually subdivided into subdistricts.
- *Subdistricts* can have different names: block, mandal, taluka, parish, circle, commune, kecamatan (Indonesia), and more. Subdistricts are further divided into villages or urban neighborhoods.
- *Villages or urban neighborhoods* may also bear many names: village, rural or urban commune, and section, among others.
- *Communities* in multisector community driven development (CDD) programs are often villages or urban neighborhoods. In sector-specific CDD programs, communities are defined by a specific common interest, such as herder's associations, irrigation associations, or associations of street vendors. Both types of programs can benefit from scaling up.
- *Elected councils and local governments* may exist at one or several of the above local levels. For example, in the Indian local government system, there are elected panchayats at all three levels: an indirectly elected district panchayat that oversees the district officials, a directly elected block, mandal, or taluka panchayat that oversees officials at these levels, and a directly elected village panchayat that also serves as the village executive.

Which Key Features of LCDD Should Be Scaled Up?

We seek to scale up the five pillars as well as the four core expected outcomes of LCDD as first articulated by the Africa Region of the World Bank in the Vision for LCDD (World Bank 2000a). See box 1.2. For a full discussion of these core expected outcomes, see chapter 3 and appendix C.

BOX 1.2

Elements of LCDD

Core expected outcomes of LCDD

- Real participation and linkage by all stakeholders
- Improved accountability
- Technical soundness
- Sustainability.

Pillars for success in an integrated LCDD approach

1. *Empower communities.* Empowering communities involves assigning functions, duties, and the corresponding authority to them, providing an institutional framework in which they elect their officials and make decisions, and assigning revenues and other fiscal resources to communities.
2. *Empower local governments.* Empowering local governments involves assigning functions, duties, and the corresponding authority to them, providing an institutional framework in which they elect their officials and make decisions, and assigning revenues and other fiscal resources to governments.
3. *Realign the center.* Realigning the center involves distributing functions and powers from central agencies and sectors to communities and local government, a process that involves both deconcentration and devolution, and shifting the mix of activities performed by central institutions so that the local community and local governments are more involved in direct service delivery and the central government is more involved in policy setting and support functions.
4. *Improve accountability.* Accountability systems need to be aligned so that accountability is to citizens and users of services (not just upward accountability from citizens and service providers to the center), adapted to the new context, and improved all around.
5. *Build capacity.* Capacity building is needed not only for community and local development participants, but also for the other co-producers, the technical sectors, the private sector, and nongovernmental organizations.

Understanding the Magnitude of Scaling Up

What does scaling up mean in terms of the magnitude of communities and people? Our example begins with an LCDD approach that has been successful in a small group of communities or villages belonging to a few subdistricts of a larger district or administrative unit. Many of the tools and approaches to be used have been developed and tested in the field, but coverage of all communities in all subdistricts has not yet been attempted; for this reason, the logistics and tools for coverage on such a large scale have not yet been developed.

While scaling up is the next logical step, this can rarely be done in one big bang at the national level. As table 1.1 shows, the numbers at a national level are just too daunting. Therefore,

- At the *national, donor, and partner levels*, policies should be synchronized with LCDD requirements.
- At the *local level*, all of the tools and logistics for scaling up should first be fully developed and tested in one district or province (as in the Borgou pilot in Benin), in a few municipalities or states (as in Mexico's Decentralization and Regional Development Projects), or in several subdistricts or kecamatans (as in Indonesia's Kecamatan Development Program, or KDP). Such field testing will quickly identify critical bottlenecks that may prevent rapid disbursement of funds and may, in turn, require legal or regulatory changes.

The pilot phase for scaling up will result in a full set of logistics, operational, and training manuals, materials, and tools, which can then be translated into other national languages and extended to and adapted to local conditions in a rollout process that ultimately covers all districts or provinces. How is such an undertaking possible? Unfortunately, scaling up is often attempted without proper guidance, preparation, and tools, leading to a frustrating experience much like reinventing the wheel. The guidance provided in this book is intended to make the process much more

Table 1.1. Magnitudes of Scaling Up: An Example

Small-scale LCDD successes	Pilot phase of scaling up	Scaled-up project
1 district or administrative center	1–4 districts or administrative centers	All districts or administrative centers
1–4 subdistricts	6–24 subdistricts	All subdistricts
5–20 community groups	100–1,000 community groups	Tens of thousands to hundreds of thousands of community groups
Fewer than 50 community projects	100–2,000 projects	Hundreds of thousands of projects
Fewer than 50,000 people	100,000 to 1 million people	Many million people

Source: Authors' compilation.

manageable and intuitive. The proof that this is possible is presented in the examples discussed in chapters 3 and 4.

Well-designed decentralization and community programs can provide and facilitate models that are easily replicated across provinces and countries. In Indonesia, the rapid expansion of KDP has been compared with that of a McDonald's franchise: *field-testing a good institutional model and then going for mass replication*. Districts not covered by KDP have petitioned the government to get the same model. Of course, this model needs adaptation in different socioeconomic conditions, just as McDonald's, through its action research and adaptive management practices, adapts burgers for different countries (in Japan it sells a teriyaki burger, in India a potato burger).

As in any franchise scheme, the overall design requires much testing and design effort, but ultimately the rules and procedures must be simple and straightforward so that people with limited skills can replicate the model in thousands of localities and communities. Complex models will not scale up quickly, and the work that goes into scaling up and making a program replicable and simple is complex (see chapter 5). These two uses of the word "complex" should not be confused.

Scaling up means more than *physical scaling up* (mass replication). It also means *social scaling up* (increasing social inclusiveness) and *conceptual scaling up* (changing the mind-set and power relations). Social scaling up can mean constant adaptations to improve the voice of the weak or special targeted programs to supplement multisectoral ones. Conceptual scaling up means going beyond the notion of LCDD as a project approach, or even a program approach, and embedding empowerment in all of the thinking and action concerning development.

Steps of Scaling Up

Well-functioning small-scale LCDD successes are a prerequisite for scaling up, but they can rarely be scaled up directly. We sometimes refer to these small-scale successes as boutiques, as they may be nice, expensive (often with specially target and unsustainable funding), and not replicable. A diagnostic phase is often necessary to establish the preconditions for a scaled-up LCDD program. In this book we recommend that this should be followed by a pilot phase in which the processes, logistics, and tools for scaling up to national levels are first developed and then fully tested. Such scaling-up pilots should cover all communities and subdistricts in at least one district of a country. The scaling-up pilot would lead to proven procedures, logistics, and tools that can be summarized in an operational manual that subsequently can be translated into local languages, rolled out for use, and further adapted in the remaining districts of a country, province, or state. This book recommends that such an operational manual be prepared to facilitate a truly scaled-up LCDD program that can cover an entire country. (These step-by-step phases are presented in box 1.3 and detailed and fully described in chapter 5).

Objectives and Structure of the Book

The LCDD scaling-up process is inherently complex: not only are there difficult political issues to be resolved, but the reform agenda and program design must involve many co-producers; significant shifts in power must also be achieved. It is not surprising that, even where successful pilot projects have existed, scaling up often has proved difficult. In addition, the magnitude of the task of developing the capacities of hundreds or even thousands of local governments and hundreds of thousands or millions of communities presents complicated design and logistics problems that have often proved insurmountable. This book is devoted to conveying how to advance the political commitment to LCDD and how to proceed in a systematic, step-by-step manner to manage successfully the complex design, logistics, and implementation tasks. It is not to be

---

BOX 1.3

Outline of the Steps to Scaling Up

- Diagnostic phase to ensure minimum conditions
- Preprogram development at the national level
- Preprogram development at the local level
- Pilot phase of scaling up
- Resource flows and accountability
- Scaling up
- Consolidation

used as a blueprint, per se, but as a starting point for country-specific adaptations. With this in mind, the book provides the following:

- A review of the history of community and local development since World War II in pioneering countries as well as within the World Bank (chapter 2)
- A summary of the findings of global project experience and a research project on how to design and scale up LCDD (chapter 3)
- A focus on the opportunities and challenges for achieving the proper fit of LCDD to the country context, using the Africa region as an example, and an assessment of the degree of decentralization and the fit of community empowerment with the institutional setup, a task that needs to be conducted in each country, which is why this chapter has global applicability (chapter 4)
- A step-by-step guide, tools, and toolkits for scaling up LCDD, addressing the activities necessary at both the national and local levels (chapter 5).

The book is intended for policy makers and practitioners of community and local development, both within countries and in donor partner agencies. Its chapters were prepared over a prolonged period of time by groups of different authors. The chapters are intended to be used as self-standing pieces, although we have tried to unify the definitions and integrate the contents, so that it is indeed an integrated book. Because the chapters also have to stand independently, some materials and conclusions are covered more than once. Practitioners will be served by chapter 5, but they will also want to read chapters 3 and 4. Policy makers might be more interested in chapters 2 and 3, but will look through chapter 4 to review the fit with the institutional context.

A growing literature evaluates LCDD programs and projects and evaluates their impacts. The findings from these two bodies of literature are summarized briefly in chapter 2. However, this book does not itself contribute to this evaluation literature, instead referring the reader to other sources. It also notes that the program and project evaluation literature is better developed than rigorous impact evaluation literature, which unfortunately is still too scarce.

The LCDD Renaissance

Although the elements of LCDD have long been understood, again and again the vision has been abandoned in practice. The inherent complexity of scaling up, impatience with participatory processes, and lack of political will to devolve power are at the root of this repeated failure.

More than 100 colonies gained independence in the three decades after World War II. These new countries faced two major challenges: how to govern and how to build their economies. Centralization was in vogue after World War II. Developing countries felt that a strong central government was essential for economic and political independence. With populations that were overwhelmingly rural and poor, rural development was another fundamental goal, but it required an inherently decentralized process.

India epitomized this duality. Mahatma Gandhi advocated highly decentralized development through what he called *village republics*, but the Indian constitution created a fairly centralized polity, a foretaste of what would happen throughout the developing world with a postcolonial era that begins with two opposite perspectives on managing the future development process and ends with finding a balance between them. India was not alone. Many newly independent countries viewed a strong center as essential to building national unity and overcoming tribal divisions. Those countries, as well as aid donors, viewed centralized government programs as the best way to introduce new technologies and modernize societies. As a consequence, developing countries became far more centralized than developed ones.

Counterbalancing centralization was another approach. Since the 1950s, dozens of nations have embarked on community development and other rural development programs, with India as the first to scale up community development over the entire country. From the late 1940s to the mid-1960s, India, Bangladesh, and other developing countries were already implementing initiatives and model programs that advanced community roles, such as the Community Development Program in India or the Comilla Rural Development Program in Bangladesh.

As discussed in chapter 2, by 1957 the core ideas of participatory local and community development were already fully developed in India and East Pakistan (now Bangladesh). Most of these programs started with similar ideals of decentralized and participatory decision making, local planning and coordination, and development of sustainable local and community institutions. Yet, for both technical and political reasons, the process in most countries stopped short of community empowerment. Most large-scale programs failed to apply their ideals of empowering local governments and communities. Power and implementation shifted back to central agencies and their technical staff. Programs became highly bureaucratic. Funding, planning, and execution of community development projects and programs rested in central bureaucracies that often pursued their own interests rather than following community priorities; rarely were they able to coordinate the executing agencies on the ground or to deliver the projects and services they promised.

In country after country, disillusionment with inadequate community-based approaches set in, and in India the entire nationwide Community Development Program and its corresponding ministry were disbanded in the 1960s. They were first replaced by sectoral and technology-based approaches in which line agencies reverted to delivering their specific services to local clients, such as the development of roads, agricultural credit, irrigation development and technologies, and technological advice (see table 1.2). One of the main achievements of these programs was the spread of the green revolution in Asia and Latin America. It quickly became evident, however, that these programs had difficulty reaching the rural poor, and many projects and programs targeted specifically to poor areas and poor groups were added.

In the 1970s the World Bank and other donor agencies entered poverty reduction and rural development in a major way via ADPs and integrated rural development programs (IRDPs). These programs focused on the same elements as the earlier community development programs: decentralization, participation, community empowerment, and the development of local institutions. In practice, however, the programs suffered the same fate as the earlier community development programs and became centralized, bureaucratic, and unable to coordinate actors on the ground. In many cases, these weaknesses were aggravated by lack of appropriate technology that

Table 1.2. Timeline of Development Approaches

Indicator	1950s	1960s	1970s–80s	1990s	2000	2005
Development approach	Centralized, decentralized	Sectoral, technology-led, green revolution, irrigation development	Special area or target group, ADP and IRDP, NGOs and private sector	CBD, social funds	CDD	LCDD
Community involvement	Minimal ⟶	Consultation⟶	Participation ⟶			Empowerment

Source: Authors' compilation.
Note: ADP, area development program; IRDP, integrated rural development program; NGO, nongovernmental organization; CBD, community-based development; CDD, community driven development; LCDD, local and community driven development.

could be readily disseminated. By the early 1990s, the approach was discredited and abandoned by the World Bank and most donors. This left the World Bank without an instrument to reach the rural poor at a time when it was beginning to place a renewed emphasis on poverty reduction (while in the midst of redressing the draconian effect on the poor of financial reform policies in that decade).

In the meantime, different sectors had improved their programs by introducing stronger community participation and collaborating with nongovernmental organizations (NGOs). Social funds were subsequently developed to transfer resources to local levels and to execute projects in a participatory manner. Community driven development programs emerged that transferred resources directly to community management, while at the same time introducing coordination at the local government level. These approaches came to be known as community driven development (CDD), with successful programs in Mexico, Brazil, Indonesia, West Africa, and elsewhere. The methods also proved applicable in emergency settings and postconflict situations.

Through these experiences, it became increasingly apparent that community development could not operate in a vacuum, but required local coordination via local government structures and technical support from the sectors. At the same time, democratization in Latin America, and later in Africa, brought about many decentralization initiatives. India and other Southeast Asian countries also started to reemphasize decentralization as they became disillusioned with strictly sectoral approaches. Based on these experiences, their experimental and adaptive management, and the learning generated, LCDD emerged as a synthesis. It is ironic that this synthesis included all of the elements that the earliest pioneers of community development presented so clearly in their vision and pilot projects.

The Importance of Committed Country Leaders and Donors

Country leaders and donors need to be committed to LCDD and able to seize opportunities when the political dynamics of a recipient country bring to power politicians genuinely committed to shifting power to the grassroots. More research is needed on the related political economy issues.

What is different, however, is that the international experience with such programs is now much better synthesized and that policy makers in countries and donor agencies can learn from previous action research done in other countries' programs. In particular, the preconditions for scaling up genuine local and community empowerment are now much better understood, and diagnostic tools to assess whether they are in place and what needs to be done are well developed (see chapter 5). How to design and sequence an LCDD program in a step-by-step manner is also better understood and is discussed in great detail in chapters 4 and 5.

However, implementation progress across the world is still limited. The centralization-decentralization dilemma remains a struggle about power. Most participants in this struggle see it as a struggle about a finite amount of power and economic and social resources. This is the wrong perspective, because LCDD can lead to greatly enhanced power at local and community levels, while at the same time providing the center with real power to guide an expanding pie of social and economic development. The gradually expanding literature on impact is providing many examples of such positive processes and their impacts.[1]

The Slow Evolution of Participatory Approaches: From Consultation to Empowerment

The first approach taken was the *community consultation model* (see table 1.2). In this model, government agencies or NGOs consulted communities, but operated as direct service providers using their own staff. This model for the sectoral provision of frontline services to rural areas was widespread and, in many cases, remains so.

The second approach was the *community participation model*. Government agencies or NGOs invited participation from communities in choosing development priorities and project design, co-financing the investments, with contributions in cash or in kind, and operating the investments once they were completed, including the levying and management of user fees. Frequently this approach used participatory assessment techniques to define the needs and aspirations of communities. The earliest pioneers of community development had this approach in mind when they talked about community development. In the 1980s, the approach was widely used again by sectors that introduced participation to enhance the effectiveness of their programs.

The third approach was the *community empowerment model*. The implementation of projects was devolved entirely to communities, along with the funds for implementation. This approach was the key advance introduced by large-scale CDD programs in the 1990s in Mexico, Brazil, and Indonesia. In these programs, participatory assessments and participatory monitoring and evaluation were used to define community priorities and implementation mechanisms as well as to monitor progress.

In Burkina Faso, as part of the sharing of central revenue, the community empowerment model provided untied funds to communities under a formula. Communities augmented those resources by providing cofinancing in cash and in kind and by collecting user fees. This empowered communities to plan and execute subprojects according to their own priorities. In this approach, government agencies and NGOs operated primarily as facilitators and trainers. Communities were involved heavily in the design and choice of technology for their chosen projects; usually communities managed the project funds and contracted directly for goods and services to implement them. The approach provided communities with ample opportunities for increasing skills in project and financial management through learning-by-doing.

Community driven development is a phrase that has had different meanings for different development agencies, covering a host of approaches ranging from community consultation to empowerment. But, as defined today by the World Bank, CDD means the community empowerment model, even if that model is not yet fully practiced in all projects due to the country context.

Devolving resources to communities required the development of new disbursement, procurement, and accountability mechanisms; otherwise, the resources would not flow. Adaptation of the usual processes used in development assistance projects was required. Through experimentation, a radically simplified set of mechanisms was developed. Instead of focusing primarily on accountability for the use of money to the funding agency or the government, the new mechanisms are built on horizontal and downward accountability of community leaders to each other and to their members. Accounts are maintained in a local language that all literate community members can read; disbursement is in tranches based on statements of expenditures; checking on physical progress and conducting random audits are the primary tools for verification; and simple competitive shopping for goods and services replaces complex procurement procedures. The success of these mechanisms is confirmed by the fact that World Bank–financed LCDD programs score well on fiduciary compliance compared with other projects. New experimentation and learning are now needed to comply with anticorruption and good governance codes.

LCDD is preferably used in multisector programs, but single-sector programs are sometimes appropriate. For community empowerment to work, giving communities the full choice of development alternatives, multisectoral LCDD would need to be put in place, but political and fiscal conditions may make that difficult. Single-sector LCDD cannot drive this process, but it can convince people that empowerment is the best way to go. In Kerala, India, incumbent local governments were reelected in all five gram panchayats (the village-level governing authority) participating in the pilot phase of the Jalanidhi Water Supply Project, whereas two-thirds of incumbents were defeated statewide. This sectoral lesson provided strong political support to the whole empowerment process. Often local governments are thinly funded, whereas sectoral schemes are well funded and attract more public participation. LCDD projects and processes can evolve together through mutual strengthening.

Co-production of sectors, local governments, and communities under the LCDD approach requires a common mind-set and vision, detailed and clear assignment of functions and responsibilities, and training of all involved. These assignments of responsibility have to be worked out in detail in a participatory manner that involves the actors that ultimately are supposed to implement LCDD at the district level and below. This is best done in a scaling-up pilot under which all processes are first implemented in all communities in one or several districts. This piloting should result in a field-tested and adaptable operational manual that spells out who has to do what, how, and with what tools and instruments. This manual then becomes the instrument through which the assignment of functions and all the other program details are clearly spelled out and can be disseminated via training. The adaptive management of the scaling-up process based on learning-by-doing is at the heart of the LCDD approach and its scaling up.

Countries differ widely in how far they have gone in implementing the LCDD agenda. Many successes have been achieved, as in Brazil, Burkina Faso, Indonesia, Mexico, Uganda, or selected states of India. The path to future success is quite clear, but most countries are still struggling with the same empowerment versus centralization dilemma that has plagued this field for so long.

World Bank project and program practice is also evolving based on constant learning. As shown by the Quality Assurance Group, the Independent Evaluation Group, and the discussion in chapter 4, different regions and team leaders, together with client countries, design programs that differ widely in how far they move the LCDD agenda forward. The task of moving decentralization and community empowerment forward is a global one, relevant across the world, from West Bank and Gaza to Brazil, Paraguay, Rwanda, and Timor-Leste. Different conditions require different approaches. Some operations are sector-specific programs that focus primarily on producing infrastructure and services with and for communities. Some countries start with decentralization and only incorporate community empowerment at a later stage. At the other extreme are programs, such as KDP in Indonesia or the CDD program in Burkina Faso, that systematically push forward the entire decentralization and community empowerment agenda. While World Bank guidance clearly articulates the LCDD vision, spells out its key elements, and provides excellent toolkits for virtually all phases of an LCDD approach, in practice the three approaches sometimes compete, and the World Bank is in both a conservative role and a leading role (see chapter 2 and, more specifically, chapter 4 for the Africa region).

A synthesis of the stock-taking exercises carried out in each region of the World Bank shows that only some progress has been made in the integration of this guidance framework, that regions are using different approaches (and not only to account for country context), and that sectoral integration is still far from the norm (Van Domelen 2008). Also, scaling up is seldom considered in the original design. Strong adaptive management is required to take advantage of the richness of experiences and to incorporate learning across the globe.

Adapting to the National and Local Context

By examining a wide range of country experiences in LCDD, we find that consensus on clear objectives and sound technical designs are vital for scaling up. Once a country is ready to engage in an LCDD process, a lot of work is needed to determine the scope and approach of the program and to establish the sequencing of actions. These preparations should involve a broad range of stakeholders, from communities and civil society to local governments, ministries of local government, ministries of finance, and donors. They should include an examination of the following questions:

- Where is the country in its processes of decentralization and of local and community empowerment?
- How can the conditions that are conducive to LCDD be established?
- How can adverse institutional barriers be overcome?
- How is LCDD sequenced?
- What is to be scaled up?
- How can total and fiscal costs be reduced?

- How can the program be financed?
- How can co-production problems be managed?
- How can LCDD be adapted to the local and national context?
- How will field-tested manuals, toolkits, and scaling-up logistics be created?

Toolkits have been developed to assemble and analyze existing information and to systematically analyze all of these questions (which are discussed especially in chapter 5 of this book). No wheels need be reinvented; they can simply be adjusted to new circumstances. Development programs must be highly adaptable to institutional conditions in an environment of low capacity at the national, state, and local levels; unstable and unpredictable policy making; and limited democratic culture and civic capacity. LCDD programs fulfill this requirement with their highly flexible design based on a few core principles and a handful of proven methodologies and with the underlying attitude that learning-by-doing or adaptive management is key.

The Key Concept: Adapting to Local Context

Program designers must make strategic choices concerning (a) the balance between improving access to services and developing local institutions and (b) the allocation of responsibilities among the central program agency, local governments, communities, and the private sector.

Because the methodological options for LCDD programs are well known and rapidly disseminated, these decisions can be based on local experience and regional or international good practice. To build on existing capacities and experiences, the final configuration can be adapted based on the context and trajectory of preexisting programs.

The criticism that LCDD programs use a cookie-cutter approach has some validity, but it is vastly exaggerated. These projects are not all designed in the same way. They do share some basic principles, but they rely on a variety of institutional strategies and management instruments. Strategic program design today reflects a contingency approach: program elements are combined based on the country-specific policy priorities, institutional contexts, and experience. Even so, learning and adaptation are still required. This reflects the challenges of implementing complex programs in, for instance, low-capacity African countries, in conflict situations, or in Middle Eastern and Northern African middle-income countries, where the trajectory to decentralization and community empowerment is different; it also reflects the path dependence of each country's reform and institutional development. Each stage of capacity building must be grounded in prior stages.

Sometimes changes in strategy reflect adjustment to changing country contexts, but sometimes leading strategies change the country contexts. Less risk-averse program designers employing leading strategies in Burkina Faso, Rwanda, and Mozambique encouraged central governments to adopt policies more friendly to decentralization and community empowerment. Similarly, intensive discussion in the Islamic Republic of Iran, Tunisia, and Lebanon on community empowerment may contribute to changing country strategies. China's visits to Indonesia, Brazil, and Africa encourage learning, but China clearly states that all CDD programs will need to be adapted to China's unique and varying regional context.

Specific Lessons

The various chapters of this book yield a reliable set of lessons and recommendations:

- *Strong political commitment to decentralization and empowerment is essential*, and national leaders and local champions often facilitate the process. They need to receive systematic and quick support from donors.
- *Committed country leaders and donors need to be opportunists*, seizing occasions when the political dynamics of a recipient country bring to power politicians genuinely committed to shifting power to the grassroots. More research is needed on the related political economy issues.
- *Successful scale-ups put money in the hands of communities to harness their latent capacity through learning-by-doing.* This is supplemented by relevant capacity building.
- *Pilot projects are useful for field-testing in different conditions.* Often countries have a broad range of existing pilots involving local governments and communities that can be used to derive best practices. As discussed, the pilots are rarely scaled up to cover all communities and local government areas even within a single district. Therefore, a pilot phase for scaling up can reveal problems and suggest adaptations and opportunities before attempting a national rollout.
- *Successful scale-ups have sound technical design.* They create context-specific procedures to be incorporated in manuals and training courses

for stakeholders. These manuals and procedures are living documents that are constantly adapted and updated in the light of new experiences and contexts.

- *Good systems are needed for sharing and spreading knowledge.* Such systems help to inform different stakeholders precisely about what their roles are and help to create common values.
- *Incentives for different stakeholders should be tailored to their new roles.* Incentives for different co-producers need to be aligned to the common objectives. Managerial incentives should reward the right processes and outcomes rather than rapid disbursement. Establishing the right processes can take time, but once they are well established, scaling up can proceed relatively quickly.
- *Success depends on training.* Tens of thousands of communities are needed to execute and manage projects and accounts. Good scaling-up logistics not only lower training costs but also improve community ownership and sustainability; so does community co-financing.
- *Scaling up is a long-haul process.* It can take as long as 15 years, and long-term commitment of governments as well as donor partners is key.

The following recommendations pertain specifically to operating in emergencies and in postconflict settings (World Bank 2008c):

- *LCDD funds can provide a quick response* in postconflict areas and areas hit by natural emergencies; they help to stabilize communities and kick-start infrastructure rehabilitation. LCDD funds use simple procedures; they need to have good management and operational autonomy with the ability and flexibility to take advantage of a wide range of available and innovative implementation capacity.
- *Responses have to be tailored to community needs* because conflicts and emergencies can affect communities in very different ways and may affect many services at once.
- *LCDD funds promote transparent and accountable institutions.* This is critical in communities plagued by mistrust and institutional breakdown. Participatory planning and consultative outreach support the demand side of good governance and social accountability.
- *Civil society organizations are often critical immediately after an emergency.* They are often the only ones still working in postconflict settings. Working with partners outside government is important to an effective response.
- *Conflict mediation is integral to the programs,* because a breakdown in trust and social cohesion risks inflaming tensions and provoking

more violence. By engaging community members in interacting with each other and with local institutions, the programs begin to reestablish social and institutional relationships, networks, and interpersonal trust—that is, social capital.

For longer-term sustainability, an effective decentralization agenda needs to be pursued, and local governments may need to be built up from zero.

Step-by-Step Approach

Given the large number of political, design, and technical difficulties that have to be overcome in scaling up LCDD, it is not surprising that programs have often run into serious bottlenecks associated with inadequate analysis, design, logistics, or training. To reduce these difficulties in future programs, we provide the tools for a systematic step-by-step approach to scaling up, starting from the diagnostic phase and moving through the consolidation phase of the program (see box 1.4 and chapter 5).

BOX 1.4

Steps to Scaling Up (Expanded)

Diagnostic phase to ensure minimum conditions

- Assess the LCDD underpinnings in the national context
- Align with the national government, donors, and other partners
- Synchronize or transform policies, regulations, and laws with LCDD
- Have national leadership and coordination

Preprogram development at the national level

- Define the program
- Select pilot districts
- Appoint a scaling-up team

Preprogram development at the local level

- Assess the LCDD underpinnings in the local context
- Achieve local buy-in
- Set up communications

(continued)

BOX 1.4

Steps to Scaling Up (Expanded) *(continued)*

Pilot phase of scaling up

- Define players and roles
- Conduct training
- Ensure that facilitation capacity and facilitators are in place to assist in participatory planning
- Conduct participatory planning
- Supply technical support

Resource flows and accountability

- Direct financing to communities
- Devise options for allocating funds
- Devise options for managing and disbursing financial resources

Scaling up

- Ensure that the necessary elements are in place
- Plan finances
- Manage bureaucratic hurdles
- Design a management system
- Focus on costs and logistics
- Devise a communications strategy
- Put in place a system for monitoring and evaluation
- Take into account special conditions
- Conduct prelaunch activities

Consolidation

- Achieve self-sustainability

Appendix B assembles a large number of individual design elements that can achieve true empowerment, smooth operation of a program, and cost-effectiveness. Neither the step-by-step approach nor the list of design elements is intended as a fixed blueprint and process; each needs to be used selectively and adapted to the specific context in which scaling up takes place. Using these tools should allow for faster and less error-prone scaling up of LCDD programs.

Agenda for the Future

For the first time in the 65-year history of LCDD, the following elements are fully developed:

- What the objectives are
- What success looks like
- A wealth of operational experience
- An understanding of the conflicts that have to be resolved
- A description of the roles of different actors and institutions, diagnostic and design tools, and fiduciary mechanisms
- Step-by-step guidance
- A review of the beginning round of impact evaluation literature, which on balance is rather positive.

Shortfalls

Some elements still fall short, however. Systematic and long-term political commitment is still shaky, both in many countries and among development partners. There are constant risks of backsliding.

Stronger central leadership is needed within the World Bank to engage in dialogue, mutual learning, harmonization, and adaptation based on the existing portfolio of LCDD operations. Each of the three approaches—sectoral, local government, and direct community support (see p. 59)—has merit, and the richness of experiences should be celebrated and built on through constant learning and adaptive action research. Review and guidance mechanisms are needed to embed the LCDD operations fully into a country-driven and fully accepted decentralization program. Existing diagnostic tools are not yet widely applied. Operations are focusing on shorter-term objectives linked to funding programs without waiting for the completion of diagnostics and policy dialogue on decentralization. Different regions have devised different solutions to the question of how to handle productive investments with regard to LCDD; those different approaches provide a score of learning to be applied and adapted in other regions. Above all, vast amounts of strong research on impacts would feed into the adaptive management required for the LCDD approach.

New Opportunities

It might be better to concentrate first on the shortfalls, but in the meantime, the application of LCDD around the world is being advanced in various ways, and strong learning should be based on these new experiments:

- Some countries are seeking to harmonize the local development platform and to transform different programs into one nationally driven LCDD program. The countries, rather than donors, are driving this agenda.
- Some large firms, such as global mining companies, as part of their social responsibility agenda, are turning to LCDD-type programs for the areas in which they operate.[2] Many establish community foundations with endowments and expect the communities to use the proceeds of the endowments to manage LCDD programs. Community foundations are also a tool to be considered for the sustainability of LCDD programs, especially in urban areas: an LCDD program may provide the initial endowment, and private sector and other programs may add to it (World Bank 2008a, 2008b).
- Social entrepreneurs also bring LCDD principles in some of their enterprises promoting social and environmental goods by working directly with and through communities.

Leveraging the social capital created in LCDD programs into economic capital is well under way in South Asia and Latin America and offers great opportunities in other regions of the world.

How to integrate social protection into the LCDD agenda is again under experimentation. This is ironic because social funds specifically started as instruments of social protection, but then veered away from these objectives. Employment generation, conditional cash transfers, and other community driven social safety nets are being experimented with. This is an agenda where strong learning and action research are being pursued.

LCDD approaches have also been used for environmental management, such as projects funded by the World Bank–Global Environment Facility. In these projects, the struggle for power among actors is also playing itself out, often in a negative way. A systematic look at the performance of such approaches with respect to the real degree of community empowerment may be needed. A particular opportunity for LCDD approaches to environmental management comes from carbon trading and climate change adaptation instruments that have been or are being developed and piloted.[3]

Communities would develop and manage new land-use options and other carbon-saving opportunities, as well as the income streams derived from them. Attitudes of major faith-based organizations are shifting toward a stronger engagement with the development agendas of local communities as part of their focus on global stewardship of the Earth as well as poverty reduction in addition to their traditional focus on spiritual matters.

In the global labor market, remittances have been important sources of income for the families and communities from which the migrant labor originated. While such remittances are used mostly for consumption, education, and health expenditures of families, migrants often form community associations in the place where they work and conduct fund-raising activities for the community back home for diverse activities, such as building and repairing schools, health clinics, mosques, and churches. Research shows that such remittances decline with the second generation and almost vanish with the third. To make the most of the remittances from the first-generation migrants, governments are starting to match remittances for investment purposes. However, another strategy would be to create community development funds or community foundations.

Notes

1. For example, in one evaluation China calls it "government-driven, community driven development" and explains that government roles are changing, but not diminishing.
2. See http://commdev.org/.
3. For more information on the Community Development Carbon Fund, see http://wbcarbonfinance.org/Router.cfm?Page=CDCF&ItemID=9709& FID=9709.

CHAPTER 2

Historical Roots and Evolution of Community Driven Development

Hans P. Binswanger-Mkhize, Swaminathan S. Anklesaria Aiyar,
Jacomina P. de Regt, Rodrigo Serrano-Berthet, Louis Helling,
Julie Van Domelen, David Warren, and Stephen Spector

This chapter traces about 60 years of thinking and experience that we now define as local and community driven development (LCDD), an approach to development that started outside the World Bank but has now become an integral part of Bank practice. One of the great ironies is that we are now embracing and applying an approach that emerged out of the post-colonial years in India as a way of helping poor rural areas to advance through decentralized governance and community empowerment. That approach, however, competed against the more expedient urge by governments to centralize power.

From the late 1940s to the mid-1960s, Bangladesh, India, and other developing countries were already implementing initiatives and model programs that advanced community roles. This was long before the broader donor community took any interest. Individuals such as Akhtar Hamid Khan in Bangladesh (the Comilla Program) and S. K. Dev in India (the Indian Community Development Plan), with their deep roots in the era's independence struggles and influenced by the ideas of Mahatma Gandhi, developed the concepts and practices that have evolved into LCDD.

Although their ideas and programs were compromised when the programs were scaled up (and, ironically, bureaucratized), the role of communities has evolved and broadened from the era when development practitioners *consulted with* communities to the era when communities *participated in* certain aspects of development programs and eventually to the era when communities *were empowered* to define and manage the programs themselves or in partnership with local government (see table 2.1). The World Bank, although a latecomer to community empowerment, now is an active proponent of shifting power, decision making, and development management away from central authority and toward local levels.

The LCDD vision has gained ground around the world. The vision focuses on community empowerment linked to effective local government with supportive central government and sector institutions. It emphasizes building institutions and capacity and learning how to manage directly the ways and means of development. The World Bank's resolve to advance LCDD, both as policy and practice, has come at a very good time for central and local governments and communities. The Bank can provide extra momentum for scaling up proven programs. As this chapter shows, the road to a coherent vision and practice of LCDD has been long and arduous. Now, as the twenty-first century begins, LCDD offers a way to make progress over the next 60 years and to do so in a more empowering, decentralized, and equitable way.

This chapter comprises two parts. The first discusses the political economy of empowerment and provides some historical examples of approaches before 1990; the second traces the evolution of community-focused approaches within the World Bank, from community-based development (CBD) through to LCDD.

Table 2.1. Timeline of Development Approaches

Indicator	1950s	1960s	1970s–80s	1990s	2000	2005
Development approach	Centralized, decentralized	Sectoral, technology-led, green revolution, irrigation development	Special area or target group, ADP and IRDP, NGOs and private sector	CBD, social funds	CDD	LCDD
Community involvement	Minimal ⟶	Consultation ⟶	Participation ⟶			Empowerment

Source: Authors' compilation.
Note: ADP, area development program; IRDP, integrated rural development program; NGO, nongovernmental organization; CBD, community-based development; CDD, community driven development; LCDD, local and community driven development.

A Sampling of Historical Experiences before 1990

More than 100 colonies gained independence in the three decades after World War II. These new countries faced two major challenges: how to govern and how to build their economy.

Local and Community Empowerment and Political Opposition to It

Centralization was in vogue after World War II. The Soviet, Keynesian, and welfare state models all posited a strong central authority as the engine of progress. Developing countries believed in dependency theory or feared neo-colonialism; they felt that a strong central government was essential for economic and political independence. With populations that were overwhelmingly rural and poor, rural development was another fundamental goal; however, quite the opposite of centralizing tendencies, it required an inherently decentralized process (see table 2.1 for the timeline of approaches).

India epitomized this duality. Mahatma Gandhi advocated highly decentralized development through what he called *village republics*, but the Indian constitution created a fairly centralized polity, a foretaste of what would happen throughout the developing world. The postcolonial era began with two opposite perspectives on managing future development and ended with a balance between them.

India was not alone. Many newly independent countries viewed a strong center as essential to building national unity and overcoming tribal divisions. These countries, as well as aid donors, viewed centralized government programs as the best way to introduce new technologies and modernize societies. Besides, many leaders in developing countries saw centralized rule as a way to thwart political rivals and stay in power. As a consequence, developing countries became far more centralized than developed ones. Initially, centralized rule by charismatic leaders who had spearheaded independence movements had widespread acceptability. But by the 1980s, corruption, inflation, aid weariness, and high debt led to disillusionment.

Counterbalancing centralization was another approach. Since the 1950s, dozens of nations have embarked on community development and rural development programs, with India as the first country to scale up community development over the entire country.

As shown in box 2.1, by 1957 the core ideas of participatory local and community development were fully developed in India. Most of these programs started with similar ideals of decentralized and participatory

BOX 2.1

India's Champions of Empowerment (1948 Onward)

When India became independent, Community Development Minister S. K. Dev was a champion of community empowerment. He piloted community development projects in 1948, using community participation approaches within a deconcentrated service delivery model to cover all aspects of rural development—agriculture, roads, animal husbandry, health, education, housing, transportation, and communications. The pilots were quickly scaled up to a nationwide community development program, and a special ministry for community development was created. Community development workers were posted in villages to assist communities with their own development priorities, but the community development ministry was disbanded.

Then, in 1957, another champion, Balwantrai Mehta, headed a committee that found centralization to be a root cause of the failure of community development. It recommended a three-tier system of *panchayati raj* (local governments at the district, development block, and village levels). However, implementation was left to state governments, and politicians in state capitals wanted to keep rather than lose power and resources to the grassroots. They held few local elections and took over the running of many municipalities. Community empowerment and democratic decentralization were minimal. By the end of the 1960s, most programs had shifted back to state governments, but this centralized service delivery yielded unimpressive results.

In 1989, Prime Minister Rajiv Gandhi became a champion of village empowerment and set in motion a constitutional amendment to provide for regular panchayat elections and for state finance commissions to suggest the transfer of sectoral programs and funds from state governments to local governments. However, weak implementation and outright sabotage by state governments were again widespread: many did not implement the recommendations. Two states (West Bengal and Kerala) ruled by the Communist Party went about decentralization in earnest, since they viewed this as a route to electoral success. Most other parties and states did not.

The current head of the ruling Congress Party, Sonia Gandhi, is also a champion of grassroots empowerment. She aims to bypass state government resistance by channeling funds directly to districts for centrally sponsored programs (notably the National Rural Employment Guarantee Program) and asking village-level local governments to implement them. But the use of such funds has been poor in some states. The struggle between champions and saboteurs of community empowerment continues.

decision making, local planning and coordination, and development of sustainable local and community institutions. Yet, for both technical and political reasons, the process in most countries stopped short of community empowerment.

Most large-scale programs failed to apply their ideals of empowering local governments and communities. Power and implementation shifted back to central agencies and their technical staff, and programs became highly bureaucratic.

The Ongoing Need to Overcome Entrenched Interests. The devolution of power to the grassroots requires legal and sometimes constitutional changes, along with substantial institutional development at the community level. Such change threatens a wide range of political, bureaucratic, and business interests that have profited from centralization. Strong political champions of community empowerment and decentralization are necessary to overcome such resistance. But, then as now, even where champions decree decentralization and community empowerment, vested interests will try to obstruct the process and reverse them unless the country or state shares the commitment and has the political will to share power.

In Bangladesh during the 1970s, community development found a champion in Akhtar Hamid Khan of the Bangladesh Academy for Rural Development. He devised the community-based Comilla model of rural development, which was later scaled up to cover the whole country (see box 2.2). Local government elections were held, but central politicians refused to transfer financial and project implementation to the grassroots, undermining the original aim of community empowerment.

Most similar experiments failed to provide fiscal and administrative decentralization along with political decentralization. Local bodies were often appointed by and accountable to the central government, not local people. They typically lacked finances and administrative powers. One study of four countries (Crook and Manor 1995) showed that decentralization succeeded only where the government was truly serious about devolving political, financial, and administrative powers (as in the state of Karnataka, India) and failed where it was not serious (as in Bangladesh, Côte d'Ivoire, and Ghana). Even in Karnataka, where Chief Minister Ramakrishna in 1983–88 championed and implemented *panchayati raj* (a three-tier system of local governments), a new chief minister recentralized power in 1990 (Hegde 2000). This pattern of creating local

BOX 2.2

The Comilla Model of Rural Development

The Comilla model of rural development was created by the Bangladesh Academy for Rural Development, led by Akhtar Hamid Khan (Banglapedia 2005). The model sought to approach rural development from the viewpoint of villagers, based on their intimate understanding of their problems. The key element of this community participation model was *the creation of an institutional base in rural society*, around which development programs could be integrated. The institutional base included local governments and a two-tier system of agricultural cooperatives for savings, credit, and extension services. It sought to create a cadre of institutional leaders in every village and to coordinate the activities of government departments and people's organizations. The Thana Irrigation Program provided irrigation through participatory planning and implementation by communities.

After a successful pilot in Comilla District, the government in 1972 created a national integrated rural development program to extend the model nationwide. This was supervised by the Bangladesh Rural Development Board, which eventually dominated rural development. In the process of scaling up, planning and coordination of programs shifted from communities and local bodies to bureaucrats. The program drifted back to the community consultation approach, with implementation through government agencies and later through NGOs. Although district assemblies were created and local elections took place, the government never transferred financial resources and implementation responsibility to the districts or to the communities. By not implementing one of the key features of the Comilla model, the original model of community empowerment was never disseminated.

governments without devolving authority and fiscal resources to them has been a common problem in many other developing countries.

Even strong international leadership is not enough. Robert McNamara, president of the World Bank (1969–81), sought to reduce poverty and the inequitable distribution of income through integrated rural development programs (IRDPs), also known as area development programs (ADPs). As discussed in a later section, his strong support was not enough. The best intentions and proclamations from leaders in the donor community were still far from the reality at the village level. Despite good intentions, the programs generally ended up top-down and unable to embrace the priorities of communities or respond to their felt needs; the programs foundered amid coordination problems among central agencies.

Sectoral Approaches. Historically, government support for rural development in most countries started with sectoral approaches. Today's big irrigation canal systems in Brazil, China, Arab Republic of Egypt, Mexico, and South Asia are the legacy of sector-specific irrigation bureaucracies, some of which were created in the nineteenth century or even earlier. From 1965 to 1986, irrigation accounted for a quarter of the Bank's agricultural and rural development lending (World Bank 1987). Other sectoral projects included agricultural research and extension services, rural roads, water supply, health, education, forestry, land administration, and targeted agricultural credit.

The sectoral approach had some successes, but many bureaucracies failed their citizens, especially the poor (World Bank 2003c). The bureaucracies were highly centralized and not accountable to users. Some engaged in rent seeking and corruption. They spent a disproportionate share of funds on staff and offices in the capitals, rarely meeting the needs of the rural poor. Centralized attempts to provide rural credit also had limited reach and missed the poor, although microfinance institutions (MFIs) are now correcting this shortcoming (see box 2.3).

In many countries, efforts are under way to make centralized agencies more accountable to users, deconcentrate their staff and services, and devolve some or all service delivery functions to local governments and community groups (such as irrigation associations, forest user groups, and drinking water groups).

Technology-Led Production Programs (1960s Onward)

India's Community Development Program failed in the 1950s, and the country became increasingly dependent on food aid. To correct this, priorities in the 1960s shifted to *technology-led change* in agriculture. Supported by the Ford Foundation, the Intensive Agricultural District Program focused money, expert staff, and agricultural inputs in a few well-endowed agricultural districts (Staples 1992). At first, the results were mixed and limited. Called the *green revolution,* a breakthrough came with the development of high-yielding dwarf varieties of rice and wheat in the mid-1960s. This required using the new seeds with reliable irrigation and high doses of fertilizer. The green revolution raised the income of farmers and

---

BOX 2.3

From Specialized Agricultural Credit to Microfinance

In the 1980s, specialized agricultural credit institutions were set up all over the world to finance rural development. India, for example, created cooperative land development banks for investment credit, along with agricultural credit cooperatives for seasonal input credit. From 1965 to 1973, a quarter of World Bank agricultural lending went to agricultural credit, mainly in Brazil, India, Mexico, Morocco, and Pakistan. Unfortunately, almost no self-sufficient institutions emerged. Most systems ended up dysfunctional and bankrupt. Moreover, most credit benefits were captured by rural elites. Therefore, the World Bank stopped supporting specialized agricultural credit institutions (World Bank 1987).

In the 1990s, the focus shifted to microfinance institutions (MFIs), which typically lend to groups of poor women, helping to improve social indicators by increasing the financial power of women within the household. Spectacular scaling up with very low payment default was first achieved by the Grameen Bank and other MFIs in Bangladesh. MFIs have since been established in dozens of developing countries and scaled up rapidly. Today, many poor households are covered, and there is a campaign to reach 175 million families through microcredit by 2015 (http://www.microcreditsummit.org/about/about_the_microcredit_summit_campaign/). The United Nations declared 2005 to be the Year of Microfinance, and the 2006 Nobel Prize for Peace was awarded to Mohammed Yunus, founder of the Grameen Bank.

---

rural laborers; it also created more jobs in transport and food processing. In time, India became self-sufficient and then produced a surplus in food for export.

The green revolution spread quickly across the world. Its success led to the creation of the Consultative Group on International Agricultural Research (CGIAR) to support research in all major tropical food crops via a string of international centers. It soon became apparent, however, that countries needed to strengthen their own research institutions to adapt internationally available varieties to local conditions. The Bank and other donors supported the green revolution, CGIAR, and other agricultural research institutions across the world.

While the green revolution fared well in irrigated areas, there was a need for crop varieties that would do well without water control. Farmers who relied on rain were unwilling to spend large sums on expensive inputs. This was especially true in Africa, where weak distribution systems led to high fertilizer prices and poor farmers had no access to credit. This exposed the limitation of technological approaches and led to experiments in programs for special areas and target groups.

Programs for Special Areas and Target Groups (1970s Onward)

Rural development programs faced the dangers of elite capture and social exclusion of minorities and the very poor. To mitigate these dangers, programs were designed to target weaker groups and poorer areas. These were typically managed by the central government or nongovernmental organizations (NGOs; see box 2.4). Using a mix of grants and subsidized credit to reach specific areas and target groups, rural employment programs and asset creation programs emerged in a big way in the 1980s. Implementation experience was mixed.

Similar programs emerged all over the world. The Bank and other donors supported a variety of programs targeting specific areas and the poor. Here again, the experience was often unsatisfactory:

- The participation of communities was limited or nonexistent.
- While targeted programs clearly had a role to play, they were managed by sectoral bureaucracies who were not accountable to the communities they were supposed to serve and could not be disciplined for shortcomings in service delivery.

BOX 2.4

A Sample of India's Target Group Programs

In the 1970s, India's central government launched many programs aimed at target groups, such as the following (Hegde 2000):

- Small Farmers' Development Agency
- Tribal Development Agency
- Marginal, Small Farmers, and Agricultural Laborers Development Agency
- Command Area Development for areas falling under each irrigation scheme
- Drought-Prone Areas Program
- Hill Areas Program.

In the 1990s, donors and governments rectified this by including communities and local governments in targeted programs.

Area Development Programs (1970s Onward)

The limitations of the green revolution inspired World Bank President Robert McNamara to promote ADPs (IRDPs). Following McNamara's famous Nairobi speech in 1973, the World Bank sharply increased its lending for agricultural and rural development. ADPs and IRDPs aimed to integrate many strands of development, from irrigation and agricultural credit to rural infrastructure, education, health, water supply, and small-scale industry. They emphasized smallholder development and aimed to reach the poor in previously neglected and degraded areas (see box 2.5). By 1992, the Bank had assisted nearly 300 such projects, 45 percent of which were in Africa.

The Bank's Rural Development Policy of 1975 emphasized that rural development should be *participatory, decentralized, embedded in a favorable agricultural policy regime, and based on good available technology*. In Mexico, the three PIDER projects (Programa Integrado de Desarrollo Rural or Integrated Rural Development Program), implemented from 1975 to 1988, were considered the cutting edge of a "social engineering" approach to participation. However, most ADPs did not follow the Bank's professed policy of decentralization and participatory planning, as such approaches would have required major, time-consuming institutional change. Many

---

BOX 2.5

Plan Puebla, Pioneer of IRDPs

In the early 1970s, the Plan Puebla was a flagship rural development project based in the valley of Puebla, Mexico, including almost 200 villages. Looking for a better way to disseminate modern agricultural techniques, the plan built a collaborative relationship between government agricultural specialists, campesinos, credit institutions, and suppliers; it also established a rural microenterprise project with village women.

Plan Puebla recognized the fundamental role played by villagers and farmers and helped them to establish community-led cooperatives and businesses. It also threatened the traditional channels of rural power and was subject to changes in political commitment and interference.

projects were prepared in a hurry by agricultural professionals with little beneficiary involvement. Implementation was entrusted to sectoral agencies, which inevitably used the limited community consultation approach to service delivery and often had the wrong priorities. Again, the central agencies involved often had major coordination problems.

In 1993, the Operations Evaluation Department (OED) of the Bank found that such projects fared poorly compared with other Bank programs, especially in Africa. The overall failure rate was half, and two-thirds of African projects failed. Projects were more successful where government commitment was strong and the agricultural policy environment was better. For the most part,

- The projects did not follow the institutional development lessons of the Comilla model.
- Their benefits were rarely sustainable. Projects had little impact on institutional development, especially where project management units were used and staffed by expatriate advisers.
- Central coordination of the sector agencies never worked.
- Locally proven technologies were often not available; project-specific technology components set up to remedy the situation usually failed.
- Monitoring and evaluation were often poor or nonexistent.

In the early 1990s, the World Bank abandoned both the ADP approach and lending for large-scale irrigation and rural credit projects. With a diminished portfolio of agricultural and rural development projects, Bank support for the poor shifted to the human development sector, seeking to create human instead of economic capital.

Nongovernmental Approaches (1970s Onward)

During the 1970s, under pressure from the failure of many state-led efforts, governments started to recognize the role of NGOs in supplementing government efforts in development activities that included relief and rehabilitation, family planning, care of mothers and children, income and employment generation, health, and sanitation. In some countries, donors viewed NGOs as less corrupt and more efficient in delivery than state agencies.

In India, the Ministry of Agriculture created the Freedom from Hunger Campaign to support voluntary organizations involved in rural development. This eventually became the Council for Advancement of People's Action and Rural Technology. Their success has encouraged many state governments to launch schemes to promote people's participation. Several centrally sponsored schemes have stipulated the development of community-based organizations to plan and implement programs (Hegde 2000). NGOs often act as contractors for government-financed programs. Ironically, in many countries such contracting has led to a new class—intermediary NGOs servicing preformulated schemes—and to an explosion of self-help groups with little connection to decentralized local or village government. The intermediary NGOs sometimes draw valuable staff away from government service and further diminish national capacity.

Most NGOs have aimed at CBD rather than community driven development (CDD): that is, they have opted for the community consultation and participation model rather than the full community empowerment model. They have tended to substitute their own staff for central staff and have had coordination problems within their own bureaucracies. Consequently, this approach has often failed to build the management and implementation capacities of communities or to reduce overhead costs. Nevertheless, by shifting from completely top-down systems to CBD, NGOs have played an important role in promoting and disseminating participatory appraisal and planning.

Participatory Appraisal and Planning (Late 1970s Onward)

In 1979 the Zacatecas State Development Plan in Mexico became the first part of the PIDER project to have a participatory methodology across an entire state. All communities participated in detailed surveys to discover and define their problems and priorities for projects. Direct consultations led to 4,029 investment proposals, with an additional 2,209 projects being proposed by government departments (Cernea 1983).

Rapid rural appraisals (RRAs) were developed in the 1970s and 1980s as a streamlined, effective method and toolset to provide a quick, high-quality understanding of community development realities without the expensive, time-consuming surveys used in Zacatecas. The RRA techniques were soon transformed into participatory rural appraisals (PRAs), and the responsibility for analyzing and planning shifted to the community level (see box 2.6).

Putting the Last First: The Case for Community Participation

Rural Development: Putting the Last First, a seminal book written by Robert Chambers in 1983, strengthened the case for community participation. Chambers showed how billions of dollars had been wasted in rural development programs without meeting community needs or reducing

---

BOX 2.6

Participatory Rural Appraisal

Participatory rural appraisal is a structured process that helps communities to understand their constraints and opportunities and to develop their own priorities (World Bank 2003d). Facilitators help communities to develop, present, and analyze information. Techniques involve (a) diagrams, maps, or quantification that are created and presented by rural people in a manner they readily understand; (b) walks across the village to gain a shared understanding of the environment; (c) household listings and wealth rankings; (d) reports on and analysis of the findings in discussions with different groups, such as men, women, youth, and marginalized groups; (e) ranking and scoring of constraints, options, opportunities, and priorities. Visualization of the results is a major element of these techniques.

Participatory appraisal and planning techniques have become essential tools all over the world. They have been applied widely to participatory planning at the level of local governments. For example, they are widely used in the pilot local development fund programs initiated by the United Nations Capital Development Fund in more than 15 developing countries (UNCDF 2005). More recently, learning and participatory monitoring and evaluation have been added, and the abbreviation PLA (participatory learning and action) is often used.

---

poverty. The problem was related not to project preparation, but to attitudes, power relations, and principal-agent issues. The top-down approach was doomed to fail because it was conceptually flawed.

Rural poverty and its roots were typically unseen or misperceived by outsiders. Researchers, scientists, administrators, and fieldworkers rarely appreciated the richness and validity of rural people's knowledge or the hidden nature of rural poverty. Despite some lip service to decentralization, most political leaders and bureaucracies resisted ceding power to the grassroots. Top-down, often patronizing approaches viewed communities as passive recipients to be led, not economic actors whose energies could be harnessed through empowerment. Such approaches viewed central experts as the most knowledgeable; in fact, only local people could know the precise nature of their key problems and possible solutions. Community participation and empowerment were essential to correct this. As Chambers wrote, "Communities should be viewed not as the last actors in the development process but [as] the first."

Many NGOs, universities, and donor agencies started putting these ideas into practice. By the late 1980s, the term *participatory rural appraisal* had emerged. The PRA repertoire includes several of the RRA techniques, and the difference between the two approaches lies not in any of the techniques, but in the emphasis that PRA places on participation. The approach has been described as "both an attitude and a methodology" (Joseph 1991: 132), as facilitators need to learn to pass the baton and have those in the community take the lead. Robert Chambers (1993) defined this approach—the *new professionalism*—as follows: "The central thrusts of the [new] paradigm . . . are decentralization and empowerment. Decentralization means that resources and discretion are devolved, turning back the inward and upward flows of resources and people. Empowerment means that people, especially poorer people, are enabled to take more control over their lives and secure a better livelihood with ownership and control of productive assets as one key element. Decentralization and empowerment enable local people to exploit the diverse complexities of their own condition and to adapt to rapid change."

Other Influences

The adoption of PRA methods and the new professional paradigm became especially widespread in NGOs. Another key contribution was made by the Ford Foundation, especially David Korten in South Asia, who pioneered the development of powerful strategies for transforming public bureaucracies into responsive support systems dedicated to strengthening community control and management of land, water, and forestry resources. Other donors and governments also realized that a paradigm shift was in order. This set the scene for shifting CBD toward CDD in the 1990s. These and many other professionals and experiences influenced the World Bank, a latecomer to this arena.

LCDD and the World Bank since 1990: A Shift away from Top-Down Approaches

By the 1990s, *public choice theory* had gained wide intellectual acceptance and showed that a strong centralized state could be predatory rather than benevolent. Economic failure and rural neglect in many countries were attributed to excessive centralization and top-down approaches. The collapse of the Soviet Union strengthened the disillusionment with command systems, and, in much of Latin America, democracies replaced military autocracies. These trends provided the political and economic impetus for decentralization, which gradually became fashionable. Some countries saw decentralization as a means of dismantling command economies, others as a tool for poverty reduction, and still others as a path to grassroots empowerment (Aiyar 1995a, 1995b).

After the debt crisis of 1982, the main focus of the World Bank shifted from poverty reduction to stabilization and structural adjustment programs via macroeconomic and sector policy reforms. However, by the end of the 1980s, the adjustment programs were yielding many unintended consequences: the stern economic discipline had imposed significant losses and suffering on the poor.

The *World Development Report 1990* returned poverty reduction to center stage among the World Bank's priorities (World Bank 1990). The new strategy rested on a dual approach of accelerated growth complemented by targeted programs for those bypassed by growth. At about this time, the area development approach to reaching the poor was abandoned because of its disappointing results). Past experience had shown the limitations of centralized sector-specific or ADPs in reducing poverty. Consequently, at a time when the World Bank most needed an acceptable and scalable model for targeting the poor, it did not have one. However, also at this time, two new factors emerged;

- The insights of Robert Chambers and other practitioners had proven the need for and practicality of involving communities and other stakeholders.
- The debt crisis itself prioritized new approaches for quick disbursal of emergency social fund programs that were targeted at poor communities.

Thus the global development agenda moved toward CBD with elements of community consultation and participation. Simultaneously, many countries moved toward decentralization and the creation or advancement of local governments.

What follows in this chapter is the story of how the Bank learned on the job to engage in programs that target the poor and to define progressively, in a step-by-step way, poverty reduction targeting, empowerment, accountability, and local governance.

The World Bank progressively incorporated these approaches in its programs, as visionary staff recognized the need to listen to beneficiaries and tailor programs to their needs (Cernea 1985; Salmen 1987). Gradually, the two ends of the continuum became clearer: CBD (where the community is consulted and involved, to varying degrees, by program managers) and CDD (where the community is the fully engaged and empowered program manager).[1]

Stakeholder Participation and Deconcentration in Sectoral Programs

Although it had been used with some success in scattered sectoral projects from the 1970s onward, community participation evolved to a new level in the 1990s (see box 2.7). A sectoral approach created opportunities to focus community participation, build capacity, and assess the impact of participation under diverse circumstances in a tangible, outcome-oriented way.

BOX 2.7

Examples of Sector Programs with Community Participation

Water resources sector. By 1995, Deepa Narayan (1995: 1, 2) was able to analyze a sample of 121 completed water supply projects with participatory mechanisms in 49 countries. The degree of participation varied widely, from user committees to direct community construction and supervision of contractors. Of the 121 projects, only 21 percent received a high rating for participation. Multiple regression analysis showed substantial benefits for participatory projects after controlling for 18 other variables. Effective participation did not occur when sectoral agencies retained control over implementation.

Urban development sector. The Kampung Improvement Program in Indonesia was an example of a government-initiated, community-based urban improvement program starting in the 1970s. Kampungs are unplanned, underserviced shanties and slums in many Indonesian cities. This program consulted beneficiary communities, who contributed part of the improvement costs. The program upgraded some 7,700 hectares of kampungs with 3 million people. Roads, footpaths, drainage canals, water supply, sanitation, solid waste disposal, schools, and health clinics were built. (For an example of the program in the city of Surabaya, see http://base.d-p-h.info/en/fiches/premierdph/fiche-premierdph-2104.html.)

Natural resource management sector. Several donors gave forestry loans to Nepal between 1971 and 1989. The World Bank supported the Second Forestry Project (1983–92) in the Terai region. The emphasis was on government plantations, which had a mortality rate of more than 80 percent for trees. No control or rights were given to communities;

(continued)

BOX 2.7

Examples of Sector Programs with Community Participation (*continued*)

timber in this region was so valuable that the Forest Department sought to control all resources. When the Bank supported the Hill Community Forestry Project (1989–99) in the degraded mid-hills, complete rights over forest produce went to anyone who used the forest, including local villagers and nomads. Implementation completion reports estimated the economic rate of return at 12 percent for the earlier project and 18 percent for the one with community control and a corresponding decrease in deforestation in the mid-hills of 0.2 percent a year, compared with a high of 1.3 percent for the overall area (Aiyar 2004).

Nutrition sector. The Tamil Nadu Integrated Nutrition Program in India (1980–90) targeted pregnant and lactating women as well as children under three and their mothers. Those found underweight were given additional nutrition through 9,000 community nutrition centers set up in the state. A little more than 40 percent of project funds went to upgrade personnel at local health facilities for the nutrition centers; appointees were selected in consultation with communities. They had to be local, educated residents, and preference was given to poor women with healthy children. The project reduced severe malnutrition by one-third to half in children ages 6–24 months and by half in children ages 6–60 months. In the next phase, the program was combined with the state's Noonday Meal Program for schoolchildren and later with the Integrated Child Development Services Program.

Breaking out of the Sectors: Social Funds and AGETIP Projects

While sectoral programs with community participation recorded some successes, this was a slow, incomplete route to rural empowerment. Most sector bureaucracies resisted such changes. A sector-by-sector approach was also too slow to deal with the adverse employment and welfare consequences of the economic reforms and adjustment programs of the 1980s. Therefore, many World Bank staff looked for better ways either to reach communities directly with a broad menu of interventions or to assist municipalities with broad programs that sector agencies were unable to deliver. The program models discussed in the rest of this chapter are directly associated with Bank initiatives, starting with social funds and AGETIP (Agence d'Exécution des Travaux d'Intérêt Public or the Agency for Public Works Management and Employment) projects, which emerged from these efforts.

Social Funds. Social funds began as emergency programs aimed at getting funds quickly to communities in need, especially poor communities bypassed in earlier programs in countries with a weak state apparatus. The funds were multisectoral and gave communities the opportunity to specify their subproject priorities. This was the start of several new experiments in community-based development using the community consultation and community participation models (see figure 2.1).

The first social fund was launched for Bolivia in 1987 and succeeded well in reaching poor communities. Social funds were soon devised for countries across all continents, and, from fiscal 1987 through fiscal 2007, $5.3 billion was committed for 142 operations. The IEG evaluation of social funds in 2005 looked at the period from fiscal 1987 to fiscal 2000 and at the results available for the 98 social funds in 58 countries with a total of $3.5 billion. The evaluation found that 96 percent of closed social funds had satisfactory outcomes, against 71 percent for all Bank projects. Social funds worked especially well in postconflict situations (such as Cambodia and Nicaragua).

IEG rated institutional development as substantial in 65 percent of projects (much better than the average of 36 percent for all Bank projects). Social funds demonstrated that they could help to build the capacity of local governments, communities, and NGOs. Their effectiveness was attributed, in part, to their autonomy from line ministries. However, IEG rated sustainability as *likely* for only 43 percent of projects, against 51 percent for all Bank projects. Maintenance responsibilities and obligations were often not clearly specified; neither was ownership after project completion. Furthermore, social funds depended on donor stamina and reliability, which cannot be assumed.

Figure 2.1. Evolution of Social Fund Objectives and Activities, 1987 to Present

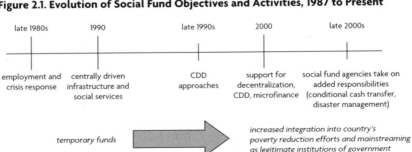

Source: de Silva and Sum 2008.

Communities participated widely in discussions on subprojects, yet community priorities were not always met. The top community-defined problem was addressed for only 27 percent of respondents in surveys in Jamaica, 34 percent in Malawi, and 22 percent in Zambia. Over time, social funds, such as the Malawi Social Action Fund (MASAF), moved from community consultation to community participation models, and, today, they mostly use the community empowerment model. They also discovered the value of having community projects coordinated and supervised by local development committees associated with local governments. The evolution of social funds parallels the evolution of empowerment, and the funds are often good examples of the LCDD approach discussed later in this chapter.

The AGETIP Approach. Starting with Senegal in 1990, many Francophone African countries created a multisectoral approach to resolving urban municipal problems called AGETIP. Local governments planned public works, such as water supply and sewage systems, roads, and markets, and then delegated the implementation and project management to AGETIPs. These agencies employed consultants and contractors to execute projects, thus creating local capacity for construction. This approach avoided cumbersome government procurement procedures and was generally efficient and timely in completing subprojects since staff were paid market-based salaries. They were effective in completing projects, but they were also dependent on donor financing and not financially sustainable; because AGETIPs were not subject to competitive bidding, they were often accused of corruption.

Although communities had only superficial involvement, AGETIP projects helped to build local government and private sector capacity. Social funds did the same, but with much more community participation. Meanwhile, decentralization became a growing institutional shift in many developing countries, and this influenced the agenda of donors. The agendas of AGETIPs, social funds, and local governments overlapped and began to converge. The Bank was learning that setting up all of these separate agencies and bypassing local governments did not work well in the long term.

Fostering Genuine Involvement: Social Development in the World Bank

According to the Task Force on Social Development of 1995 (see Davis 2004), "People are the ends and the means of development, and the impact

of development on people and their societies is the measure of its success."
In parallel, the Bank was learning about participation. In 1991, a World
Bank group led by David Beckmann and Aubrey Williams reviewed the
Bank's experiences with participatory approaches and prepared a report
(World Bank 1994). Lewis T. Preston, World Bank president (1991–95),
included a note urging, "Systematic client consultation and stakeholder
involvement, particularly the poor, should become a part of the [World
Bank's] approach to developing successful policies and projects."

The group's report identified several impediments to promoting participatory approaches in the Bank's institutional make-up and practices and
suggested remedial measures. Among the institutional impediments were
the Bank's own procurement guidelines, lack of participatory approaches
within the upstream work of the Bank, including economic and sector
work, and a lack of borrower-government efforts to promote a more
enabling environment (World Bank 1994). This resulted in the creation of
the social development perspective at the World Bank and the Social Development Network that has been responsible for advancing it.

To change mind-sets and practices, the Social Development Network
issued the *World Bank Participation Sourcebook* in 1996 (World Bank
1996). Intended primarily for Bank task managers, the sourcebook drew
on the experience of Bank staff who had pioneered efforts to adapt participatory approaches to their work, mainly, but not exclusively, in development projects. The sourcebook covered several areas:

- Reflections on what participatory development is and what it means
  to use participatory processes
- Shared experiences (examples, presented in the first person, of how
  Bank staff used or helped others to use participatory approaches in
  Bank-supported operations)
- Practice pointers in participatory planning and decision making
- Practice pointers in enabling the poor to participate
- Methods and tools.

The sourcebook team established a steady continuum of progress toward
greater, genuine community participation and empowerment.

Decentralization Approaches to Local Development

In addition, and also in parallel, the Bank was learning about decentralization. In the early 1990s, the World Bank conducted several decentralization studies, including a global study of 14 countries and five provinces

in large countries (Aiyar 1995a, 1995b, 1996; McLean and others 1998; Piriou-Sall 2007).[2] It looked at several sectors and the powers of local institutions over service delivery.[3]

The studies showed that the best performers are more decentralized than the low performers. Jiangxi Province, in strongly decentralized China, topped the list, followed by other decentralizers—Colombia, the Philippines, and Poland (see figure 2.2). The lowest scorers had little or no decentralization: Imo State in Nigeria, Côte d'Ivoire, Burkina Faso, and Senegal.

Those studies and others encouraged the Bank in the 1990s to support decentralization projects in several countries, such as Brazil, Colombia, and Mexico. From a study of Colombia's decentralization, Fiszbein (1997) concluded that competition for political office resulted in accountable and innovative local governments that improved service delivery and reduced corruption. Faguet (1997) showed how decentralization improved accountability and reduced poverty in Bolivia. However, Tendler (1999) showed that some Latin American social funds were supply driven in fair measure and were not fully participatory.

Figure 2.2. Index of Sector Decentralization in 19 Countries, 1990s

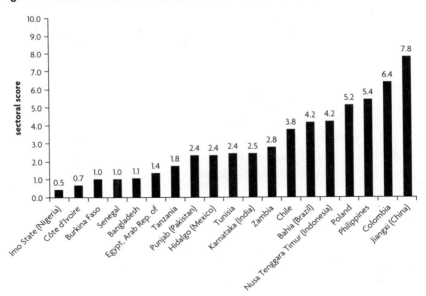

Sources: Aiyar 1995a, 1995c; McLean and others 1998; Piriou-Sall 2007.

Crook and Manor (1998) showed that decentralization yielded good results only if there was

- Strong government ownership
- Appropriate legal, administrative, and fiscal arrangements
- Local elections
- Sufficient and reliable funding
- Freedom for communities to choose projects.

World Bank (2000b) concluded that decentralization had great promise, but only when it was tailored to reach the poor and backed by adequate finance and autonomy.

Community Driven Development in a Decentralization Context

Community participation and decentralization were often introduced in a country independently of one another, even though they clearly needed to be integrated in order to improve sustainability and maximize synergies. In the 1990s, major projects in Mexico, Brazil, and Indonesia adopted this approach (see boxes 2.8–2.10). This integrated approach empowered both local communities *and* governments with untied funds and new powers. These programs successfully pioneered the addition of *local* to *community driven development*. In all three countries, local governments already existed, and the programs sought to include them as actors from the beginning. In other countries, either local governments did not exist and programs were aimed at communities or local governments were included as community programs grew. Applying the subsidiarity principle—bringing government decision making to the lowest possible level because that is the level where the most knowledge is available about local circumstances—is a powerful argument for either starting to decentralize and bring in local governments for local empowerment programs or aiming to empower both the local communities and local governments.

Toward the Synthesis

During James Wolfensohn's presidency of the World Bank (1995–2005), Wolfensohn reaffirmed Lewis Preston's vision that *poverty reduction would be the institution's overriding policy*. This meant a new focus on rural development and on initiatives to overcome the problems that had hobbled IRDPs since the 1970s. A review of Bank lending experience again verified that community participation, community empowerment,

---

BOX 2.8

The Integrated Approach in Mexico

Between 1990 and 2002, Mexico implemented two decentralized regional development projects (DRD I and II) supported by the Bank. These provided municipal funds and addressed the weaknesses of earlier projects through several innovations. Rural municipalities obtained untied funds based on a formula targeting poor municipalities. These funds were only for investment projects identified and executed by communities within the municipality; they could not be used for recurrent municipal expenditures.

Project priorities were set by communities, which contributed 20–40 percent of project costs. Municipal development councils headed by elected mayors selected the projects to be financed and supervised the communities' execution and fund management. The program invented simplified procurement and disbursement procedures that are now used in CDD projects throughout the world.

Municipal fund activities used a learning-by-doing approach across all levels of operation—federal, state, municipal, and community. As a consequence of the new approaches to procurement and disbursement, the project executed 17,000 community projects in the first nine months after money was transferred to municipalities, demonstrating massive scalability for the first time. Half a million projects were implemented between 1990 and 2002. These were in line with community priorities, generally of good quality, and at a cost 30 percent less than the cost of similar projects of state agencies.

BOX 2.9

The Integrated Approach in Brazil

Before 1993, the Bank supported IRDPs in the poor northeast region of Brazil. They were implemented by state governments (without involving local governments) and drifted from crisis to crisis. But they contained one successful component that provided matching grants to rural communities, along the lines of the Mexican municipal funds. This became the basis of one of the largest and most successful CDD programs in the World Bank, disbursing $1.43 billion and benefiting 37,592 communities with 2,540,733 families over 12 years. Funds actually reaching the communities have risen from 45 percent to more than 90 percent, while costs per subproject have fallen 30 percent (Barboza and

(continued)

BOX 2.9

The Integrated Approach in Brazil (*continued*)

others 2006). As in Mexico, the program is well targeted at poor municipalities and poor communities, although it does not generally reach the poorest of the poor.

A recent rigorous impact evaluation shows that the program has achieved significant improvements in water supply and electrification, reduced infant mortality and the incidence of several communicable diseases, and sustainably increased social capital at the community level. The assets of community members also grew, but the increase was not statistically significant. At this time, the final evaluation is forthcoming (World Bank 2009).

Brazil implemented CDD cautiously, and the number of projects implemented under the program was much smaller than in Mexico. It provided fewer fiscal resources to the municipal level and did not mainstream the approach into the intergovernmental fiscal system. The challenge for Brazil and the World Bank is finding a way to institutionalize the basic approach fully at all levels.

BOX 2.10

The Integrated Approach in Indonesia

The Kecamatan Development Program (KDP) of Indonesia started in 1998, a time of tremendous political upheaval and financial crisis (see also box 3.5). With a focus on Indonesia's poorest rural communities, KDP aimed to improve local governance and reduce poverty and corruption by channeling funds directly to local government and community institutions. In its third phase, ending in 2009, the program provides block grants of approximately Rp 500 million to Rp 1.5 billion (approximately $50,000 to $150,000) to subdistricts (kecamatan) depending on population size. Villagers allocate those resources for their self-defined development needs and priorities.

Under the program, communities discuss their priorities from an open menu (meaning they can address any problem, only subject to a small negative list) and then propose projects to the kecamatan level. This sparks competition between communities for the limited funds. The kecamatans then choose the best projects, ask the communities to contribute part of the funds, and provide matching grants. KDP emphasizes transparency and information sharing throughout the project cycle. Decision making and financial management are open and occur at the local level. There are no complex rules that would make communities overly dependent on NGOs or consultants.

and decentralization yielded better outcomes than top-down centralized approaches. The next step was to synthesize the many strands of community empowerment and local development and to create a new development paradigm (Helling, Serrano, and Warren 2005).

Wolfensohn, in his many country visits, had seen firsthand what community participation could achieve.[4] But he was bewildered by the wide variety of community-based approaches used. In 1999 a cross-sectoral Working Group on Community Driven Development brought together all practitioners of community empowerment and decentralization approaches to review the many programs and approaches applied in the World Bank. The group became the instrument for building consensus and integrating approaches.

The Africa Region's CDD working group articulated a new vision (World Bank 2000a),[5] which was, initially, not universally accepted because the opportunities for greater decentralization and for working with local governments as well as communities were less available in some regions of the world.

In order to track World Bank support, the Bank-wide CDD working group came up with clear definitions of different approaches to CDD and matched them to Bank lending data. CBD was defined as *community consultation and participation*, whereas CDD was defined as *community empowerment*, with community control over projects and resources. Efforts to reform the institutional environment, including decentralization and capacity building, were also tracked and categorized as CDD. From fiscal 2000 through fiscal 2008, the International Development Association (IDA) portfolio of CDD lending for activities financed totaled approximately $12 billion for 468 activities (see table 2.2). This was almost three-quarters of total World Bank/IDA lending toward CDD for this period, which was approximately $16.3 billion. Overall, between fiscal 2000 and fiscal 2008, a period of nine fiscal years, $16 billion was lent for 637 operations, or about 9 percent of total lending of the World Bank Group. For IDA lending, this percentage was higher, about 16 percent. The internal quality assurance process rated 97 percent of the CDD operations reviewed for fiscal 2007 as moderate to highly satisfactory through the design stage.

Guidance and Implementation. Along with defining how the Bank had been supporting CDD, a second major task for the World Bank's CDD working group was to develop guidance on how best to implement

Table 2.2. Progress of World Bank/IDA Support to CDD, 2000–08
US$ billions unless otherwise noted

Fiscal year	Total lending		CDD lending[a]		
	World Bank Group[b]	IDA	World Bank Group[b]	IDA	CDD as % of IDA lending
2000	15.3	4.4	1.0	0.6	14
2001	17.3	6.8	2.2	1.6	24
2002	19.5	8.1	1.8	1.1	14
2003	18.5	7.3	1.6	0.9	12
2004	20.1	9.0	2.0	1.9	21
2005	22.3	8.7	1.6	1.3	15
2006	23.6	9.5	1.8	1.1	12
2007	24.7	11.9	2.2	1.6	13
2008	24.7	11.2	2.1	1.9	17

Source: Authors' compilation.
a. Excluding enabling environment.
b. International Bank for Reconstruction and Development and International Development Association.

CDD. The working group laid down key design principles, listed in box 2.11.

Members of the CDD group developed implementation tools, which are accessible from the World Bank's Web site, with regard to economic, social, and gender issues, information and communications, monitoring and evaluation, targeting and selection, direct financing and contracting, institutional options, safeguards, and community mobilization and capacity building.

The group also assembled the existing experience of CDD in postconflict settings and in urban development (World Bank 2003a, 2004b). CDD was adapted and used for combating HIV/AIDS (human immunodeficiency virus/acquired immune deficiency syndrome) and for managing natural resources. The *World Bank Participation Sourcebook* (World Bank 2003d) provides a comprehensive overview of methods to enlist the participation of all stakeholders, from the community level to the local, municipal, and national levels. The chapters in this book also compile much of the group's experience and lessons learned.

The Development of Community-Based Disbursement and Procurement Mechanisms. The progressive shift from central sectoral programs to community consultation and participation and then to community empowerment would not have been possible using the classical disbursement and procurement mechanisms of the World Bank and other donors. Bank staff,[6] Mexican counterparts, and specialists of the Latin America and the

BOX 2.11

World Bank Guidance on Key Design Principles for CDD

- Establish an enabling environment through relevant institutional and policy reform
- Make investment responsive to informed demand, by providing knowledge about options and requiring community contributions to investment and recurrent costs
- Build participatory mechanisms for community control and stakeholder involvement by providing community groups with knowledge, control, and authority over decisions and resources
- Ensure social and gender inclusion
- Invest in capacity building for community-based organizations
- Facilitate community access to information
- Develop simple rules and strong incentives, supported by monitoring and evaluation
- Maintain flexibility in the design of arrangements
- Design for scaling up
- Invest in an exit strategy that establishes project sustainability, including permanent institutional and financing arrangements (that are fiscally affordable).
  See Dongier and others (2003: 321).

Caribbean Region of the World Bank pioneered a series of new systems that balanced disbursement efficiency and practical accountability for community programs (see box 2.12).

Proper application of these rules implies a radical and progressive shift away from upward accountability to program authorities and toward horizontal and downward accountability to community members.

Upward accountability remains, but in sharply simplified form. At first, the concept of transferring funds directly to communities met with widespread resistance from all quarters: Bank staff, governments, and NGOs. It took more than 10 years for the innovative procedures from Mexico to gain full acceptance. With increased emphasis on anticorruption, this practice is again coming under attack and meeting with great resistance, even though independent studies show that the level of corruption in these community-level programs is very low. The direct transfer of funds to communities is based on trusting communities that have the social capital to check corruption through existing measures of horizontal social

Six Innovations in Direct Financing of Community Subprojects

De Silva (2002) highlights innovations in six areas:

1. *Legal ownership of the funds.* Funds transferred to communities are considered matching grants and therefore become *the property of the communities* rather than the executing agency of the program or the World Bank. As with credit from a bank, the spending of these funds is the privilege and responsibility of the community.
2. *Replacement of detailed accounting for the funds by a contract with the community.* The contract for a small community project specifies what will be done with the money and how it will be used as well as the technical details of the subproject to be financed. It is a four- to six-page contract between the executing agency, the community, and sometimes a facilitator or technical agent. At the end of implementation, the community signs a *certificate of completion or handover* of the project certifying that the project has been executed properly and the funds accounted for. Rather than having to produce receipts for each individual expense, this certificate of completion serves as the "receipt" for accounting purposes of the executing agency and the World Bank. The implementing agency or outside auditors can then verify that a road or a classroom has been constructed and is in operation.
3. *Direct transfer of the matching grants into the accounts of the community.* This is usually done in tranches, the first of which follows signing of the contract and the second or third of which depends on demonstrating progress in execution of the project.
4. *Purchase of technical support by the community.* The community can select any capable supplier and use a portion of the matching grant, usually on the order of 8 percent, to pay for the technical services.
5. *Local shopping for both goods and services.* The traditional distinction between services and goods in the community procurement rules is surpressed. Local shopping is the main procurement system of communities for small contracts and quantities of supplies. Local shopping rules mean that the community obtains offers from three suppliers and its finance or management committee chooses from these three offers. Competitive bidding is still required if the community enters into larger contracts where this method is justified.
6. *Transparency at the community level.* Communities elect finance committees that are in charge of day-to-day spending. Checks must be signed by at least two members of the committee. The committee has to present all accounts to the general assembly, which often also elects a committee to audit accounts, purchases, stocks, and their uses.

accountability. Furthermore, many downward and horizontal account-ability mechanisms can be introduced to strengthen such practices.[7] The learning is ongoing.

Implementing the Vision and the Tools of CDD. Integrating sector-specific approaches, social funds, AGETIP projects, and CDD programs into a coherent framework was slow and complicated:

• Widely different approaches in projects in different sectors confused country teams and borrowers.
• Other development partners also experimented with CBD and CDD, but rarely coordinated their efforts with Bank-supported projects.
• The distinction between CBD and CDD was often not clear, as they lie on a continuum and there was not always progress from the CBD end of the continuum to the CDD end.
• Governments were often not willing to devolve resources (especially untied resources), significant powers, or responsibilities to communi-ties or local governments.
• Many projects were driven by sector specialists and did not tackle the underlying issues of the institutional, social, and economic policy environment.

As amply illustrated in a recent Independent Evaluation Group (IEG) review, this reduced the impact and sustainability of many projects (World Bank 2005).[8] According to the review, during 1989–2003, the share of Bank projects with CBD or CDD components grew from 2 to 25 percent, with a progressive shift from CBD to CDD. The outcome ratings of CBD or CDD projects were better, but sustainability ratings were worse than for other projects.

Sustainability ratings improved over time, possibly because of the shift from CBD to CDD. Interventions initially failed to provide either the con-sistent, long-term support or the institutional changes needed for sustain-ability. The projects fared better in meeting quantitative goals (such as construction of infrastructure) than qualitative goals (such as enhance-ment of capacity). The best projects built on indigenously matured par-ticipatory efforts. Projects where the Bank provided long-term support to communities beyond the length of a single subproject also fared better in capacity enhancement. By design, these programs were not always aimed at reaching the poorest, and therefore not all members of the communities benefited (see table 2.3).

Table 2.3. Overview of Strengths and Weaknesses of CBD/CDD Projects

Strengths	Weaknesses
Outcome ratings are generally better for CBD/CDD than for non-CBD/CDD projects. Much more success has been achieved in CBD/CDD projects on quantitative goals, such as the construction of infrastructure, than on qualitative goals, such as capacity enhancement or quality of training.	The Bank's project monitoring and evaluation systems do not allow systematic assessment of the capacity-enhancing impact of CBD/CDD interventions. It is often assumed that meeting the quantitative goals will automatically fulfill the qualitative goal—for example, holding a certain number of training courses is expected to enhance capacity.
Borrower officials believe that a participatory approach can contribute to poverty alleviation.	Borrower officials do not necessarily believe that community control over decisions and resources in a subproject is the best means of engaging communities.
CBD/CDD projects help to lower the cost to government of delivering infrastructure.	Communities bear an increased share of the burden for service delivery infrastructure.
CBD/CDD projects increase access for remote communities to service delivery infrastructure such as schools, health centers, and the like.	The poorest may not always benefit from CBD/CDD projects.
Capacity enhancement effort in a CBD/CDD project has been more successful when a Bank project supports indigenously matured efforts or provides sustained, long-term support to communities beyond a Bank subproject cycle.	The individual subproject cycle is too short to sustain community capacity where it is weak or does not exist.
Sustainability ratings have improved over time.	Infrastructure and services have been difficult to sustain beyond the Bank presence because of a lack of resources from the government and communities to ensure their operation and maintenance.
CBD/CDD projects have enhanced government capacity to implement participatory interventions.	Few governments appear to have adopted the CBD/CDD approach in their own development programs.
Adaptation of Bank policies and decentralization to field offices has enhanced Bank capacity to implement CBD/CDD projects.	More changes are needed to improve fiduciary and safeguard compliance in CBD/CDD projects.

Source: World Bank 2005.
Note: While the table combines CBD and CDD without differentiating which approach has which weaknesses, the IEG conclusions bring up important issues for all proponents and practitioners of LCDD. It is a *positive criticism*, a tool to keep LCDD on the right course.

The empirical evidence and analysis of CDD gained by the World Bank is growing, including a set of recent case studies covering programs in Africa, East Asia, South Asia, and Central America (see appendix A to this chapter). Rigorous impact evaluation studies, although still too few, have also been conducted, addressing the lack of *hard evidence* on the impact of projects on poverty reduction and community capacity.

In March 2005, the Bank's Quality Assurance Group carried out a portfolio review based on a sampling of 90 operations for quality at entry and quality of supervision. The results highlighted that social fund and CDD operations are a strong cohort (better satisfactory outcomes and quality of supervision than Bank-wide averages), despite being designed and implemented under challenging country circumstances (Garg 2006):

- *Development effectiveness:* better ratings on development effectiveness as compared with Bank-wide ratings
- *Outcomes:* lower percentage of unsatisfactory outcomes compared with Bank-wide ratings
- *Sustainability:* more likely to be sustainable than the Bank-wide averages
- *Institutional development:* substantially stronger institutional development compared with Bank-wide averages
- *Portfolio management:* better ability to recognize risks than Bank-wide projects, as reflected in high realism and pro-activity ratings
- *Quality at entry:* on par with Bank-wide projects for strategic relevance and approach, technical, financial, and economic aspects, poverty and social aspects, fiduciary aspects, policy and institutional aspects, and risk assessment
- *Quality of supervision:* higher overall ratings than Bank-wide projects on performance
- *Monitoring and evaluation:* improvements still needed in monitoring and evaluation and in assessments of social risks.

There are obvious islands of success amid oceans of indifference or sectoral self-interest. Projects have enhanced the capacity of government institutions to implement participatory interventions, but few governments have adopted the approach more widely in their development program. A key recommendation of the IEG report is that CBD/CDD projects still need to be better integrated into an overall country assistance strategy (a policy issue that is covered in chapter 5). Until 2003, the project portfolio fell well short of implementing the design principles presented in box 2.11. The Bank experience clearly demonstrates that, where the design principles are fundamental to a program, it succeeds; where they are compromised, it founders.

With the exception of a few projects and programs, the most glaring shortcomings are in the areas of institutional reform, full empowerment of communities, monitoring and evaluation, failure to scale up, and development of exit strategies. Much has been achieved to spread participatory approaches, but the ideal design principles for CDD are still not fully implemented.

One problem identified by the IEG report is that community support programs can undercut local government development. Ironically, projects channeling funds directly to communities through parallel structures *can* lead to a neglect of local government capacity building, thus jeopardizing the long-term sustainability of such projects. While CDD may be catalyzed by external factors, it can be nourished or starved by local, sectoral, or national dynamics. The linchpin of the process—the integration of those dynamics—is a work in progress. IEG points out that such integration is not yet being done systematically, and this has to be addressed.

The LCDD Consensus: A Proactive Agenda for the Future

Starting around 2004, a consensus has been built through the comparison of LCDD experiences around the world. Despite the diverse roles that LCDD plays in development programs, locations, and circumstances, a consistency in outcomes points to the integrity of the design principles and the role of linkage. The concept of linkage was the outcome of analysis by Louis Helling, Rodrigo Serrano, and David Warren (Helling, Serrano, and Warren 2005; see figure 2.3).

Figure 2.3. Linked Approaches

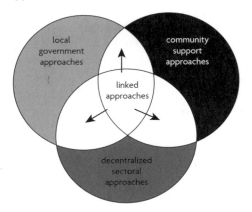

Source: Helling, Serrano, and Warren 2005.

The concept begins with the observation that *community empowerment* does not take place in a vacuum: it is affected by *local government development* and *sectoral programs of national governments*. The three alternative approaches to local development emphasize many of the same principles: empowerment of the poor and other marginalized groups; responsiveness to beneficiary demand; autonomy of local institutions associated with greater downward accountability (from the center to the community level); and enhancement of local capacities. However, the approaches go about things differently:

- *Sectoral approaches,* defined through functional specialization—the services they provide—tend to be better at mobilizing technical capacity but less responsive to local demand and conditions and cross-sectoral considerations.
- *Local government approaches,* organized through the institutions of territorial governance, commonly ensure clear formal autonomy and accountability of local decision makers but are often more politicized and less effective in managing service provision.
- *Direct community support approaches* are organized around social groups that, traditionally or voluntarily, make collective decisions. Because they enhance empowerment and responsiveness to local priorities and conditions, their entry point through community structure and processes often complicates coordination with public sector organizations, on the one hand, and local government institutions, on the other.

Each approach has generated a distinct body of theory and practice. Many countries use all three approaches. This can lead to confusion, unproductive competition, and duplication. But it also can lead to synergy that builds on the strengths of each approach. Bringing these approaches together in the right way is *linkage*.

The International Conference on Local Development held in Washington in June 2004 discussed the emerging consensus on local development and found that CDD (that is, the community alone) is not an adequate description. The conclusion from the conference was that the appropriate term is *local and community driven development*. This new framework links all three organizational structures and sees them as co-producers of local development. The framework promises to improve coordination, synergy, efficiency, and responsiveness in local development processes, and it becomes the foundation for the next step: scaling up.

The World Bank's LCDD Challenge: Facilitating the Framework, Continuing the Integration

Linking the approaches can capitalize on the comparative advantages of each, complementing its contributions with methods drawn from other approaches. However, significant synergies and tensions can arise when linking these approaches. The World Bank's challenge is to facilitate a local development framework that draws on concepts underpinning the decentralized and participatory methods employed by practitioners of the three approaches, while achieving the buy-in of all participants and honoring the different context in each country.

Buy-in must occur at two levels:

- The *national government level,* so that policies, regulations, and commitments (the co-productive efforts) by government and sector management are made to synchronize with LCDD efforts
- The *local government or community level,* so that buy-in is explicitly developed to diagnose and move forward all LCDD approaches simultaneously to a proper co-production model.

To assist this process, the World Bank sponsored the production of two toolkits—*Community Driven Development: Toolkit for National Stocktaking and Review* (Heemskerk and Baltissen 2005) and *Scaling Up LCDD: A Step-by-Step Guide* (Binswanger and Nguyen 2005)—which are the focus of chapter 5.

Sectoral experience on how to organize, manage, and deliver services effectively at the local level is linked to the systems of decentralized governance associated with local governments: multisectoral planning, resource mobilization and management, and mechanisms of democratic accountability. Such public sector approaches are complemented by methods drawn from community support approaches for (a) promoting more consequential and inclusive empowerment and (b) strengthening grassroots participation and social capital for governance, collective action, and infrastructure and service co-production. Context-appropriate institutional arrangements and capacities that build on the contributions of each of these approaches can improve governance, public services, and the welfare of households and communities.

A local development framework does not eliminate the tensions and challenges associated with linking alternative approaches or the operational problems associated with institutional reform, capacity building, governance, and service delivery at the local level. The framework's promise is more modest: to provide a more coherent and consistent way to analyze and understand the challenges that confront policy makers and program managers in supporting local development and to assist in organizing knowledge to help them to formulate and coordinate sectoral, local government, and community-focused initiatives to meet those challenges.

Julie Van Domelen (2008), in her synthesis of the LCDD portfolio reviews carried out in each region, shows that within the World Bank only some progress has been made in the integration of this framework: in different regions of the world, there are marked differences in approaches, sectoral integration is still far from the norm, and scaling up is rarely considered.[9]

Grounding in Countries' Strategies and the Future

While it is important to move toward linking the different approaches into an LCDD approach, this cannot be done without a deep understanding of the fundamental dynamics of community, local government, and sector approaches in each country. In fact, governments themselves need to have local and community empowerment as a goal in their overarching strategic documents, such as poverty reduction strategies or similar long-range plans for the future. For instance, Indonesia has announced that by 2009, the KDP approach will be fully scaled up to the whole country and will serve as the national poverty reduction program. As both the donor community and governments mature in their thinking toward such long-range goals, this process allows the programmatic approach toward LCDD to emerge. Documents such as the country assistance strategy used in the World Bank or joint donor-country strategies should also reflect these programmatic LCDD approaches (see box 2.13). Nigeria's

---

BOX 2.13

CBD/CDD: An Important Part of the Bank Strategy

An IEG review of 62 country assistance strategies found that CBD/CDD operations are an important part of the Bank's strategy in more than 74 percent of countries. Over time, Bank lending has placed increasing emphasis on greater community participation in decision making and resource allocation.

multidonor Country Partnership Strategy (2005–09) did have such an emphasis (World Bank and DFID 2005).

Countries approaching national coverage of LCDD programs or attempting to put in place the conditions necessary for such national programs to emerge should consider such programs not as "projects" but as national programs being financed through the budget. Such a programmatic approach would allow them to tackle broader LCDD initiatives such as institutional reforms to improve accountability and efficiency at the local level. However, the programmatic approach toward LCDD progresses at different paces in different countries and different country teams within the Bank. Having national programs allows governments to move toward financing such programs as sector-wide approaches (SWAps) in which donor and government funds are pooled. Bank and other donor funding to such SWAps can be treated as investment funding but also as budget support funding for the country. As of 2008, the Bank had financed LCDD programs through budget support (development policy loans, DPLs, as the lending instruments) in only six countries. Such national programs with budget support would also impose one approach across different donor agencies and end practices such as the use of different manuals, different levels of per diem payments, and so forth.

The Morocco case is illuminating. In May 2005, the king announced the National Initiative for Human Development, a $1.2 billion program over five years (2006–10) based on LCDD principles (a new concept in a highly centralized country accustomed to top-down, single-sector programs). The World Bank support to this SWAp is only $100 million; other donors and realigned sectoral programs in the country are supposed to contribute the bulk of the financing, although the government would have preferred this to be financed by the World Bank as a DPL. Morocco is using its own procurement and financial management systems. The program has had remarkable success because of the high-level leadership, with 3 million beneficiaries and the financing of 12,000 community projects. These projects were selected within a six-month period of time because everyone was on board (Fruman 2008)!

Similarly, the successor to KDP in Indonesia, a national poverty reduction program called PNPM (Program Nasional Pemberdayaan Masyarakat), launched in 2007, is financed by the government with the support of a donor trust fund in which all development partners participate.

Similar SWAps have been established in Senegal for the Participatory Local Development Program and in Vietnam for the Support to Ethnic Minority Communities in Remote and Mountainous Areas.[10]

While the past 60 years have seen remarkable progress toward more decentralized development, with local government and community actors having more say and power over resources, more can be done, both by governments at all levels and by development partners. The synthesis of the regional stocktaking efforts presented many positive results in LCDD project performance as well as areas for improvement (Van Domelen 2008; see appendix B to this chapter and box 2.14).

The next obvious question for practitioners, development planners, and the donor community is, What next? Since 2000, the understanding and consensus of how to empower communities and local governments for their own development have grown enormously, and the tools for analyzing social, economic, and institutional situations in a country are well developed, as are the guidelines and tools for designing complex LCDD programs. The volume of Bank resources for LCDD programs has increased sharply. However, generalizing LCDD into institutions and fiscal systems, transferring real power, resources, and accountability to local and community levels, and developing the implementation capacities for

---

BOX 2.14

Trends in Project Performance

According to Van Domelen (2008), CDD projects generally

1. Reach poor communities
2. Involve communities in decision making and implementation
3. Demonstrate a fair amount of participation (with the exception of the Middle East and North Africa, where participation and community contracting experience are very limited)
4. Deliver infrastructure in a cost-effective, high-quality manner
5. Increase incomes of participant communities (although better data are needed)
6. Improve the dynamics of how communities interact with local government and create social capital.

The evidence on sustainable operations and maintenance (O&M) is mixed. There is no evidence that better links to local government result in better maintenance, as O&M is routinely underfunded and of little interest to local government and sector ministries. Community ownership is not enough incentive by itself to create a successful maintenance regime within communities.

such programs are not well advanced in most countries. This agenda will require consistent long-term leadership, effective policies, and analytical and financial support from the World Bank and other donors.

LCDD programs fit well with the governance agenda, because well-designed programs strengthen both transparency and accountability at the local level and in communities as well as the accountability of service providers to their clients. LCDD approaches have been widely used in postconflict settings to assist with rebuilding community infrastructure, restoring services, and building social capital. Broadening the agenda to LCDD, as has been done in Sierra Leone, is a natural way of strengthening weak postconflict states from below and building a local cadre of politicians who can exert pressure on behalf of their local constituencies; it also complements other activities to rebuild the central state. Chapter 4 presents significant examples of LCDD in Africa and how projects can be effectively adapted to complex national circumstances.

At the same time, Bank-driven and -financed LCDD programs cannot be a panacea for poverty reduction if they remain islands of success or cannot be sustained. The devil is in the details, and only superior analytical work and high-quality program design, implementation, and monitoring and evaluation can prevent a drift of such programs toward capture by local, rather than national, elites. These programs are the underpinnings, at the community level, required for scaling up. While the underpinnings are the local context, coordinated efforts are needed at the national and institutional levels, too. Such quality can only be sustained if national leadership is fully behind the approach, if other donors assist with design, implementation, and finance, and if governments' own fiscal resources, both national and local, become the main source of LCDD programs. Improved macroeconomic management, debt reduction, and growth in many countries are helpful developments in this regard.

With all of these factors in place, a solid foundation can be prepared for sustainable local development that can be scaled up, achieving LCDD that multiplies community empowerment on the national and global scale.

Annex 2A. Some Recent Impact Studies

Senegal: Arcand and Bassole (2007), in an independent impact evaluation, study the impact of the CDD project in Senegal, Programme National d'Infrastructures Rurales (PNIR), on access to basic services, household expenditures, and child anthropometrics. Using a multidimensional panel data set, the authors find a significant improvement in access to clean water and health services and a decrease in child malnutrition. The income-generating agricultural infrastructure projects and enhanced primary education opportunities significantly increased household expenditures per capita, while hydraulic and health projects did not. Village chiefs and subregional politics were shown to play an important role in determining which villages had access to the project.

Philippines: Labonne and Chase (2007) examine ex ante preferences of elected village leaders and community members in the Philippines concerning which project proposals received funding. The findings show that the degree of involvement of households in communal activities influenced the likelihood that their preferences would be represented in the village proposals and that, within a municipality, resources flowed to the poorest and more politically active villages. Controlling for poverty, the more unequal villages were more likely to receive funding because the elected officials were more likely to override community preferences and to influence the intervillage competition such that resources flowed to their villages.

Labonne and Chase (2008) compare communities in the Philippines that received grants with control communities, finding that participation in village assemblies, the frequency with which local officials meet with residents, and trust toward strangers increased as a result of the project. However, group membership and participation in informal collective action activities declined. The declines may have been due to time constraints or to improvements in the efficiency of formal forms of social capital, which meant that households had to rely less on informal forms of social capital.

Brazil: Barboza and others (2006) use a quasi-experimental design and also draw from earlier evaluation studies of a rural poverty reduction program in northeastern Brazil (Amazonas and others 2006). They find that the program significantly increased access to water and electricity services and that some 60 percent of new connections came through this program, on average costing 30 percent less than similar public programs. Households that gained this access would not otherwise have done so. This increased access had significant effects on infant mortality and morbidity. The program was well targeted (75 percent earning under $1 a day) and improved targeting over time, now focusing specifically on women, indigenous people, and *quilombola* (descendents of runaway slaves). Satisfaction with the program was high (more than 90 percent), and infrastructure was sustainable (more than 80 percent of projects were still running after three to five years). However, productive projects need outside markets to become sustainable, and data on income and physical capital accumulation are not conclusive or statistically significant.

The program had a positive and sustainable impact on social capital, transforming it into new social and political spheres. Transparent mechanisms minimized political interference and elite capture. Social capital generated in communities and municipalities continued to increase even after project implementation. The program's wide-ranging and effective mechanisms to channel funds have been copied in other states and other programs, but could be used much more widely if federal, state, and municipal budgets would also adopt the LCDD mechanisms.

Malawi: JIMAT Consult, ITAD LMT, and O and M Associates (2008) find a marked reduction in the prevalence of underweight children under five in the MASAF villages in Malawi and a statistically significant difference in improved access to water sources and sanitation in the villages that had road projects, with no explanation for any causal link.

Indonesia: McLaughlin, Satu, and Hoppe (2007) seek to determine whether KDP influenced local governance practices and community empowerment in Indonesia. They compare communities in KDP and controls as well as different development programs within the same communities. Much depended on the location and local culture, as Indonesia is very large and diverse, but the role of the village head is crucial. Much more could be done to train the village head and villagers in more long-term development planning, so that the majority vote would not rule against smaller, more marginal groups, but rather would allow their proposals to be considered later. On the whole, compared with other development programs in the villages, KDP projects were well implemented, more accountable, and less corrupt; KDP projects answered the needs of the people, although women were still mostly marginalized. Projects decreased poverty overall.

Voss (2008) uses household panel data in KDP 2 and control kecamatan and finds that, compared with the control areas, in KDP 2 areas, the gains in real per capita consumption were 11 points higher in poor households, the proportion of households moving out of poverty in poor kecamatan was 9.2 percent higher, vulnerable households near the poverty line were less at risk of falling into poverty, the proportion of household heads gaining access to outpatient care was 11.5 percent higher, and unemployment was 1.5 percent lower. Moreover, households in less poor kecamatan saw either no benefit or negative benefit, and KDP 2 had no impact on school enrollment rates.

Annex 2B. Regional CDD Stocktaking Reviews

To date, regional community driven development (CDD) stocktaking reviews have been conducted in six regions: Africa (World Bank 2008c), East Asia (World Bank 2007c), Europe and Central Asia (World Bank 2007d), Latin America and the Caribbean (World Bank 2007a), Middle East and North Africa (World Bank 2007f), and South Asia (World Bank 2006). This appendix summarizes the findings for all but Africa, which is covered in detail in chapter 4 of this volume.

In *East Asia and the Pacific*, there is evidence of the following:

1. CDD operations in East Asia successfully target poor areas, but do less well at reaching poor groups within communities. Most East Asian CDD operations support public infrastructure that benefits all members of the community.
2. CDD operations involve communities in decision making and implementation much more broadly than traditional approaches. This particularly benefits disadvantaged groups and women.
3. CDD operations deliver cost-effective, quality infrastructure, mostly because local labor and materials are used and local contractors charge within agreed budgets.
4. Operations and maintenance of CDD operations are better integrated in local government systems, but CDD operations often fall short of the standards established for CDD operations (functioning infrastructure, active maintenance groups, active maintenance plans). No data are available to compare against traditional investment operations in the World Bank.

5. CDD approaches raise the incomes of participant communities. Economic internal rates of return are 52.7 percent for Indonesia's KDP and 20 percent for the Philippines' Kapitbisig Laban sa Kahirapan (Linking Arms against Poverty) operation. In Indonesia, impact evaluation also showed that the longer a village participates, the higher its rate of return.
6. CDD approaches change the dynamics of how communities interact with local governments. Increased citizen participation changes local institutions by increasing the flow of information.

In *Europe and Central Asia*, the study reviewed whether social funds are still a useful tool for the region, constructing a typology by purpose of the social fund: infrastructure management, local governance, emergency, or social inclusion. It concluded that, for the future, two objectives are still relevant: improving local governance and infrastructure provision and addressing vulnerability and social inclusion, as long as these objectives fit into the country context. The review concluded that social funds can help countries in the region to achieve their transition and accession toward becoming part of the European Union.

In *Latin America and the Caribbean*, the review encompassed large mature CDD programs (Brazil, Mexico) as well as smaller and more recent ones (Haiti), yielding the following lessons:

1. It is important to have a clear understanding of the sociopolitical context in order to promote collective decision making and inclusion of vulnerable groups.
2. Beware of preconceived notions of the overused term "community." Most communities are heterogeneous and often have internal tensions. Experience indicates that resolving conflicts at the community level is more effective than creating new or parallel structures.
3. Participation is not a panacea. There is no one-size-fits-all template for conducting an effective participatory process. Rather, there are a tested set of principles, such as promoting access to information, enabling the disenfranchised and vulnerable members of a community to gain a voice in community affairs, maintaining an open dialogue with elected and spontaneous leaders, and strengthening the capacity of community organizations to engage in participatory processes at the local and regional level.
4. Greater attention must be given to integrating local community initiatives into a national policy framework that promotes a

decentralized approach to meeting community preferences. Policy integration is an important prerequisite for the sustainability of any CDD program.

In the *Middle East and North Africa*, the CDD approach to strengthening local institutions would fit very well with the region's acute need for institutional enhancement and job creation. However, the CDD portfolio of the region is small and lacks clear business lines; it is increasingly focused on youth, gender, and employment creation as well as on social accountability and local governance. Qualitatively, the participatory framework and local level of CDD operations appear insufficient. CDD programs are mostly concentrated in Morocco and Republic of Yemen, where the scaling up is going well, because the operations are large and long term, with national-level programs.

For *South Asia*, a review undertaken in India offers the following preliminary lessons:

1. Quality of leadership is crucial, with commitments to long-term listening to the poor and placing the poor at the center so that they can take progressive control of decision making.
2. Livelihood activities are best managed by organizations of the poor themselves rather than *panchyati raj* institutions, which, as representative institutions, are best at managing public goods. If the panchyat institutions are asked to manage livelihoods, the risk of elite capture is great.
3. Projects must be focused on the poor, with targeting and livelihoods development at their core.
4. Sequencing is very important: facilitation in the form of capacity building, training, and group building should be given high priority and precede or go hand in hand with large-scale financing.
5. Empowerment is a lengthy process: decades of commitment are necessary.
6. Markets and marketing must be an important part of livelihoods development, and these linkages should be facilitated.
7. Seed capital should be provided as a grant. This approach worked extremely well in Andhra Pradesh, with the gradual hardening of terms and maturities as the grant was lent farther down the chain.
8. Interest rates should be reasonable so that commercial lenders and microfinance institutions can move in and establish linkages with creditworthy groups.

9. Cross-learning should be encouraged through peer visits.
10. It is important to keep the scheme simple and resist adding in infrastructure development when the goal is livelihoods improvement.

Notes

1. The term *community driven development* was coined by Deepa Narayan and Hans Binswanger in 1995 to denote the integration of participatory approaches with decentralization and direct community empowerment. The term *community development* was rejected because it was identified too closely with the failed community development program in India or the community development programs in the United States (which mostly used the *service delivery* or *intermediary* models for working with communities rather than the *empowerment* model).
2. The study was headed by Hans Binswanger, and the team at various times included Keith McLean, Graham Kerr, Andrew Parker, Suzanne Piriou-Sall, Johan van Zyl, and Melissa Williams. See Aiyar (1995c); Aiyar, McLean, and Piriou-Sall (1996); Aiyar and Piriou-Sall (1996); Piriou-Sall (1996).
3. The study constructed a decentralization index ranging from 0 to 10 based on data collected from World Bank sector specialists who had worked intensively in the respective countries, states, and provinces. It was based on answers to the following questions: (1) Where is the smallest management unit for rural sector service delivery physically located? (2) Which level of government is responsible for the conditions of service of civil servants in the smallest management unit? (3) How important are elected bodies in service delivery, policy formulation, and funding of each sector? (4) Which level of government pays the salaries of staff in the smallest administrative unit? (5) What proportion of sector expenditures of the smallest administrative unit is derived from the budgets of local governments? (6) What proportion of sector expenditures of the smallest administrative unit is derived from user charges, in-kind contributions, and other beneficiary cost-recovery schemes? (7) Who determines the budget of the smallest sector management unit?
4. Mr. Wolfensohn's decision to call for the formation of this working group resulted from a meeting between him and the following staff from the Africa Region: Daniel Benor (senior adviser), Callisto Madavo (vice president), Jean-Louis Sarbib (vice president), and Hans Binswanger (director of the Environmentally Socially Sustainable Development sector). The group presented Mr. Wolfensohn with an initial version of the Africa CDD vision and proposed that it become a major operational thrust in the Africa Region.
5. The members of this working group were Hans Binswanger, Jacomina de Regt, Jan Weetjens, Laura Frigenti, Brian Levy, Willem Zijp, Helene

Grandvoinnet, and Catherine D. Farvacque-Vitkovic. The statement was written by Swaminathan Aiyar. In 2001, the Africa Region followed with a *Sourcebook for Community Driven Development for Africa* (World Bank 2001). Shortly thereafter, a similarly comprehensive vision was presented in Dongier and others (2003: ch. 9). The Africa Vision states (p. 9), "The five main dimensions of CDD are empowering communities; empowering local governments; realigning the center (decentralization); improving account-ability; and building capacity (learning-by-doing).

6. Jean-Claude Sallier, a World Bank CDD team member and engineer.

7. For more about accountability, see http://www.capacity.org/en/publications/ world_bank_sourcebook_on_social_accountability_strengthening_the_ demand_side_of_governance_and_service_delivery.

8. IEG could not apply the four-way classification developed by the CDD group, because prior to 2000 the classification did not exist and thus could not be applied to projects prior to then.

9. A recent notable exception is a community-level program in the sanitation sector in Ethiopia, called the Learning-by-Doing for At-Scale Hygiene and Sanitation. The initiative uses local leaders and health extension workers to catalyze collective changes in hygiene and sanitation behavior. These efforts are integrated into actions at multiple levels, across multiple sectors, and using multiple channels of communication, such as face-to-face meetings, community events, religious institutions, school curricula, mass media, and advocacy. In all, 10 districts have been "ignited" for total behavior change in hygiene and sanitation, with estimates that some 600,000 people have been reached by the program. The vision is to reach the whole regional pop-ulation of 20 million and to achieve a complete change in behavior regard-ing hygiene and sanitation by 2012. The At-Scale Initiative is documented in a district resource book for community-led behavior change in hygiene and sanitation, and practical training manuals have been developed for use in Amhara and for adoption and replication in other regions of the country. The Amhara Regional Health Bureau (Addis Ababa, Ethiopia) is supported by the World Bank Water and Sanitation Program and the U.S. Agency for International Development–funded Hygiene Improvement Project. More information is available at www.worldbank.org/wsp.

10. More information can be downloaded at http://web.worldbank.org/WBSITE/ EXTERNAL/COUNTRIES/EASTASIAPACIFICEXT/VIETNAMEXTN/0,, contentMDK:21705492~menuPK:3949587~pagePK:1497618~piPK:217854 ~theSitePK:387565,00.html.

CHAPTER 3

Scaling Up Community Driven Development: Underpinnings and Program Design Implications

*Hans P. Binswanger-Mkhize, Swaminathan S. Anklesaria Aiyar,
Jacomina P. de Regt, Deborah Davis, and Tuu-Van Nguyen*

Local and community driven development (LCDD) is not a project; it is
an approach that aims to *empower* both communities and local governments with the resources and authority to use them flexibly, thus taking
control of their development. *Empowerment* means the expansion of
assets and capabilities of poor people to participate in, negotiate with, and
hold accountable institutions that affect their lives. It means giving people
access to voice and information, greater social inclusion and participation,
greater accountability, and organizational strength. LCDD aims to harness
social capital through empowerment and to increase social capital through
scaling up.

Well-functioning small-scale LCDD successes are a prerequisite for scaling up, but how scaling up proceeds from there depends on the context of
the intended location and country. While each situation is unique, the core
philosophical underpinnings (the values, elements, overall processes, and
goals) of LCDD are, essentially, universal. However, the goal is to adapt
LCDD to and within the local context without undermining the universal
philosophical underpinnings.

The complexities of scaling up, even for experienced practitioners, are
multidimensional, daunting, challenging, and fascinating. Many readers
will come to this chapter with experience at a nongovernmental organization (NGO), a donor agency, or a public sector organization; some may

have successfully scaled up a specific sectoral intervention (see box 3.1). The tendency is to stick to the approach or toolkit used effectively in a previous effort, instead of exploring a fuller set of options that may be more appropriate. This chapter provides examples and approaches that help the reader to envision a much broader set of options in any given circumstance. In chapter 5, the design process is developed further in a step-by-step approach that addresses the requirements for scaling up LCDD at both the national and local levels.

After reviewing the LCDD features that need to be scaled up, the chapter reviews lessons from global experience and discusses political commitment and well-designed decentralization, followed by how to overcome the adverse institutional environments when the conducive conditions are lacking. It then reviews ways to reduce economic and fiscal costs of the program, how to overcome lack of political will, problems of working with many co-producers in a single program, unfavorable social conditions, and poorly designed decentralization and addresses the common challenges of adapting to the local context, development and testing of manuals and toolkits, sequencing, and pre-program diagnostics and design. Lessons are brought together in the concluding section.

BOX 3.1

Leveraging Success without Reinventing the Wheel

Many development organizations are addressing empowerment and scaling up as a way to leverage successful projects. The process of preparing Poverty Reduction Strategy Papers (PRSPs) in many highly indebted poor countries aims to strengthen communities and reduce poverty within a framework of good macroeconomic and sectoral policies. In 1999 the World Bank introduced PRSPs as the framework through which low-income countries receive concessional lending from it and the International Monetary Fund. A PRSP describes a country's "macroeconomic, structural, and social policies and programs to promote growth and reduce poverty, as well as associated external financing needs." It is prepared by national governments, in consultation with civil society groups and external donors (see millenniuminstitute.net). The following are among the important documents advancing empowerment and scaling up: World Bank (2002a, 2002b, 2004e); de Silva (2002); Hancock (2003).

Islands of Success amid Oceans of Travail:
Why Is Scaling up LCDD So Difficult?

We all are familiar with islands of success in community driven development (CDD). These empower a few villages, urban neighborhoods, or producer organizations in a country. How wonderful if they could be scaled up to cover all communities in a province or nation! But there are preciously few scaling-up successes. Five key problems explain why.

First, the institutional setting may be hostile to LCDD. The central government, or vested interests in the status quo, may fear the political consequences of empowering communities, local governments, and even NGOs. The laws and regulations of national governments and donors may not allow money to be disbursed directly to communities. The central government may not authorize local governments or communities to provide their own services (education, primary health) or to levy user fees or taxes. Locally generated revenues may be centralized, rather than left for local use. The social environment may deprive women and minorities of voice. Ethnic, religious, and class conflict may undermine real participation by all (World Bank 2000a).

Second, total costs, fiscal costs, or both may be too high. Some LCDD islands of success are inherently not replicable because, like many boutiques, they are too costly for the masses. Total costs per community member may be high because the project relies on expensive technology, inputs, staff, and advisers. Mobilizing and training community members is less expensive: communities and local governments do not have to travel over long distances or charge management fees. Costly boutiques have excessive overhead costs and poor transfer efficiency: too low a proportion of program costs relate to actual work at the community level. Even if costs per unit are reasonable, national scaling up may lead to excessive fiscal cost because the approach fails to mobilize sufficient co-financing from communities and local governments. Donors that support boutiques may not be willing to support national scaling up.

Third, difficulties arising from co-production may not be mastered. Scaling up LCDD implies the co-production of investments, outputs, and services by many stakeholders at many levels: community workers, local government officials, NGOs, the private sector, technical specialists at all levels, administrators, program managers, bureaucrats, politicians, and aid agency personnel. Three problems afflict co-production:

- *Incompatible incentives of co-producers.* Co-producers lacking compatible incentives will either produce low-priority outputs that bring them rewards (such as reports or workshops) or obstruct the program. Different levels of government are co-producers, but they may act as rivals rather than as collaborators. Public sector workers, such as teachers or extension agents, may not gain from the program. Technical specialists may lack incentives to produce the specific inputs required. Communities may lack incentives to co-finance the program. The central politician, bureaucrat, or sector manager may lose budgets and staff by devolving power. Where political resistance is strong, scaling up should not be attempted, as the risks are too high. Where political conditions are conducive, a field-tested rollout of logistics in a pilot—maybe in a single district—can reveal all of these incentive issues and inform the design of an incentive-compatible operational manual.

- *Differences in values and experience of co-producers.* Community workers and local NGOs often do not understand how higher levels or sector specialists operate or can contribute. Sector specialists often underestimate the latent capacity of the community. Higher-level administrators are used to strict controls and cannot understand how social capital can enable communities to hold their leaders accountable. Until program participants learn to adhere to a common set of values and approaches, scaling up will remain difficult.
- *No clear assignment of functions to different co-producers.* Scaling up requires the precise assignment of a long list of functions to specific actors at different levels and clear instructions on what to do, how to do it, and what tools to use (including forms, questionnaires, technical approaches, and training materials). The problem is compounded in multisectoral programs, where all sectors need to follow common rules and procedures, while using sectoral best practices and norms. A field-tested operational manual is often missing or incomplete, that is, it does not contain submanuals, tools, critical functions, or levels. Operational manuals are too often designed in an office, not in the field.

Fourth, adaptation to the local context may be missing. What looks like best practice in some contexts may fail in others. Pilots may succeed because of special circumstances relating to geography or the sociopolitical context. Scaling up should be adapted to each context. Ideally, process monitoring should provide continuous feedback that enables the scaling-up process to be constantly improved.

Fifth, scaling-up logistics may be lacking. Scaling up can cover tens of thousands of widely dispersed communities, so logistics must be designed to train tens of thousands of program participants and disburse resources to tens of thousands of communities, an issue that does not arise in successful pilots. Scaling-up logistics must control costs; otherwise fleets of jeeps, enormous travel allowances, and expensive training equipment can make national scaling up fiscally impossible. Not enough scaling-up programs design and field-test logistics carefully and cost-effectively.

Box 3.2 provides an example in which many of these challenges were successfully overcome in the context of fast food. In LCDD programs, scaling up is rarely so well designed. When programs are approved without resolving these five issues, the newly appointed program managers bear the consequences. They rarely understand fully the need for a

---

BOX 3.2

Lessons from the Teriyaki Burger

Scaling up LCDD is very different from scaling up a fast food franchise. Yet fast food chains and LCDD planners have a similar goal: scaling up to cover entire countries quickly. To date, McDonald's has been more successful at this than have most governments of developing countries.

The franchise model used by fast food chains uses sophisticated action research into production and organizational methods to maximize efficiency and consumer satisfaction. It carefully defines the products, assigns functions, develops the logistics, and puts these into operational and training manuals. Once the design is finalized, its execution is facilitated by simple, transparent rules that can be replicated easily by franchisees and unskilled workers. The logistics of mass replication are worked out in detail; costs are also reduced by training local employees instead of using expensive supervisors.

McDonald's is often accused of banal uniformity in its menu, but in different countries, McDonald's studies local tastes and adapts its menu accordingly. In Japan it sells a teriyaki burger. In India Hindus do not eat beef, so McDonald's experimented with lamb burgers, but pilots showed that chicken burgers and potato burgers would attract the most clients. The menu was adapted accordingly before scaling up.

LCDD also needs the same adaptive management style: thoughtful design and adaptations to different contexts (the teriyaki burger approach rather than Big Mac uniformity). It also needs simple rules and procedures to facilitate mass replication. There are huge differences between McDonald's and LCDD. Although McDonald's does not aim to empower its local branches with resources and authority to use them, LCDD can learn something from the franchise model.

phase of detailed design and testing. Untested programs quickly run into bottlenecks, which often are associated with unresolved issues related to the flow of funds or procurement. Typically, the donor sends out a supervision mission to fix the bottleneck rather than operating at a more strategic level. Once the problem is resolved, the program cranks up, but quickly runs into more bottlenecks; more missions come to the rescue, and the vicious cycle continues. *Fatigue sets in, lack of capacity is blamed for the failure to reach cruising speed, and willingness to pay for scaling up fades away.*

This chapter and the rest of the book present practical ways to avoid the failure syndrome and to overcome these five classes of problems. These pages advocate embracing that complexity and offer the following aids:

- *A framework* to underpin program design for scaling up and the steps for completing phases of the process. As presented in box 1.3 and detailed in box 1.4 in chapter 1, the steps to scaling up comprise seven categories of activities, each with various tasks, challenges, and outcomes.
- *A systematic compilation of cases* that suggests design options for scaling up, creating a global base of knowledge that makes cross-regional and cross-sectoral learning possible and enables programs to anticipate and avoid problems and to build improvements into program design.
- *Practical ways of overcoming the five key of problems* typically encountered, including (a) a systematic approach to check program design for completeness, (b) an approach to design and field-test the logistics, and (c) a diagnostic toolkit for new or existing programs.

Having presented the difficulties involved, the chapter addresses what can be achieved by scaling up.

Which Core Features of LCDD Do We Seek to Scale Up?

We seek to scale up the five pillars and four core features of the LCDD approach, as shown in box 3.3. These pillars and core features were first articulated in 2000 by the Africa Region of the World Bank in the Vision for CDD (World Bank 2000a).

Real participation and genuine linkage concern the collaborative decision-making process. These features have a theoretical underpinning

---

BOX 3.3

Pillars and Core Expected Outcomes of LCDD to Be Scaled Up

Core expected outcomes of LCDD

- Real participation and linkage by all stakeholders
- Improved accountability
- Technical soundness
- Sustainability.

Pillars for success in an integrated LCDD approach

1. *Empower communities.* Empowering communities involves assigning functions, duties, and the corresponding authority to them, providing an institutional framework in which they elect their officials and make decisions, and assigning revenues and other fiscal resources to them.

2. *Empower local governments.* Empowering local governments involves assigning functions, duties, and the corresponding authority to them, providing an institutional framework in which they elect their officials and make decisions, and assigning revenues and other fiscal resources to them.

3. *Realign the center.* Realigning the center involves distributing functions and powers from central agencies and sectors to communities and local government, a process that involves both deconcentration and devolution; it also involves shifting the mix of activities performed by central institutions so that the local community is more involved in direct service delivery and the central government is more involved in policy setting and support functions.

4. *Improve accountability.* Accountability systems need to be aligned so that accountability is to citizens and the users of services (not just upward accountability from citizens and service providers to the center), adapted to the new context, and improved all around.

5. *Build capacity.* Capacity building is needed not only for community and local development participants, but also for the other co-producers, the technical sectors, the private sector, and nongovernmental organizations.

---

in bargaining models of public choice. The models provide powerful reasons to foster real participation and empowerment in communities or governments—at local, district, and national levels—where collective choices are made regarding development plans and expenditures. The reasons for this bargaining are well known and have been especially well developed by Gary Becker, the Nobel Laureate in Economics, who proved that bargaining can benefit all stakeholders.

According to Becker, bargaining will lead to decisions and outcomes that will benefit all stakeholders or pressure groups if all the following conditions hold (Pareto/welfare-improving choices):

- All pressure groups have correct and equal information about the consequences of each option for each stakeholder group.
- All pressure groups have equal lobbying power or technology.
- All decisions and associated expenditures have to be evaluated against a single aggregate budget constraint.
- Redistribution is costly.
- The usual properties of mathematical convexity ensure that there is a unique solution for the bargaining problem.

The logic is simple. If all groups are fully informed and have equal bargaining power, no group can secure unanimity on proposals that benefit it alone. So the bargaining process will drive participants toward proposals that benefit all stakeholders. The common budget constraint means that every approved proposal has to be financed from the common budget rather than from other sources; therefore, some other proposals will have to be dropped. Consequently, the common budget constraint connects the decisions to each other and ensures that decisions improve welfare for all groups.

Of course, these are ideal conditions, not the reality encountered on the ground. Traditionally, dominant groups have not given equal voice to others, but good legal provisions and features of the program design can increase equality of voice, help to bring about equal access to information, and create a common budget constraint. Program design features can also promote single budget constraints, such as via a program design in which funds are fungible between uses. Where inequality persists, interventions targeted at disempowered groups (such as the very poor or historically oppressed groups) can be appropriate supplements. The step-by-step guide in chapter 5 describes how the bargaining and decision-making process is introduced and how it works in practice.

The key principles that lead to welfare-enhancing social decisions also enhance sustainability. In a setting in which all stakeholders are well informed about the financial, social, and environmental consequences of the development options discussed and make their decision against a unified budget constraint, the choices will also ensure environmental, financial, social, and fiscal sustainability. Real participation enhances efficiency and sustainability. Environmental and social safeguards are needed when these ideal conditions for social choice are not met—for example, when information is lacking or poorly distributed or when key stakeholders are excluded from the decision-making process.

Keeping these principles in mind, we now examine and draw lessons from global examples of successful scaling up.

Lessons from Global Experience

Map 3.1 and the information in tables 3.1 and 3.2 show the geographic and programmatic diversity of projects that make up some of the global LCDD experience from which a body of analytical and empirical work on LCDD has taken form (see, for example, Hancock 2003; Narayan 2002). The map provides a quick overview of significant LCDD projects, and the tables provide a snapshot of their starting point and their scale-up impact.

In 2002–03, researchers from the Africa Region conducted a global study on the scaling up of CDD projects.[1] An early version of this chapter provided the analytical framework for the study. Case studies were conducted of scaled-up programs in six countries—Benin, India, Indonesia, Mexico, Uganda, and Zambia—representing four regions (Africa, East Asia, Latin America, and South Asia), constituting the first comparative survey of CDD projects. The findings of the field research were discussed at a two-day international review workshop in June 2003. Combined with earlier insights of the researchers, the findings of the study yielded a reliable set of lessons and recommendations:

- *Strong political commitment to decentralization and empowerment is essential,* often facilitated by local champions who need immediate support from donors.
- *Successful scale-ups put money in the hands of communities* to harness their latent capacity through learning-by-doing. This is supplemented by relevant capacity building.
- *Pilot projects are useful for field-testing in different conditions.* They reveal problems and suggest adaptations before scaling up.
- *Successful scale-ups have sound technical design.* They create context-specific procedures, incorporated in manuals and training courses for

Map 3.1. The LCDD Global Experience

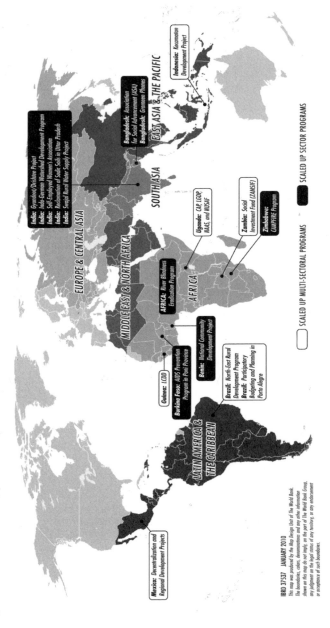

India: Gyandow/Drishtee Project
India: Indo-German Watershed Development Program
India: Self-Employed Women's Association
India: Reclamation of Sodic Soils in Uttar Pradesh
India: Swajal Rural Water Supply Project

Bangladesh: Association for Social Advancement (ASA)
Bangladesh: Grameen Phones

EUROPE & CENTRAL ASIA

SOUTH ASIA

EAST ASIA & THE PACIFIC

Indonesia: Kecamatan Development Project

MIDDLE EAST & NORTH AFRICA

AFRICA

AFRICA: River Blindness Eradication Program

Uganda: CAP, LGDP, NAAS, and NUSAF

Zambia: Social Investment Fund (ZAMSIF)

Zimbabwe: CAMPFIRE Program

Guinea: LCDD

Burkina Faso: AIDS Prevention Program in Poni Province

Benin: National Community Development Project

Brazil: North-East Rural Development Program
Brazil: Participatory Budgeting and Planning in Porto Alegre

LATIN AMERICA & THE CARIBBEAN

Mexico: Decentralization and Regional Development Projects

SCALED UP MULTI-SECTORAL PROGRAMS   SCALED UP SECTOR PROGRAMS

IBRD 37537   JANUARY 2010
This map was produced by the Map Design Unit of The World Bank.
The boundaries, colors, denominations and any other information
shown on this map do not imply, on the part of The World Bank Group,
any judgment on the legal status of any territory, or any endorsement
or acceptance of such boundaries.

Source: Authors' compilation.
Note: CAMPFIRE, Communal Areas Management Program for Indigenous Resources; CAP, Community Action Plan; DRD, decentralized regional development; KDP, Kecamatan Development Project; LGDP, Local Government Development Program; NAAS, National Agricultural Advisory Services; NUSAF, Northern Uganda Social Action Fund.

Table 3.1. Examples of Scaling Up Sector-Specific Programs

Country, program, and year started	Description	Coverage
Africa, various countries: River Blindness Eradication Program, 1975	A program to eradicate disease-bearing black flies in West Africa that coordinated government efforts (spraying) with local community management of collecting, distributing, and administering medicine	11 countries, 40 million people; during 2001–07, scaled up to 19 other countries with 65 million people
Bangladesh: Association for Social Advancement, 1990s	A microcredit program and savings program for the poor that offers an alternative financial resource that is transparent and not exploitive	In 2002, 1,121 branches with 4,000 credit officers serving 1.68 million customers (mainly rural women); scaling up in other countries: Rep. of Yemen, Philippines, Nigeria
Bangladesh: Grameen Village Phones, 1997	A microcredit program developing capacity among poor local entrepreneurs (usually women), setting them up to provide affordable cell phone services to rural villages	In August 2008, 20 million customers; in 2006, 255,000 village phones in operation in 55,000 villages around Bangladesh. The program has been replicated in Uganda and Rwanda
Burkina Faso: AIDS Prevention, Program, 1999–2005	An AIDS education and prevention program developed with provincial and local government to train and empower local AIDS educators from villages and urban neighborhoods	Pilot program in Poni Province with 500 locations and 2,000 trained village specialists. In 2008, scaled up nationwide
India: Gyandoot/Drishtee Project, 2000	A project bringing Internet service kiosks to empower villagers by providing electronic access to government records and services and the ability to use the Web for marketing crops and products	In 2007, 1,500 kiosks in 12 states
India: Indo-German Watershed Development Program, 1980s	A project using participatory process for sustainable watershed management that started by working with *harmonious communities* to establish participatory capacity and watershed management	200,000 people; 146 watersheds; in 2008, active in 896 villages located throughout four Indian states.

(continued)

Table 3.1. Examples of Scaling Up Sector-Specific Programs *(continued)*

Country, program, and year started	Description	Coverage
India: Self-Employed Women's Association, 1972	Began as an NGO quasi trade union supporting the rights of self-employed women, but evolved to be a significant trade organization facilitating a broad range of services for members; represents the convergence of labor, women, and cooperative movements	In 2002, 212,000 members, 4,500 self-help groups, 101 cooperatives, 11 federations across India. In 2007, 1.2 million members
India: reclamation of sodic soils, Uttar Pradesh, 1993	A community-based program focusing on training and capacity building in participatory processes and extension services aimed at restoring and managing soil quality	Includes 45,600 people; 974 site committees; 69,000 hectares of improved land
India: Swajal, Rural Water Supply, Uttar Pradesh, 1996	A participatory approach to providing and managing rural water services based on the creation of village water and sanitation committees	Started with some 350 villages and was expanded to 3,900 villages. The Swajal approach is being applied in several states, including the Kerala Water Project.
Zimbabwe: CAMPFIRE, 1989	A model wildlife and resource conservation program that involves local communities	From two districts, in 1989, CAMPFIRE spread to 25 rural district councils, reuniting about 2 million people with traditions as well as earning them millions of dollars. The elephant population had doubled by 2006. The Global Environment Facility has adopted a similar approach in almost all of the programs dealing with communal management of biodiversity resources. Five neighboring countries have also adapted the CAMPFIRE approach.

Source: Authors' compilation.

Table 3.2. Examples of Scaled-Up Multisectoral Programs

Country, program, and year started	Description	Coverage
Benin, National Community Development Project, 1998	A national program designed to support Benin's transition to economic liberalization and democratization after the fall of the authoritarian regime in 1989. Seven initiatives addressed problems of essential services, employment, and local capacity building. NGOs, in most cases, controlled project funds and acted as technical and social facilitators. Elected broad-based village committees received training in leadership, monitoring and evaluation, organizing and conducting meetings, and financial record keeping	In 2004, adoption of a national CDD program
Brazil: participatory budgeting and planning in Porto Alegre, 1989	Empowerment of municipalities through participatory budget planning by citizens' associations across the city's regional groups	In Porto Alegre, covered 16 regions and districts; in 2000, scaled up to more than 100 municipalities in five states; in 2007, adopted by 140 municipalities in Brazil and some 200 cities worldwide
Brazil: Northeast Rural Development Program, 1980s	A program that has steadily expanded the participation of communities in project selection, funds management, and project supervision and also built local governance capacity	As of 2007, in 1,500 of 1,686 municipalities, reaching 11 million people
Guinea, Village Community Support Project, 1999	A program to build local government and community capacity in planning, funding and procurement, implementation of projects, and accountability	Supposed to be scaled up gradually to the whole country; a rural infrastructure project with local governments was in place as of 2008
Indonesia: KDP, 1998	Considered one of the best-practice examples, this has been a three-phase scale-up of community empowerment	10 million people in 20,000 villages; 2008 phase, 20 million to 30 million people
Mexico: Empowerment of municipalities and communities, 1970s	A long, evolving, and maturing regional development and decentralization project that emphasizes community participation, local government empowerment, and genuine community-based procurement and disbursement for needed projects and services	A completely mainstreamed program

(continued)

Table 3.2. Examples of Scaled-Up Multisectoral Programs (continued)

Country, program, and year started	Description	Coverage
Uganda: four projects, 1990s and 2000s	Four projects or programs designed to strengthen social capital and support the decentralization of institutions and financial systems mandated by the constitution and the Local Governments Act of 1997. CDD principles are part of the four projects	LCDP has become a dominant, national program, operating fully through budgetary support
CAP	A plan to improve community-level infrastructure, with a focus on education, water, and health	
LGDP, 1999	A program to develop the capacity of local governments for participatory planning, sustainable service provision, monitoring and evaluation, and documentation of lessons learned, as inputs for scaling up the program countrywide	
NAAS	A program to bring private sector assistance to farmers in the areas of productivity enhancement, soil conservation, entrepreneurship, financial management, marketing, and agro-processing, with local government providing oversight and quality control	
NUSAF, 2002	An autonomous unit created to respond flexibly to community demands in a variety of sectors, beyond the mandate of local governments, while aligning community needs with available support, and providing direct funding to community-level project committees in conflict-torn northern Uganda	
Zambia: ZAMSIF, 1990s	Originally a traditional social investment fund, this project transformed itself from a parallel institution that bypassed established structures in order to channel money directly to communities, to one that seeks to integrate community development into mainstream development planning. ZAMSIF has developed two separate funding mechanisms: a community investment fund (CIF) and a district investment fund (DIF), which aims to build the capacity of local governments to support CIF activities	Closed and supposedly fully integrated in a decentralization strategy

Source: Authors' compilation.

Note: KDP, Kecamatan Development Project; CAP, Community Action Plan; LGDP, Local Government Development Program; NAAS, National Agricultural Advisory Services; NUSAF, Northern Uganda Social Action Fund; ZAMSIF, Zambia Social Investment Fund; community investment fund (CIF); district investment fund (DIF).

stakeholders. These manuals and procedures are living documents that are constantly adapted in the light of new experiences and contexts.

- *Good systems for sharing and spreading knowledge help to inform different stakeholders* about precisely what their roles are and to create common values.
- *Incentives for different stakeholders should be tailored to their new roles.* Managerial incentives should reward the right processes and outcomes rather than rapid disbursement. Establishing the right processes can take time, but once they are well established, scaling up can be rapid.
- *Scaling up means more than physical scaling up (mass replication).* It also means social scaling up (making the process more inclusive) and conceptual scaling up (moving beyond participation to embedding empowerment in the entire development process).
- *Success depends on training tens of thousands of communities to execute and manage projects and accounts.* Good scaling-up logistics not only lower costs but also improve community ownership and hence sustainability. So does community co-financing.
- *Scaling up is a long-haul process.* It can take as long as 15 years.
- *Ease of replication is a key to rapid scaling up.* Rules and procedures must be designed carefully, yet be so simple and transparent that they can be replicated easily in tens of thousands of communities.

The following sections expand these lessons, first by emphasizing how important an enabling climate is and then by considering the five classes of remedies for the five problems identified earlier.

Conducive Conditions

Simply put, conditions conducive to LCDD include strong political commitment from the top and well-designed decentralization. This represents a government in active support of LCDD, and the outcome of these two conditions advances the other factors that make LCDD possible (see box 3.4).

Political Commitment

Strong political commitment alone can ensure that power actually shifts from the top to the bottom. In many countries, the impetus for change has

BOX 3.4

Steps for Scaling Up: Diagnostics

Diagnostic phase to ensure minimum conditions

- Assess the LCDD underpinnings in the nation
- Align with the national government, donors, and other partners
- Synchronize and transform policies, regulations, and laws with LCDD
- Have national leadership and coordination.

Preprogram development at the national level

- Define the program
- Select pilot districts
- Appoint a scaling-up team.

Preprogram development at the local level

- Select districts
- Assess the LCDD underpinnings in the local context
- Achieve local buy-in
- Set up communications.

come from the very top, but in other cases it has come from state governors or chief ministers. For example,

- In Brazil, the necessary political commitment came from state governors.
- In the province of Poni, Burkina Faso, it came from the provincial governor.
- In Mexico, it came initially from the federal government, with the success of the municipal funds program, but also from state governors.
- In Malawi, the political commitment came from the minister of agriculture and his management team.
- In Indonesia, it came from the president.
- In Morocco, it came from the king.
- In India, the constitution was amended in 1993 to make local governments mandatory. Yet in practice local governments were empowered only when the state government was committed to the concept, as in Karnataka, Kerala, Madhya Pradesh, and West Bengal.

However, political commitment is not created in a vacuum; it needs an enabling climate. Every country needs a lively and empowered civil society, accountability to citizens through elections, free media, and strong NGOs. Major institutional change is required in some countries to create and nourish such institutions.

In Indonesia, a change in political leadership led to a model of LCDD (see box 3.5). The Indonesia case is a best-practice example of how the LCDD pillars can serve as a framework for channeling resources rapidly to communities, while minimizing the risk that the resources will be misappropriated. What made the change possible was a new political era with a commitment to reforms.

The Indonesia case also illustrates the kind of progress that can occur when the LCDD framework is used as a mechanism for addressing corruption, which had been the single greatest constraint to the success of

---

BOX 3.5

Indonesia: Findings and Lessons in 2003

The Kecamatan Development Project (KDP) was initiated in the late 1990s, a few months before the overthrow of the authoritarian Suharto regime (Davis 2003). KDP 1 and KDP 2 were designed to promote village empowerment and reduce official corruption as key elements in poverty reduction, by (a) making block grants directly to subdistricts instead of channeling money through line agencies and (b) providing intense social and technical facilitation to build village-level capacity and promote participation, transparency, and accountability in community driven activities.

The following are the key findings from the project:

- Requiring villagers to compete for KDP resources promoted the development of high-quality project proposals. Cultural discomfort with the idea of competition often led those with winning proposals to fold in elements of losing proposals.
- The project's emphasis on fighting corruption as a key element of empowerment and its established mechanism for reporting abuses made it possible for villagers to minimize the leakage of project funds and assert their power vis-à-vis local officials. The rapid response by project managers and local police, often leading to arrest and prosecution, had a dramatic effect on villagers' belief in the justice system and their own legal rights.

(continued)

BOX 3.5

Indonesia: Findings and Lessons in 2003 (*continued*)

- The direct transfer of funds to subdistricts and villages enabled villages to be autonomous in their development activities, but it also created the risk that activities will be unsustainable because of a lack of outside support. This problem is being addressed under KDP 3.
- Marginal individuals generally have not benefited from project activities, except in a few cases where village-level financial units hired facilitators to work intensively with very poor and vulnerable persons outside of normal project channels.
- The microenterprise component is generally considered unsuccessful due to low rates of repayment. However, some financial units earned enough through interest payments to fund activities outside of normal project channels. Further, some units declared themselves independent entities, with the intention of functioning as microfinance institutions after the project ended. KDP 3 will help to link these entities with local banks.

For a short summary of KDP's current status (as of 2008), see worldbank.org/id/kdp.

---

community-level development efforts until the Kecamatan Development Project (KDP). The broad scope of the *empowerment pillar*—which included not only the development of project-related skills through learning-by-doing, but also training in democratic decision making, a public posting of project accounts, and intensive building of awareness about villagers' legal rights—resulted in a shift in power between communities and local government.

This shift was enforced by the *transparency and accountability* pillar, which enabled communities to identify and report abuses by local officials. Project staff quickly acted on complaints, thereby reinforcing the sense of community empowerment. The success of the LCDD framework led the government to request that it be rapidly scaled up to prepare local governments and communities for their responsibilities under the new decentralization program.

KDP's innovative funding mechanism, based on a simple set of rules for community-level disbursement, has been successfully replicated in thousands of villages in Indonesia and is now the model for many government programs. It has also influenced the design of poverty alle-viation and empowerment programs in a number of other countries. The third phase of the project, KDP 3, designed as the country was undergoing a deep decentralization in 2003, has shifted its focus from poverty reduction to governance, with the aims of (a) building local government capacity to support CDD and (b) supporting the devel-opment of permanent intervillage bodies to implement multivillage projects, mediate disputes, and give villages a stronger voice vis-à-vis higher levels of government.

In September 2006, the government of Indonesia began a new nation-wide program to accelerate poverty reduction based on the CDD approach: the PNPM-Maniri (Program Nasional Pemberdayaan Masyarakat or National Program for Community Empowerment). PNPM Rural will cover all rural kecamatan by 2009. Baseline data were gathered in 2007 to evaluate the impact of this program on household welfare, poverty, and access to services and employment against those in matched kecamatan not yet in the program. These baseline data point to the need for targeted implementation strategies—for example, to ensure the inclusion of disad-vantaged groups—and a special program for female-headed households has been designed. PNPM Urban will reach 10,700 urban kecamatan by 2009. The funds will be used to provide microcredit loans to groups of urban poor, strengthen community organizations, and improve access to basic infrastructure and services by the communities. This program shows the continued commitment of political leadership and the continued sup-port of development partners.

The opportunity for LCDD in Indonesia came with the end of the Suharto era and the beginning of improved democracy and governance. Donors cannot successfully impose LCDD on any country. Politicians and officials at different levels can sabotage the best-designed schemes. *The main approach of donors must be opportunistic: to seize opportunities that arise when political changes produce leaders willing to shift power to the grassroots.* More research is required on the best strategies under different political conditions.

Well-Designed Decentralization

The historical experience of decentralization is mixed. Sometimes rulers have aimed to empower the grassroots, while at others they have diverted international attention away from the lack of democracy at the central level. Too often local governments have been created without administrative authority or fiscal resources. Decentralization has three key dimensions—political, administrative, and fiscal—and all three need to be harmonized to work well. Reporting on decentralization experiments in the 1980s, Crook and Manor (1995, 1998) find that the outcomes were poor in Bangladesh, Côte d'Ivoire, and Ghana, but satisfactory in the state of Karnataka, India. In the first three cases, the local councilors or local assembly presidents were not elected, were accountable to central governments rather than the people they served, and lacked enough fiscal means to make a real difference. Decentralization worked in Karnataka because the chief minister was serious and provided ample fiscal resources.

Key stakeholder participation and some sector programs can be scaled up without waiting for all three dimensions of decentralization, but full national coverage will, at some point, require all elements to be in place.

The Mexico case is a powerful example of how the five LCDD pillars can serve as a framework for fiscal decentralization, by establishing the mechanisms, local capacities, and principles of accountability and transparency necessary for decentralization to succeed (see box 3.6).

The intensive technical assistance provided to support the local government capacity-building and community empowerment pillars was crucial to the success of the government's effort. These pillars, in turn, benefited from the learning-by-doing pillar, which allowed both the government and the World Bank to become comfortable with community empowerment as a new approach to poverty reduction and to scale up this approach to the national level.

The Mexico case study focuses on the municipal fund components of two successive decentralized regional development (DRD I and DRD II) projects carried out in the 1990s, during the country's transition to broader political participation and decentralization. Although the projects accounted for only a small percentage of the national budget for poverty reduction, the government's own poverty program adopted cutting-edge procedures in DRD I (1990–94) for formula-based poverty targeting and participatory planning.

Subsequently, the operations manual for DRD II (1995–2000) and many of the project's design characteristics became the basis for the far-reaching Fiscal Coordination Law of 1997, which devolved responsibility and resources for social and infrastructure development to the municipalities and required them to engage with communities in participatory development. Thus, what was perceived originally as a very risky social investment experiment, carried out in the context

---

Mexico: Findings and Lessons in 2003

The federal government–driven municipal funds helped to make decentralization possible in the absence of local social capital by undertaking the following (Manoukian 2003):

- Using funding formulas (based on observed poverty characteristics) to target investment funds toward the poorest municipalities, which helped to reduce the risk of political manipulation of project funds
- Introducing action plans for the decentralization of government services
- Developing participatory approaches for communities to identify their needs and implement their own projects.

A key lesson is that, as decentralization deepens, LCDD activities need to focus more intensively on local government capacity building and community empowerment. In Mexico, before the Fiscal Coordination Law was in place, the decentralized regional development projects (DRD I and II) had a broad-based approach that encompassed federal and state capacity building, environmental protection, cultural site restoration, and poverty alleviation as components of participatory development.

As decentralization progressed, the municipal funds were simplified to focus only on the most basic sectors—water supply, rural roads, and income-generating activities—and on creating social capital at the lowest levels.

The innovative nature of the municipal fund made learning-by-doing essential and feasible at all levels; the learning-by-doing pillar was the single most important factor in the LCDD approach being institutionalized countrywide.

The willingness of the World Bank to adapt its procurement, disbursement, and planning procedures to the (then) radical new LCDD framework and to respond flexibly to the changing political situation in Mexico was crucial in the LCDD experiment not only succeeding and being scaled up in Mexico but also being adapted to many countries around the world.

---

of institutional restructuring, became an integral part of the country's resource transfer system. The federal government was the initial champion and risk-assuming entity, but as the success of the approach became more apparent, other champions emerged at the state and civil society levels.

In 2004, Mexico passed a Social Development Law, codifying the experiences of poor people participating in project planning, implementation, and supervision and allocating some responsibilities to state and municipal levels. The two projects, in part, contributed to the change in perceptions about the role that poor people and municipalities could play. The National Program for Indigenous Peoples (2001–06), a $1.7 billion program, is based on LCDD principles and the experiences of those earlier programs.

Overcoming Adverse Institutional Barriers

Even where conducive conditions exist, scaling up can be difficult because of the various problems listed earlier. We now consider the five classes of remedies: (a) overcoming adverse institutional barriers; (b) reducing economic and fiscal costs; (c) overcoming problems associated with co-production; (d) using pilots, feedback, and adaptation to improve technical design; and (e) designing and field-testing operational manuals, toolkits, and scaling-up logistics.

The political and social institutions in many countries are not conducive to shifting power to the grassroots. Top-down paternalism for decades has created structures that resist downward empowerment. Some regimes fear that decentralization may create political complications. Social conditions in some countries are so adverse that they have escalated into violent conflict and civil war.

Even where decentralization has taken place, it has yielded mixed results. The results have been poor where local governments are accountable to central authorities rather than to citizens, where public sector reforms did not take place to realign the functions and powers of the central bureaucracy, where local communities were not empowered to discipline local officials, and where local governments were not granted a reliable, adequate share of central revenue or the authority to levy and keep taxes (see box 3.7).

Zambia: Problems Encountered

The Zambia Social Investment Fund (ZAMSIF) exemplifies the problems that can occur when an LCDD project is carried out in the absence of two of the five basic conditions for LCDD: democratic decentralization and capacity building of local government. Indeed, in Zambia, subdistrict structures do not even exist.

Buy-In through Head Tax

In Tanzania, local governments are supposed to collect a head tax and transfer 80 percent of that to district headquarters, from which it rarely returns. A much happier experience comes from Guinea, where the collection of head tax has improved and become more timely because it is available for local use.

In 2000, ZAMSIF transformed itself from a parallel institution that bypassed established structures in order to channel money directly to communities into an institution that sought to integrate community development into mainstream development planning. To this end, ZAMSIF developed two separate funding mechanisms: a community investment fund (CIF) and a district investment fund (DIF), which aims to build the capacity of local governments to support CIF activities. The DIF uses the concept of a capacity-building ladder to support the progressive scaling up of local government capacity. The concept calls for giving districts more funding and responsibility as they accomplish the following:

- Gain the ability to facilitate community access to funding (level 1)
- Achieve the capacity to facilitate participatory identification processes, monitor and evaluate community projects, implement DIF projects, and account for project funds (level 2)
- Adopt a district development and poverty reduction strategy and are able to show that community-based projects reach those targeted by the strategy and acquire proven design and financial management skills (level 3)
- Show continued satisfactory performance in all phases of the community project cycle, including approval of funding for community projects, but not disbursements (level 4)
- Show consistently good performance of district councils for more than one year, existence of a basic poverty information system, and evidence of some subdistrict planning (level 5).

But the ideal did not match the reality. In the absence of democratic decentralization and local government capacity building, the performance of LCDD projects was inhibited in several areas, including commitments, disbursements, and number of projects approved (see box 3.8). The lack of local government capacity building, in particular, constrained the ability of local government to progress to higher levels of responsibility, which was crucial for ZAMSIF to be scaled up to a successful national program.

BOX 3.8

Zambia: Findings and Lessons in 2003

Despite ZAMSIF's innovative approach to capacity building for local governments, operational barriers to achieving that goal had emerged by mid-2003 (Kwofie 2003):

- Inadequate organizational structures at the district level, contributing to duplication of efforts and poor planning
- Lack of financial autonomy of district councils and lack of control over locally gener-ated tax revenues
- Lack of accountability of district-level line departments to the local authority
- Absence of structures at the subdistrict level that are legally recognized and embed-ded in the policy framework
- Existence of multiple project committees at the community level, many with no clear institutional framework or mandate, contributing to lack of accountability
- Lack of a reliable funding mechanism for the districts, with no dedicated allocation from the national budget, no access to local tax revenues, and no ability to access loans for commercially viable services
- Limited community participation and lack of direct community access to or control of project funds
- Inefficient use of human, material, and financial resources
- Different approaches and funding conditions among donors and NGOs.

The political framework under which ZAMSIF was carried out made it difficult for communities and local governments to adhere to LCDD principles. The fund's poor performance under these circumstances may indicate that programs unable to support the pillars of decentralization and local government empowerment will not succeed.

The capacity-building ladder for local governments is an important innovation that can be used in a variety of settings. The phased approach to capacity building helps to ensure that expectations regarding local governments are realistic, from the point of view of both communities and the center; it also enables project managers to address weaknesses and gaps in knowledge as they come to light.

After 2003, the government and the Bank restructured the program, scaling down significantly the number of programs to be managed through the DIF and increasing the number of projects to be managed through the CIF. The completion report of 2006 mentions the same main constraint: implementation of the decentralization policy was a prerequisite for the project activities to have their intended impact. The ZAMSIF implementation experience demonstrates that failure in public sector management can pose a serious constraint for the achievement of intended project outcomes.

By 2005, 18 districts were at level 1, 26 were at level 2, 21 were at level 3, three were at level 4, and four were at level 5, of which two had sustained this level for two years. As discussed in chapter 4, political commitment was lacking for a decentralization operation that would have incorporated the investment fund. Subsequent data show that districts have a hard time maintaining their newly acquired skills, as the support unit has also been disbanded. So, while this was an ideal case of scaling up from a separate social fund at the community level to a national program, including a 10-year exit strategy, cutting the program short after 5 years did not allow this fully integrated, scaled-up version of LCDD to mature.

Benin: Problems Overcome

The LCDD activities in Benin illustrate how scaling up can be inhibited by the lack of democratic decentralization, the failure to build the capacity of local government, and the failure to empower communities through participatory methodologies and learning-by-doing. The LCDD activities also show how the deficits can be corrected.

The seven LCDD projects or programs considered in this 2003 case study were designed to support Benin's transition to economic liberalization and democratization after the fall of the authoritarian regime in 1989. All seven initiatives addressed problems of essential services, employment, and local capacity building. NGOs, in most cases, controlled project funds, acted as technical and social facilitators, and provided training in leadership, monitoring and evaluation, organizing and conducting meetings, and financial record-keeping to broad-based, elected village committees. None of the projects had a specific scaling-up strategy; scaling up was perceived as an increase in the number of villages benefiting from project support. Efforts to reach other villages were carried out largely through rural radio networks, which widely disseminated information about LCDD activities and encouraged communities to prepare their own proposals for funding. However, only one of the projects focused on developing the linkages between villages and local governments that were needed to ensure the sustainability and scaling up of LCDD activities.

The Benin case shows the linkage between the pillars of decentralization, local government capacity building, learning-by-doing, and community empowerment and how the absence of one or more of these pillars can constrain LCDD projects from scaling up. In particular, the lack of decentralization in 2003 left local governments without the legal or financial means to support CDD projects, which, if they existed at all, were generally supported by NGOs and not integrated into regular government planning or sustained by regular government funding. Under such conditions, community empowerment was negatively affected by the difficulty of adapting centrally designed methodologies—even best-practice participatory methodologies—to local conditions. This difficulty constrained buy-in, learning-by-doing, project performance, and thus the sustainability of LCDD projects. Under such conditions, communities were unable to develop their voice or to influence local government decisions that affect them, both of which are necessary for scaling up (see box 3.9).

Benin's 1999 Decentralization Law became effective with local elections in 2002, effectively creating local governments in 2003. The Benin LCDD case improved tremendously. In 2005, the National Community Development Project was approved. By 2008, the program had successfully been implemented nationwide. The role of the new local governments was carefully tailored and supported by a learning-by-doing program, and local governments, as in Zambia, are expected to progress on a capacity ladder of three rungs before they can be fully in charge of LCDD programs in their municipality.

A review of legislation is under way to align the sectoral services with the new decentralized local governments and align the rules and regulations that govern the use of public funds, to allow both the local government and the communities to utilize, contract, and account for public funds. This experience shows that remedies to barriers will have to be tailored to the local context in each case. Some possibilities are considered below.

Unfavorable Political Conditions

Where the political conditions are unfavorable and commitment to empowerment is lacking, the following strategies can be considered:

- Establish pilot programs as examples of success. Meanwhile, canvass support for LCDD as an ideal. Enter into a dialogue with the government, opposition parties, think tanks, and civil society.

BOX 3.9

Benin: Findings and Lessons in 2003

In general, up to 2003, the CDD activities in Benin adhered only partly to LCDD principles (Wennink and Baltissen 2003):

- Community empowerment was constrained by the fact that villagers were often assigned roles based on gender and that facilitators tended to give preference to the more dominant, better-organized village groups, while passing over the more marginalized.
- Well-organized community groups were instrumental in mobilizing co-funding, and villagers considered the quality of their local co-financing mechanisms to be related directly to rapid and transparent funding of project proposals. However, the success of local development initiatives was less dependent on accessing funds than on the dynamics of village organization and the accessibility of project services and intermediation.
- NGOs laid the groundwork for scaling up by facilitating contacts among villages and between villages and service providers. The government supported community empowerment by harmonizing approaches to participatory appraisals and by providing broad-based training of trainers. However, the application of participatory methodologies considered to be best practice were often applied mechanically, not adapted to local circumstances, and detached from a strategic vision and core LCDD values. The methodologies did not help to build skills, create awareness, promote ownership, or incorporate learning processes. Community learning was negatively affected by inadequate monitoring and evaluation tools.
- There was no effort, except in one project, to establish dialogue between villages and local governments or to build local government capacity. Horizontal scaling up (wider coverage) was achieved by creating parallel structures and procedures, which did nothing to ensure the financial and institutional sustainability of the activities or to give communities the ability to affect the institutional and policy environment, both of which depend on vertical linkages with local government and other existing institutions.

The project yielded several lessons. At the community level, there is tension between the need to work with better-organized groups to mobilize activities and co-financing and the need to include the more vulnerable and marginalized. Best-practice methodologies should not be assumed to be best practice in all circumstances; they need to be dynamically adapted to the local context. Creating parallel structures and working with NGOs to carry out LCDD activities, rather than integrating LCDD into existing institutions, limit the ability of communities to affect the institutional and policy environments.

- Where central governments do not favor local governments, make a start with participatory appraisal and planning by communities, to which there is typically less resistance.
- Where there is resistance to free media, disseminate project information through community radio in pilot projects. This can be designed to be interactive and so provide voice to local people (CIMA, Community Radio Working Group 2007). Empowerment via information can also be strengthened by Internet kiosks that provide market and other information, advice, training, and e-governance support.[2]
- Help to create and strengthen user groups and producer groups. Where possible, bring about coalitions of such groups.
- Liberalize economic policy and increase the space for entrepreneurs. These actions will help to diffuse centralized power and create more economic freedom and empowerment for buyers, sellers, and intermediaries.
- Seize opportunities for empowerment created by political changes.

Unfavorable Social Conditions

Many countries have deep gender and social divisions. Empowerment requires bridging social divides and ensuring participation by all. A thorough analysis of social and political conditions needs to guide program design. Ways of overcoming elite capture and social exclusion should be worked into the design. The participatory process itself is a means of accomplishing this.[3]

Remedies in every country will have to be tailored to local conditions. Some possible strategies include the following:

- Using the participatory approach, attempt to create sustainable partnerships between all stakeholders, including majority and minority groups, NGOs, and different levels of government.
- In the initial stage, avoid the most faction-ridden villages and focus on the relatively harmonious ones, as was done by the Indo-German Watershed Development Program.
- Where women or minorities have traditionally not been allowed to participate in village councils, institutionalize separate meetings of these groups prior to council meetings. Separate meetings will help them to articulate their needs and gain organizational strength. The groups will then be in a better position to overcome traditional social inhibitions and gradually be accepted as full partners.

- Improve awareness of nontraditional roles that women can perform.
- Empower producer groups of women and minorities. This typically will attract less social resistance than some other forms of empowerment. Women's microcredit societies have gained rapid social acceptance in many male-dominated societies. The Self-Employed Women's Association in India is an outstanding example.
- Many ethnic or social groups may produce the same commodity. Creating and empowering producer groups can create social glue between different religious, ethnic, or caste groups.
- Where the participatory approach fails to bridge social divides, consider special programs targeted at those most excluded.

Some countries such as India have reserved a certain proportion of seats in local governments for women and historically disadvantaged minorities. This will overcome traditional taboos only if the proportion reserved is substantial, a quarter to one-third of seats. Even then, social pressures may undermine the effectiveness of this approach.[4]

Poor Decentralization Design

Even where political and social conditions are not favorable, poorly designed decentralization may leave major institutional barriers in place. To overcome this, LCDD proponents should undertake the following actions:

- Provide technical assistance from an early stage of decentralization. Some central authorities are not convinced that local governments and communities have the capacity and accountability to use untied funds well. The case studies highlighted in this chapter show otherwise.
- Emphasize that the political, administrative, and fiscal components of decentralization must move together in harmony.
- Emphasize subsidiarity. Functions should be devolved to the lowest level where they can be performed efficiently, and fiscal powers and administrative resources should then be realigned with the new functions. Local taxes or user charges should be used locally.
- Emphasize learning-by-doing by local governments and communities to acquire skills. This needs to be supported by training and capacity building.
- Advance a mandate for a fixed share of central resources to go to local governments (as in Mexico). This will ensure regular, reliable funding.

Reducing Economic and Fiscal Costs

Sometimes, successful pilots cannot be scaled up for three financial reasons: excessive economic cost, poor transfer efficiency, and excessive fiscal cost. Economic cost per beneficiary may be too high because a program depends on expensive staff (sometimes expatriates), costly transport (such as fleets of jeeps), expensive materials (sometimes imported), and costly designs or technology (often created for a different context). Funds may travel through several bureaucratic levels before reaching a community, projects may have to be cleared at several levels, and excessive paperwork may be required in the donor's language. High overhead costs reduce the transfer efficiency of funds: too little of the project money actually gets through to communities in the form of goods and services. In one project in Togo, overhead expenses amounted to almost 90 percent of the budget.[5] In Northeast Brazil, overhead costs declined to around 7 percent after local empowerment.

There are various ways to cut economic costs and improve transfer efficiency:

- Devolve authority based on subsidiarity. Putting the appropriate level in charge will lower costs.
- Empower communities and local governments to choose, implement, and monitor projects. Such empowerment induces innovations using low-cost designs appropriate for local conditions. The use of local materials and contractors cuts costs further. Oversight by communities and local government is less expensive than oversight by government agencies. The case studies presented in this book show that LCDD can cut the costs of individual subprojects by 20–40 percent.
- Operations and maintenance (O&M) are typically cheaper, more efficient, and more sustainable if done by communities on the principle of subsidiarity. Communities, however, may not have the skills or funds to tend to O&M, and, overall, the financing and management of O&M will remain an area where new, effective strategies will need to be designed.[6]
- Training or facilitation by outsiders, especially foreigners, is expensive when tens of thousands of communities are targeted. The aim must be to develop and use training teams from the provinces and districts to train community members and other program participants. Another effective strategy is to train local community specialists, chosen by the communities themselves, to acquire specialized skills. In successful pilots, communities and their trained community specialists can become trainers of other communities (just as successful farmers can spread

good practices through farmer-to-farmer contacts). Harnessing and developing local skills can both cut costs and accelerate scaling up.
- Well-designed logistics can reduce costs. Such designs can ensure that local people can reach training and supply points on foot rather than having to travel long distances in jeeps. Community meetings, training sessions, and the like should be arranged at locations convenient by means of local transport. Good logistics cut the cost of information sharing and cash management and simultaneously improve accountability and transparency.

Even if the cost per beneficiary is reasonable, the fiscal cost may be too high for national scaling up. Central governments and donors may lack funds. LCDD can bring down fiscal costs in several ways:

- Communities can be asked to contribute 15–40 percent of subproject costs in cash or in kind, depending on the nature of the project. Communities are more willing to share in costs when more power and resources are devolved to them.
- Communities and local governments can be authorized to levy user charges or local taxes. This typically increases the fiscal base.
- Local empowerment can improve tax compliance. Citizens are more willing to pay taxes or charges if the taxes and charges are used for local facilities than if they go to national or provincial capitals (as shown in box 3.7 for Guinea).

Overcoming Problems Associated with Co-production

Empowerment should not pit communities and local governments against central governments or line ministries. Development needs to be seen as the co-production of outputs in a joint venture of central governments, local governments, and communities, with support from the private sector and civil society. This co-production requires major institutional reform and a new collaborative mind-set. Keeping in mind that the following topics are determined by the program leaders, overcoming co-production problems requires three steps:

1. Fostering a common culture and vision among stakeholders
2. Assigning and describing program functions unambiguously to different participants and providing practical handbooks and operational manuals
3. Providing incentives compatible with program objectives.

Fostering a Common Vision and Culture

By changing entrenched attitudes and the mind-sets of co-producers, LCDD proponents aim to create widespread acceptance of a new vision and cultural attitude. This difficult task requires painstaking dialogue, communication, and negotiation; it also requires reaching agreement and commitment from all co-producers on a new participatory approach that provides voice and space for all stakeholders and a common appreciation of the new roles and powers of each stakeholder group.

Based on social and institutional analysis, a common vision can be achieved by bringing stakeholders together to accomplish the following:

- Examine how best they can use the resources and authority they will get from LCDD.
- Appreciate how important social inclusion is and how traditional attitudes to women and minorities need to give way to a new approach.
- Use the entire participatory process to try and create shared values.

Well-designed LCDD will enable traditionally voiceless groups to gain voice and assist in the emergence of a new set of shared values. Communities that function regularly in the new participatory manner will find traditional discriminatory attitudes changing.

Assigning and Describing Functions Clearly

The major changes in institutions and mind-set required by LCDD require clear-cut agreement on precisely what each stakeholder will do. Central coordination is essential, and these commitments should be formalized in the initiative's participation action plan. The participation action plan should be reviewed and upgraded periodically by key stakeholders. It should equip stakeholders with the relevant training and tools.

Providing Incentives Compatible with Program Objectives

Compatible incentives are required in any program, but more so in a program that aims to change mind-sets and institutions. Field-tested rollout logistics can help to unearth incentive issues and to design an incentive-compatible operational manual. Chapter 5 presents the steps for facilitating these problem-solving activities.

Adapting to the Local Context

The very fact that successful pilots have not automatically scaled up shows that, whatever their merits, the pilots may require adaptation to succeed in different contexts. What appears to be best practice in one setting may be poor practice in another.

The Swajal Rural Water Supply Project in Uttar Pradesh, India, experienced much greater success in the Himalayan region than in the flat Bundelkhand area. Perennial streams and springs provided cheap water in the former area, whereas the latter required expensive, deep tube wells or hand pumps whose sustainability is in doubt. Also, caste divisions posed much greater social obstacles in Bundelkhand than in the Himalayan area. This illustrates how geography and social issues can yield very different results within the same state.

The Swajal project was not linked directly to local governments, which were weakly developed in Uttar Pradesh. But the next major Bank-supported project in this sector was launched in the state of Kerala, where the panchayat system is strong and supported by firm political commitment. Adapting to the new context, the Kerala project routed funds and technical assistance to communities through local governments.

The India case illustrates how the five LCDD pillars, along with strong political commitment to reform, can bring about profound and rapid change at the local and community levels.

This 2003 case study assesses the Rural Water Supply and Sanitation Project in the state of Kerala, which transferred responsibility for rural drinking water from the public utility to the gram panchayats (lowest level of local government) in the 1990s. The project, designed as an LCDD scheme, is being carried out under very favorable conditions for LCDD: political commitment; a decentralized political, financial, and administrative framework; and the availability of high-level, low-cost technical skills.

The Kerala project is structured essentially as a partnership among the stakeholders: (a) the gram panchayats, which compete to receive project funds and are responsible for organizing beneficiary groups to upgrade and expand existing water schemes; (b) technical consultants, who conduct participatory needs assessments and participatory planning with the beneficiary groups and train them to take charge of O&M, collect dues, maintain books, monitor and evaluate their water schemes, and fulfill auditing and reporting requirements; and (c) the water utility, which trains the gram panchayats to oversee the water schemes and cooperates with the technical consultants in training beneficiaries. The project excludes beneficiaries who do not pay for water, but requires that women, the disadvantaged, and scheduled castes and tribes be included in beneficiary groups. A cascading training plan provides for learning-by-doing, with the gram panchayats and beneficiaries who received earlier training serving as resources for those who come later. The project is fully integrated with the gram panchayats' overall water plans (see box 3.10).

By 2008, almost at the end of the project, most of the objectives had been realized. By changing the rules of the game for entrenched local players and providing the mechanisms for establishing new relationships, the India case provides strong evidence that the five LCDD pillars serve as an appropriate framework for realizing reforms mandated under decentralization. In particular,

- The local capacity-building pillar enabled the transfer of responsibility for service provision from the state-owned water utility to local government.
- The community empowerment pillar, in addition to ensuring that the water schemes would be sustainable, also helped to prevent them from being captured by local elites.

BOX 3.10

India: Findings and Implications in 2003

According to Aiyar (2003),

- Existing social capital enabled the project to have immediate social and political effects.
- Gender sensitivity was inherent in the nature of the project. Women have been a driving force behind the water schemes, which have reduced their burden of carrying water and lessened tensions in the home. Many women have sold their gold to raise their share of the capital costs.
- Communities reelected gram panchayat heads who supported the LCDD scheme and defeated those who did not. In addition, beneficiary groups are diversifying into other community-based activities such as roads and street lighting. However, communities need continuous recharging to keep their sense of cohesion; the reasons for this require more study.
- Social capital and trust in local leadership seem to be as important as rules and procedures for ensuring participation and transparency.
- While corruption is common in other projects, it has not been a problem in the LCDD water scheme due to community contracting and to beneficiaries' vigilance in protecting the water they pay for.

(continued)

BOX 3.10

India: Findings and Implications in 2003 (*continued*)

- The stakeholder partnership has been negatively affected by the water utility's resistance to reform. In addition, there are tensions between the gram panchayats and technical consultants over the need for and cost of technical support.
- Many communities, especially in tribal areas, are very dependent on technical consultants, and their community activities seem to be consultant driven. This approach does not help to develop the social capital and skills needed for the community empowerment pillar to take hold in marginalized areas and almost guarantees that the LCDD activities will not be sustainable or able to scale up. More study is needed on how to provide intensive technical assistance to communities that require it, without consultants dominating the process. For example, enabling communities to purchase their own technical assistance from the co-financed project funds has been successful in Brazil.
- The project has experienced problems of exclusion. There are no provisions for covering poor people who cannot pay; further, people who first opted out and now want to join are not permitted to do so.
- The project's quarterly healthy home surveys, which track the health benefits of the water scheme, are an important contribution to LCDD practice and help to establish data on impact.

The project shows the relationship between LCDD water schemes and community empowerment. Such schemes have the potential to change the local political landscape by taking the control of drinking water out of the hands of politicians and freeing communities of the need to bribe officials for water. For the same reason, however, the schemes are vulnerable to capture by a new group of elites. Care must be taken to start small and achieve solid successes before scaling up, so that the LCDD approach cannot be discredited. This political risk is significant.

The cascade approach to training helps to ensure that knowledge is continually incorporated as successive batches of gram panchayats and beneficiary groups are trained. It also prevents the disbursement of large sums ahead of capacity building.

Even normally apathetic communities will participate in projects that provide the communities with sufficient funds and sufficient choices to make a difference in their lives.

Social capital can be a more than adequate substitute for conventional audits in LCDD projects, since communities are vigilant about ensuring the proper use of their resources.

The learning-by-doing and transparency and accountability pillars were crucial to the capacity-building and empowerment pillars, which, in turn, were essential for the decentralization effort.

Field-Testing, Manuals, Toolkits, and Scaling-Up Logistics

The examples in map 3.1 and tables 3.1 and 3.2 demonstrate that pilots should be used in a wide variety of settings to field-test what works best in what situations. Such field-testing makes it possible to develop operational manuals, toolkits, and instruments tailored to the local context. These become the maps to guide everyone participating in scaling up.

Process monitoring and participatory M&E are vital to provide feedback that enables the design of programs to be improved continuously. In the Kerala Rural Water Supply and Sanitation Project, the overall design provides for a rollout in different communities in overlapping phases. Lessons learned from the early phases are incorporated in subsequent ones. Evaluation is required and ongoing throughout a project, not just at its end. The manuals in Kerala are field-tested, but they are also living documents that are constantly modified in the light of experience. The Association for Social Advancement in Bangladesh has used a similar approach very successfully.

Any scaling-up exercise will have to tackle the huge logistical problem of training thousands of people and managing thousands of community and local government accounts. Consequently, every program needs a logistics management system, and this should be included in a scaling-up manual. This is different from the technical manuals, which are the responsibility of the relevant technical ministries or organizations. The logistics management system needs to be based on logistics field-testing.

As in the Poni AIDS Prevention Program, a pilot program should field-test a draft scaling-up manual in an entire district or province. The many problems that arise should be sorted out at the pilot stage, and their analysis should be used to update the draft manual, which can then become a finished, field-tested manual.

The scaling-up manual needs to incorporate several components such as the following:

- The logistical system to train all communities, associations, and other co-producers
- The logistical systems for disbursements, financial accountability, and random auditing, including all of the forms that are needed in these processes

- The logistical systems for contracting, procurement, and distribution of goods and services for the program, including the forms needed
- The training manuals, forms, and other tools required for scaling up
- The logistical framework and timetable for the scaling-up effort
- The templates for the project preparation and monitoring documents, including those related to participatory M&E, and performance-based contracts to be used in the scaling-up effort
- The processes for recruiting and training the training teams.

Chapter 5 presents the steps for facilitating these activities.

Sequencing

Ideal conditions may not exist for scaling up in all countries. Some typical problems include the following:

- The top leadership may not be interested in decentralization or even in enhanced participation.
- Decentralized structures may not be based on the principle of subsidiarity.
- Local leaders who manage funds may not be accountable to their own people.
- The investment climate may not allow local entrepreneurs to take up contracts.
- Technical capacity may be inadequate in many areas.
- Major public sector reforms may be needed for scaling up. In many countries this process has not begun. Where it has, it may be a long, complex process.
- Many countries suffer from deep social and gender divides, leading to elite capture and social exclusion. In some countries, ethnic strife has escalated into civil war.
- Gender discrimination may be widespread and entrenched.

Once the decentralization pillar is fully in place, the LCDD framework can create an environment for sustainable development.

The Uganda case study—a quantitative approach to assessing CDD—considers four projects or programs designed to strengthen social capital and support the decentralization of institutions and financial systems mandated by the constitution and the Local Governments Act of 1997. While not formulated with LCDD principles in mind, the four projects addressed the following key LCDD goals:

1. The *Community Action Plan (CAP)* sought to improve community-level infrastructure, with a focus on education, water, and health.
2. The *Local Government Development Program (LGDP)*, now called *Local Government Management and Services Delivery Program (LGMSDP)*, sought to develop the capacity of local governments to undertake participatory planning, sustainable service provision, M&E, and documentation of lessons learned as inputs for scaling up the program countrywide.
3. The *National Agricultural Advisory Services (NAAS)* sought to bring private sector assistance to farmers in the areas of productivity enhancement, soil conservation, entrepreneurship, financial management, marketing, and agro-processing, with local government providing oversight and quality control.
4. The *Northern Uganda Social Action Fund (NUSAF)* sought to create an autonomous unit to respond flexibly to community demands in a variety of sectors, beyond the mandate of local governments, while aligning community needs with available support and providing direct funding to community-level project committees in conflict-torn northern Uganda.

The Uganda case shows that a decentralized system that channels the largest portion of uncommitted resources downward, combined with the provision of intensive technical assistance, creates a strong environment for the development of the pillars of local capacity building and community empowerment (see box 3.11). It also shows that the sustainability of those two pillars is, in turn, crucially dependent on

---

BOX 3.11

Uganda: Findings, Lessons, and Implications from Four Programs in 2003

The case study correlated the scores of the Community Action Plan, Local Government Development Program, National Agricultural Advisory Services, and Northern Uganda Social Action Fund on community and local government empowerment, realignment of government, accountability and transparency, and learning-by-doing with project performance (Onyach-Olaa and others 2003).

(continued)

BOX 3.11

Uganda: Findings, Lessons, and Implications from Four Programs in 2003
(*continued*)

CAP scored high on community and local government empowerment and on learning-by-doing, but low on realignment of government and on accountability and transparency. Community-level project committees managed community contributions and were responsible for contracting and verifying the quality of goods and services. Social infrastructure microprojects were handed to local governments, recognizing their growing capacity and allowing CAP to focus on empowerment. The project facilitated community-level development activities and trained community facilitators in participatory techniques. However, the project was centrally designed, due largely to the lack of a self-help tradition in the project area and to the absence of NGOs capable of mobilizing community development. The community had no control over project funds.

LGDP scored high on community and local government empowerment and on learning-by-doing, but low on realignment of government and on accountability and transparency. Communities received the largest share of LGDP resources, along with intensive, demand-driven technical assistance. Three-year rolling capacity-building plans for district governments included extensive, demand-driven technical assistance and efforts to transform local governments into financially sustainable "respected entities" and "intelligent clients" of private service delivery. The project played a key role in developing the procedures and institutional arrangements governing the transfer of responsibility for services to local governments. However, the system of rewarding well-performing local governments and sanctioning poor performers was perceived as unfair by poor performers. There was also dissatisfaction with the transfer of taxes levied by subdistricts upward to the districts. Consultation with community project committees was limited during the project's design, beneficiaries were not consulted during project identification and implementation, and communities were not involved in selecting service delivery agents or disseminating information on resource allocation.

NAAS scored high on all dimensions, although community empowerment was low for marginalized groups and accountability and transparency were low in one district. Although there was no community consultation during the design phase, there was an unconditional flow of resources from the center. NGOs assisted with the formation of farmers' groups, which carried out participatory appraisals and planning and were the focus of efforts to modernize and commercialize agriculture. Resources flowed from the center, and farmers' forums created at the subdistrict level hired and supervised private service providers, including farm advisers, on behalf of the farmers' groups.

(*continued*)

BOX 3.11

Uganda: Findings, Lessons, and Implications from Four Programs in 2003
(*continued*)

There was no consultation with local government during the design phase, but strong civil society lobby groups, in existence before the project, empowered local government by demanding resources and support from the center. A well-functioning, decentralized structure supported the autonomy of local governments and created an enabling environment for cooperating private sector actors and donors. Accountability and transparency were high in two districts, for reasons not apparent from the report, but low in one district, due to poor flow of information to communities from the NAAS secretariat and the farmers' forums. The project undertook extensive training and facilitation in modern farming methods and the development of market linkages.

In NUSAF, communities received unrestricted funds, participated in all phases of the project cycle, managed resources and procurement, and monitored progress at each stage. Facilitation focused on strengthening community participation, leadership, and resource mobilization. Local governments were strengthened in the areas of technical design, procurement, financial management, participatory processes, M&E, and communications, which increased popular participation in local governments. Districts were rewarded for good performance with higher allocations, which had to be sent downward to communities. District, not government, officials resisted transferring money and authority to the communities. Information flowed downward to the community, and communities were accountable for project performance. Communities and local governments participated with facilitators in pretesting the construction of community-based infrastructure, paying special attention to vulnerable groups. In conflict areas, the project used traditional and cultural leaders to facilitate participatory conflict resolution.

The use of quantitative methods to test a project's adherence to the LCDD process rather than its outcomes is an important contribution to the LCDD toolkit and is useful in a variety of settings. This approach revealed a positive correlation between adherence to the LCDD process and the satisfaction of beneficiaries; it did not establish a correlation between beneficiaries' perception of their own empowerment and the level or quality of scaling up. A methodology for researching that question needs to be developed. Empowerment may create new tensions between communities and local government with regard to control of resources. A productive relationship between the two entities may need to be facilitated. The emphasis in some projects on empowerment through community groups often excluded marginal individuals who were unable to participate in community life. Special efforts must be made to include them.

the pillars of transparency and accountability and learning-by-doing. Further, the Uganda case explicitly shows how the capacity-building and empowerment pillars help to stimulate local economic activity by enabling the development of farmers' groups, market linkages, relationships with private suppliers, and so on—all of which are important for the LCDD framework to be scaled up and made a part of longer-term development planning.

Since 2003, Uganda has further deepened its decentralization. Under the National Local Government Development Program (a sector-wide approach funded by an adaptable program loan (APL) from the World Bank), local governments have created community development funds. National rules have also been adopted for communities to participate in the local government participatory planning process.

Three Stages of LCDD

Every country needs to consider its specific historical, social, and economic circumstances and tailor LCDD accordingly. In doing so, countries may find it useful to consider three stages of CDD: *initiation, scaling up, and consolidation*. Conditions vary vastly across countries. Where conditions are ripe for scaling up, it is possible to proceed quickly. In other cases, it may be necessary first to create the necessary preconditions.

Initiation Stage. Countries with successful LCDD programs have already achieved their initiation stage. Other countries have little or no experience with participation or decentralization. Their empowerment can be initiated on three fronts: (a) enhancing real participation, (b) targeting specific groups (such as people affected by HIV/AIDS) (human immunodeficiency virus / acquired immune deficiency syndrome), women, ethnic minorities), and (c) starting a dialogue with stakeholders on decentralization.

Where no decentralization or local funds exist, pilot projects can be initiated. Small learning-by-doing grants to communities or the lowest level of local government (as small as $5,000 to $10,000 per community) can kick-start the process. Participatory appraisal and planning can begin using existing resources. In the Borgou region of Benin, half of the 500 villages were covered by a participatory appraisal within six months using only existing resources and facilitators. A similar approach achieved good results in Malawi. This implies that entire countries can be covered fairly rapidly using modest external resources.

Pilots should be tailored to climatic, ecological, and social contexts. If pilots have been conducted only in a small part of a country, further pilots are required to establish what works in what conditions.

Many countries are not keen on decentralization. In such cases reformers need to initiate a dialogue with the government and mobilize public opinion. While that dialogue proceeds, a start can be made with participation. Enhanced participation is the first building block of CDD, whose foundation must be laid quickly even if decentralization seems some way off.

Scaling-Up Stage. Where pilots have already succeeded, scaling up is the next logical step. This rarely can be done in one big bang at the national level. All of the tools and logistics for scaling up should first be refined and tested in one district of a province, as in the Borgou pilot. Such field-testing will quickly identify critical bottlenecks that may, for example, prevent rapid disbursement and may require legal or regulatory changes. The field-tested operational manuals, tools, training manuals, and scaling-up logistics can then be extended and adapted to local conditions in a rollout process that ultimately covers all districts or provinces.

Sectoral successes can be scaled up without waiting for the creation of local governments. The Swajal Rural Water Supply Project in India, the River Blindness Eradication Program in West Africa, and the Self-Employed Women's Association in India have scaled up with little or no help from local governments.

Consolidation Stage. When countries have scaled up in some sectors or regions, they can move toward consolidation, as Uganda is doing. This can include (a) integrating participation and decentralization, (b) scaling up provincial programs to full national coverage, (c) improving LCDD design in the light of experience, (d) improving technical and organizational capability, and (e) expanding targeted programs to tackle issues that communities may have neglected. For instance, communities may give excessive priority to curative health and not enough to disease prevention measures like improved stoves, hygiene education, and malaria control awareness. Gaps left by community action can be filled in the consolidation phase. LCDD typically focuses on rural areas in the early stages, but urban areas should be covered in the consolidation stage, if not earlier. Much more can be learned and documented about urban LCDD experiences.

When strong communities and local governments have emerged, official support needs to assist the formation of networks and federations of stakeholders. Brazil provides a good example of communities federating to link up with export markets. India, Mexico, and Turkey have created successful water users' associations. The emergence of federations of communities can be regarded as the climax of the consolidation stage.

Time Horizon for Sequencing

Each country needs to take stock of its institutions and stage of development to determine its current position in this three-stage framework and decide how best to proceed. There can be no single blueprint; every country will need a separate action plan tailored to its circumstances.

Many sorts of partnerships between stakeholders are possible. Appendix C gives a list of diverse partnerships in the Integrated Development Plan of Mangaung, South Africa. Countries need to consider which sorts of partnerships are best for their circumstances.

Allowing lots of time up front for careful preparation is a good practice; pressure for rapid disbursement is not. Sequencing should allow time for participatory processes to be established and running before scaling up. Once the processes are in position, conditions will have been created for more rapid disbursement. Process monitoring is all-important. Feedback is required from the field to know what is working and what is not and to improve program design accordingly.

A sufficient time horizon is essential for programs to be scaled up successfully. Many important processes will take time, including conducting the initial social and stakeholder analysis, getting the participatory process right, strengthening the framework for decentralization, fostering political commitment, implementing and evaluating pilots in different social and geographic conditions, and so forth.

In countries where there is little experience with decentralization and community development, the best course may be *a phased program, spread over perhaps 10–15 years*. This can be financed by an APL. In Niger, for example, the World Bank has embarked on an APL spread over 15 years in four phases. Triggers have been devised for moving from one phase to the next. If trigger conditions are not fulfilled, the program will not move to the next stage. The key feature of this model is to phase in the program over a long period of time in order to allow the preconditions for national scaling up to develop (World Bank 2003b). In Indonesia KDP shows such long-term sequencing. The national program (PNPM) started in 2007 and is expected to reach all rural and urban kecamatan; by 2009, all rural keca-matan had been covered.

Design, Preprogram, and Maintenance Diagnostics

The scaling-up framework goes from concept to reality based on the integrity of the design, which, in turn, is defined by a set of preprogram diagnostics and maintained by program maintenance diagnostics. Preprogram diagnostics are inherent to understanding the pillars, values, and elements of LCDD in a country prior to scaling up. The preprogram diagnostic review shows what is strong and what is weak.

Such a review resembles a report that an environmental or geologic engineer prepares prior to designing a structure—the diagnostic review guides the program's design, pointing to where efforts need to be focused, where extra investments or policies are required, and what sequencing may be necessary. The diagnosis of program maintenance measures key aspects of the LCDD initiative to determine if the program design and implementation plan are operating as intended or if adjustments are required.

The data for these diagnostics come from three main sources: the program's M&E component, independent evaluations, and special-purpose studies (see box 3.12). These are often reviewed as part of the annual program review. A clear diagnosis of what needs to be improved comes out of these evaluations. When a program has good supervision, the diagnosis leads to an action plan and pro-active improvements that fix problems before they compromise the program.

What often happens in large, long-term programs is that evaluations are done in order to move from one stage to another. These evaluations, by independent outsiders, include beneficiary satisfaction, process and

---

BOX 3.12

KDP's Research Program

Indonesia's KDP is a prime example of an active research program that forms part of its maintenance diagnostics. Its Web site presents the studies done under the last KDP that help in the design of the next phase.

management audits, and evaluation studies. For instance, in Malawi, before moving to APL phase 2 of the Malawi Social Action Fund (MASAF), an independent impact evaluation, beneficiary assessments, and a review of the organizational structure were undertaken. As a result, and with the objective of gradually moving away from an independent agency and into regular government structures, the MASAF unit was disbanded, and staff were moved to the Ministry of Finance, where they will advise on parts of the program that are their expertise: community engagement, planning, and implementation as well as linkages with sectors, local governments, and social protection programs. Other government agencies will deal with the strengthening of local governments and fiscal decentralization.

Appendixes B and C provide a variety of program design and diagnostic tools. These can be used during program preparation, but are useful throughout program implementation, implementation support, and the restructuring of poorly performing programs.

Conclusions

The underpinnings for scaling up LCDD, based on economic theory and global experience, help to guide planners and proponents in determining the following:

- What is to be scaled up
- The conditions that are conducive to LCDD
- How to overcome adverse institutional barriers
- How to reduce total and fiscal costs
- How to overcome co-production problems
- How to adapt to the local contex
- How to create field-tested manuals, toolkits, and scaling-up logistics
- How to sequence LCDD.

The underpinnings have also established a set of practical tools to check the soundness of program design and diagnostics intended to help planners and proponents to adjust and maintain the LCDD scaling-up process.

A wide range of country experiences in LCDD shows that political commitment and sound technical design are vital for scaling up. Without political commitment, LCDD is easily sabotaged by vested interests, and donor conditionalities are no guarantee of real empowerment. Co-production difficulties can sometimes be a euphemism for political sabotage. Governments and donors need to be opportunists, seizing occasions when the political dynamics of a country bring to power politicians genuinely committed to shifting power to the grassroots. More research is needed on the related political economy issues.

Well-designed decentralization and programs can facilitate models that are easily replicated across provinces and countries. In Indonesia, the rapid expansion of KDP has been compared with that of a McDonald's franchise: field-testing a good institutional model and then going for mass replication. Districts not covered by KDP have petitioned the government for the same model. This model needs adaptation in different socioeconomic conditions, just as McDonald's adapts burgers for different countries. As in any franchise scheme, the overall design requires much testing and design effort, but ultimately the rules and procedures must be so simple that people with limited skills can replicate the model in thousands of communities. Complex models will not scale up quickly; the work going into scaling up and making a program replicable and simple is complex. These two uses of the word "complex" should not be confused.

Scaling up means more than *physical scaling up* (mass replication). It also means *social scaling up* (increasing social inclusiveness) and *conceptual scaling up* (changing the mind-set and power relations). Social scaling up can mean constant adaptations to improve the voice of the weak or special targeted programs to supplement multisectoral ones. Conceptual scaling up means going beyond the notion of LCDD as a project approach, or even a program approach, and embedding empowerment in all of the thinking and action concerning development.

What are the pros and cons of LCDD projects versus processes? Both approaches can be appropriate. Ideally, we need multisectoral CDD, but the political and fiscal conditions may make that difficult. Single-sector LCDD cannot drive the process, but it can have a vital demonstration effect in convincing people that empowerment is the best way to go. In Kerala, incumbent local governments were reelected in all five gram panchayats participating in the pilot phase of Jalanidhi, whereas two-thirds of incumbents were defeated statewide, and this sectoral lesson provided strong political support for the empowerment process. Often local governments are thinly funded, whereas sectoral schemes are well funded and attract more public participation. So LCDD *projects and processes can evolve together through mutual strengthening.*

The underpinnings of LCDD go from concept to reality and then to practice. Chapter 4 offers recommendations based on direct review and analysis of the context for improved public services through LCDD in the context of one region, Africa. Chapter 5 provides a toolkit or guide for synchronizing government and donor-partner policy with LCDD and a step-by-step guide for getting the operational details and logistics organized for scaling up. These chapters bring a sense of the complexity and inherent practicality of LCDD, as well as support this book's adaptive guidelines and observations.

Notes

1. Hans P. Binswanger-Mkhize and Jacomina de Regt, with field research conducted by Swaminathan Aiyar, Gerard Baltissen, Deborah Davis, Kwame M. Kwofie, Timothy Lubanga, Violeta Manoukian, Mwalimu Musheshe, Suleiman Namara, Martin Onyach-Olaa, and Bertus Wennink. Deborah Davis (2004) summarizes the key findings of these studies.
2. Kendall and Singh (2006). Microsoft and Hughes India will also roll out several thousand kiosks, in public-private partnership arrangements or in totally private franchise arrangements.
3. Details are available at the World Bank's participation Web site, http://www .worldbank/org/participation.
4. Often women will be represented by their husbands or fathers. Powerful elites will try to ensure that minorities cannot effectively wield power. In the Indian state of Tamil Nadu, elections have not taken place for some village panchayats (councils) where top posts have been reserved for scheduled castes: no member of the scheduled castes dares to file a nomination for fear of violence from upper castes. In the village of Melavalavu, the scheduled-caste panchayat president, vice president, and five others were killed for standing for and winning the local election (*The Hindu*, October 31, 2002). Despite such horrendous problems, reservations have improved upward social mobility.
5. Personal conversation with task team leader, 2002.
6. Many programs have come full circle on O&M. From community management of O&M with the assumptions that community associations would themselves take care of maintenance, the trend is now toward ensuring that communities manage the funds for O&M but contract out to competent (micro) enterprises. This may also require some level of subsidy, but it is, on the whole, still more economical than having O&M done by central institutions.

CHAPTER 4

Lessons from Africa

Rodrigo Serrano-Berthet, Louis Helling, Julie Van Domelen, Warren Van Wicklin, Dan Owen, Maria Poli, and Ravindra Cherukupalli

Chapter 3 presented the key elements and phases of the design of local and community driven development (LCDD) programs and introduced the fundamentals of country diagnostics and the need to assure that LCDD is customized to the country context (the national political and governance situation). This chapter focuses on the experience of the World Bank in the Africa Region with assessing country context and adjusting program design and funding mechanisms so that LCDD can work in a variety of complex political and national scenarios. While assessments have been done in other regions, the Africa Region assessment is especially illuminating.

A Contingency Approach to Assessing Fit between Empowerment Strategies and Country Context

The evolution of the World Bank's project portfolio toward participatory local government raises new strategic and operational challenges for LCDD program designers. The variety of objectives, strategies, and field approaches employed in programs across the continent reflects the diversity of the contexts in which LCDD programs are designed and implemented, both regarding the problems they are meant to address and the opportunities and constraints that characterize the policy and institutional environments within which they are set.

The Africa portfolio shows that appropriate LCDD roles can be effectively defined if the country context is understood and accommodated for.

The key is using a contingency approach based on the fit between key features of the country context and various options for improving planning, resource management, subproject implementation, and service delivery.

Characterizing Country Contexts for LCDD Design

Assessing the strategic fit between LCDD design and country context requires a concise, consistent characterization of the country context. For local and community development programs, variables related to decentralization and governance are the most relevant. Country context can be characterized by two main variables: the quality of national governance and the status of national decentralization. Where the public sector is insufficiently responsive to community needs and priorities, the problem lies in two structural factors: deficits in the quality of governance and highly centralized planning, resource allocation, service delivery management, and accountability.

This chapter uses the World Bank's country policy and institutional assessment (CPIA) cluster of governance variables (cluster D) as a proxy measure of the quality of national governance. This index averages variables characterizing property rights and rule-based governance; quality of budgetary and financial management; efficiency of revenue mobilization; quality of public administration; and transparency, accountability,[1] and corruption in the public sector. Low CPIA cluster D values (less than 2.5) correspond to countries widely perceived as deficient in national governance.

No widely employed and tested proxy for the degree of decentralization is available, so this review uses three variables:

- The legal and political autonomy of local governments (whether there are statutory, elected local governments)
- The fiscal basis of local government autonomy (whether there is an on-budget, intergovernmental capital transfer)
- The administrative significance of local government autonomy (whether there has been devolution of the responsibility for basic transport services and basic social services such as primary health, primary education, and potable water supply).

Although focusing on only two independent variables results in a highly stylized, reductionist characterization, this approach is simple and economical. Table 4.1 describes four idealized types of country context that provide the basis for subsequent discussions of fit.

Table 4.1. Classification of Country Context

Description	Low-functioning intergovernmental system		High-functioning intergovernmental system	
	Dysfunctional government	Deconcentrated system	Incipient decentralization	Consolidating decentralization
Characteristics	CPIA cluster D is less than 2.5	Local state bodies are upwardly accountable, but not elected	Decentralization law creates local governments with some autonomy in resource management, and local elections are held	Conditions for incipient decentralization are met, combined with fiscal decentralization and devolution of service delivery
Countries	Angola, Chad, Dem. Rep. of Congo, Rep. of Congo, Liberia, Sudan	Mauritania, Mozambique, Niger, São Tomé and Principe	Benin, Burkina Faso, Cameroon, The Gambia, Guinea, Kenya, Madagascar, Malawi, Mali, Nigeria, Rwanda, Senegal, Sierra Leone, Zambia	Ethiopia, Ghana, Tanzania, Uganda

Source: Authors' compilation.
Note: Categories are based on 2006 data and include only countries with a relevant World Bank project.

A Panorama of Country Contexts from Dysfunctional to Functional

Dysfunctional government characterizes countries that are rated low or very low for the quality of national governance; they do not provide legitimate, credible public decision making and resource management. In general, national decentralization policies are not relevant given such widespread and systemic institutional failure. Most of these countries have suffered from internal conflict in the past decade and are transitioning to stable, postconflict governments. In countries without conflict, dysfunction may result from the nontransparent, weakly accountable, and frequently opportunistic behavior of public bodies and officials. Chad, contemporary Zimbabwe, the Central African Republic, and the nonconflict regions of northern Sudan are such endogenous dysfunctional regimes. In other cases, as in Angola, the end of conflict does not always bring significant short-term improvements in national governance.

Deconcentration characterizes centralized states. These have moderate or even good national governance, but decision making and accountability remain dominated by national government bodies or their regionally delegated authorities. There are no statutory, elected local governments.[2] Several countries with emergency, postconflict, and poor governance contexts also lack significant decentralization. They are expected to advance into the group of deconcentrated states as they move toward stability and good governance.

Incipient decentralization characterizes moderately well-governed countries in which the government has adopted national decentralization policies and basic laws, but the basic elements of political, fiscal, and administrative decentralization are not fully implemented. After the passage of enabling legislation, local elections are held and local government councils and executives are constituted in at least some part of many countries, often beginning in cities and towns. But decentralization often remains only incipient: territorially limited, fiscally constrained by insufficient transfers from the central government, and lacking own-source revenues. Decentralization also remains functionally constrained because responsibilities for delivering important public services—especially basic health, education, water provision, and road maintenance—are retained by the central government and its deconcentrated structures.

Consolidating decentralization refers to moderately well-governed countries in which three pillars of local governance are being implemented, even if incompletely or ambivalently. The countries have achieved the following:

- The legal and political empowerment of local governments
- Access for local governments to significant fiscal resources through intergovernmental transfers and own-source revenues
- Administrative responsibility for local governments to deliver the basic services contributing to local social and economic development.

Few countries in Africa have reached this phase in their decentralization process. Some of the countries included in this category have more consolidated systems (Botswana, South Africa), and others are less consolidated (Ethiopia, Ghana, Tanzania, Uganda).

The Fit between Country Context and LCDD Strategy

The toolkit discussed in chapter 5 is intended to fit LCDD design strategies to the country context. Such a design strategy involves two steps:

- A static institutional analysis of how a strategy for strengthening local governance takes advantage of the opportunities or constraints presented by country context

- A dynamic risk analysis of how much confidence LCDD design teams can have in future reforms of the policy environment (*policy risk*) and in local governments' performance in executing their responsibilities (*performance risk*).

Static Institutional Analysis of Strategic Fit. Based on the assessment of a given country at a particular time, designers of community driven development (CDD) and LCDD programs can choose institutional strategies that match, are more conservative than, or lead the country context when determining the role of local government.

Matching strategies adjust program design to take advantage of opportunities in a country's policy and institutional environment to advance the dual goals of service delivery and local governance, without assuming extraordinary risks. If a deconcentrated context is suited to increasing local responsiveness by introducing local planning, a strategy with local government planning and community-based subproject management would be a matching strategy—neither too cautious nor too ambitious compared with the situation.

Conservative or lagging strategies deliberately adopt more conservative postures compared with the country context, not taking full advantage of the opportunities to promote the role of local government in program implementation, either through local capacity building or policy reform. This caution expresses a reluctance to entrust local governments with full authority to set priorities, manage resources, and implement subprojects. In certain (often controversial) contexts, programs adopting conservative strategies may even hinder or conflict with the roles and powers ascribed to local governments under national policy, due to an assessment that local governments are likely to perform poorly.

Leading strategies use LCDD programs' institutional designs to push the boundaries of the institutional environment and accelerate change in the political, fiscal, administrative, or social aspects of local governance. The additional risk may be justified by confidence that policy champions in government or dynamic leaders in civil society will support ongoing changes that link local development to broader national reforms. Table 4.2 identifies, in an abstract case, when institutional strategies lead, match, or are conservative with respect to country context.

As governance and decentralization contexts improve, greater responsibility can be entrusted to local governments for fund implementation in collaboration with community programs. As country contexts improve, the

Table 4.2. Assessing Strategic Fit between Country Context and Institutional Strategies

Country context	Agency managed (A1)	NGO managed (A2)	Community managed (B1)	Local government planned and community managed (B2)	Local government and community co-managed (C1)	Local government managed (C2)	Intergovernmental fiscal management (D)
Dysfunctional government							
Deconcentrated system							
Incipient decentralization							
Consolidating decentralization							

Source: Authors' compilation.

Note: Dark gray designates a conservative strategy; medium gray designates a matching strategy, and light gray designates a leading strategy.

zone where strategies match context shifts from pure community management (column B1 in table 4.2), through community management with local government planning and oversight (column B2), and toward either hybrid or predominantly local government management (columns C1 and C2).

This approach allows program designers to enhance the sustainability of improvements in governance and service delivery by shifting pure community-based programs toward stronger links to and partnership with local governments. The implicit bias toward a bigger role for local governments does not seek to marginalize communities:[3] hybrid strategies involving the community and local government *are* the goal.

Adopting matching, conservative, or leading strategies reflects a calculation of the expected costs and benefits of taking risks. These categories should be seen less as a prescriptive argument about what is right and wrong with a country and more as a measure of risk aversion. Leading and conservative strategies do not mean that development programs or funding mechanisms have been poorly designed; rather, the strategies represent a decision that factors beyond national governance and decentralization need to be taken into account. What might these factors be?

Dynamic Risk Analysis of Strategic Fit. Assessing risk is essential to avoid applying context-strategy matching too mechanically. Defining context, though a useful starting point, is structural and static, so it must be complemented by a more nuanced and dynamic assessment of risks. By assessing policy risk and performance risk in the local government system, program designers can make better decisions about whether to adopt a leading (a bias toward local government) or a conservative (a bias toward community) posture compared with country context.

Policy risk measures uncertainty about whether government policies and institutions—as approved and as implemented—will be conducive to decentralized, downwardly accountable, and beneficiary-responsive local governance and public management. Are policies that favor centralization or less accountability likely to be adopted? Might influential central government officials or bodies impede pro-decentralization and pro–local governance policies? Greater policy risk implies a higher probability that centrally defined rules and procedures will make LCDD programs reliant on local governments less likely to produce the desired results.[4]

Performance risk measures uncertainty about whether local public officials and organizations will make decisions, manage resources, and provide services not in the interests of the intended beneficiaries but instead in their own interest or in that of their families, friends, or associates. Greater performance risk implies a higher probability that local officials will adopt decisions and behavior that make programs reliant on local governments less likely to produce the desired results.

These risk assessments will shape decisions on institutional strategies. Significant policy risk may make program designers reluctant to adopt leading strategies, while low policy risk may spur designers to enhance the role of local governments in planning, resource management, and subproject implementation because the future prospects for decentralized governance are good. Similar considerations apply to performance risk.

Risk Assessments and the Four Stylized Types of Countries

The sequential logic can be applied to typical situations associated within each of the four country contexts (see box 4.1 and table 4.3).

In countries with *dysfunctional government,* the structural constraint is government incapacity to manage public resources and increase access to local public services. In this situation, national decentralization policy is a minor factor. The predominant concern is the need for alternative management arrangements to support local service delivery—bypassing government planning, finance, and management systems that do not meet minimum fiduciary and governance standards.

Classic methods of CDD—including community-level subproject planning and co-implementation, financial flows outside public budgets and government disbursement channels, and fund agency–administered procurement and fiduciary arrangements—have proven effective for community investment and capacity building. Even in difficult contexts, good practice for local and community development programs includes significant roles for beneficiary communities in project identification, infrastructure co-production, implementation oversight, and operations and maintenance.

BOX 4.1

The Sequential Logic

Static institutional assessment of fit between   ➲   Nuanced and dynamic
program strategy and country context   assessment of risk

Table 4.3. Alternative Responses to Risks Associated with LCDD Implementation via Local Government

Strategy	Dysfunctional government	Deconcentrated system	Incipient decentralization	Consolidating decentralization
Matching	Employ parallel mechanisms to channel resources with community participation (B1)	Introduce local participatory planning and oversight mechanisms of deconcentrated bodies (B2)	Use project-funded block grants to local governments to demonstrate viability of intergovernmental transfers and increased mandate for service delivery by local governments	Promote greater roles for local government in intergovernmental system; institutionalize CDD and participatory practices in local government systems
Leading	Demonstrate engagement of local governments in LCDD program planning and oversight via pilots (B2 or C)	Promote and provide resources to participatory councils to demonstrate advantages of accountable local governments	Support reform of intergovernmental system and more local government capacity and accountability to devolve functions and resources to local governments; pass community resource flows through local governments (hybrid strategy)	Enhance civic engagement, local government transparency, and community co-production to increase local government accountability
Conservative	Strengthen central agency control and external oversight of local resource use	Maintain resource flows directly to communities, with local government roles limited to coordination and consultation	Limit resources allocated to local governments, maintain some direct resource flow to communities (mixed strategy, CI), and ensure strong oversight of local governments	Limit local government discretion in resource allocation, enhance community roles in subproject co-management, and ensure strong oversight of local governments

Source: Authors' compilation.

Note: Dysfunctional government indicates a central government that cannot reliably, fairly, and transparently channel resources to local levels. A deconcentrated system indicates low responsiveness and downward accountability of deconcentrated bodies. Incipient decentralization indicates disempowered or weak elected local governments, with few resources and capacities to deliver. Consolidating decentralization indicates an underperforming intergovernmental system, with inadequate central government support to local governments and weak accountability for local governments. Matching strategy indicates acceptable assessed risks. Leading strategy indicates low assessed risks, and conservative strategy indicates high assessed risks.

Community management (strategy B1) is thus the strategic option that matches dysfunctional country contexts. If performance risk is low, LCDD programs may begin to create a modest role for local governments to build local capacities and demonstrate the potential of accountable, decentralized governance even where national institutions are troubled. If performance risk is high, LCDD programs will likely seek to mitigate fiduciary risk by relying on agency or nongovernmental organization (NGO) resource management and direct-to-community implementation arrangements.

In countries with *deconcentrated systems,* planning, resource allocation, and management systems remain centralized, and the lines of accountability flow upward to the capital. Local authorities thus tend toward limited responsiveness to community priorities. A matching strategy for local and community development programs would rely on community institutions for subproject implementation. But it would also introduce local government–led participatory planning to integrate the LCDD program's investments with local investment plans and recurrent-cost budgets and to increase their responsiveness (strategy B2).

If policy risk is low, LCDD programs may gradually enhance the role of deconcentrated institutions of governance, even though they have no statutory autonomy and are formally accountable only to the central government (a leading strategy). If policy or performance risk is high, designers may limit deconcentrated local administrators to coordinating and consultative roles, continuing to channel resources directly to communities until capacity and accountability among local public managers satisfy minimum standards.

In countries with *incipient decentralization,* the powers, resources, and capacities of local governments are modest compared with those retained by national officials and bodies. A matching strategy for LCDD programs would allocate at least some resources for planning and management under the local government, often also maintaining resource flows to beneficiary communities. Where the performance risk remains high, conservative strategies may continue to disburse grants directly to communities to mitigate the fiduciary risks. Where central government has a strong, clear commitment to decentralization and local governance is good (low policy risk), a leading strategy may enhance the role and resource base of local authorities before the intergovernmental fiscal transfer system is consolidated and befo re sectoral service responsibilities are devolved.

In countries with *consolidating decentralization,* LCDD program strategies usually support local government management, while retaining significant community participation in planning, oversight, and in some cases co-production. Where policy or performance risk is high, conservative or mixed strategies may maintain a dedicated flow of grants to communities, while making investments to enhance the accountability and capacity of local governments.

Fitting to Context: Opportunities to Improve Local Governance and Leverage Community Capacity

The challenge for LCDD programs is to deliver benefits in the short term and strengthen the state capacities for promoting and sustaining local development benefits in the long term. Based on the framework introduced in chapter 3, this section assesses how African local and community development programs supported by the World Bank have fared. It focuses on two questions:

- How well do the institutional strategies selected by African local and community development programs fit with their country contexts? Do they match, lead, or adopt a conservative posture?
- How effectively have local and community development programs promoted local governance institutions?

The contingent approach to program design fits Africa's continuing local and community development challenges—low state capacity (national and local), unstable and unpredictable policy making, and weak democratic and civic political culture.

Taking Advantage of Opportunities: Design Strategies and Country Fit

In recent years many LCDD programs in Africa have moved toward strategies that strengthen the role of local governments in community driven local development. A review of the diversity of program designs in the Africa region shows the extent to which these strategies can be understood as contingent responses to the challenges of fit between program design and country context. Table 4.4 applies the contingent program design framework to the portfolio of active LCDD programs and shows the distribution of programs by country context (on the vertical dimension) and by institutional strategy (on the horizontal dimension).

Table 4.4. Strategies of Active Operations in the Africa Region, by Country Context

Context and country	Community management (B1)	Local government planning and community management (B2)	Local government and community co-management (C1)	Local government management (C2)	Intergovernmental fiscal management (D)
Dysfunctional government					
Angola	Social Action Fund (P)				
Chad			Social Action Fund (S)		
Congo, Dem. Rep. of	social fund	Local Development Support Program			
Congo, Rep. of					
Liberia	Community Empowerment Project				
Sudan	Community Development Fund (P)	Community Development Fund (S)			
Deconcentrated system					
Mauritania	Community-Based Rural Development Program				
Mozambique		CAP			
Niger	social fund				
São Tomé and Principe					
Incipient decentralization					
Benin			National Community-Development Project	District Planning and Finance Program	
Burkina Faso			CBRD		

Country			
Burundi			
Cameroon	Community Development Program Support Project (I)	Community and Social Development Project; Community Development Program Support Project (2)	
Gambia, The			
Guinea		Community Driven Development Project; VCSP	
Kenya	Western Kenya Community Driven Development	Arid Lands Resource Management	
Madagascar	Community Development Project (P)		Community Development Project (S)
Malawi	MASAF (P)	MASAF (S)	
Mali		Rural Community Development Project	
Nigeria	LEEMP	Decentralization and Community Development Project	
Rwanda	Community Poverty Reduction Project	Participatory Local Development Program	
Senegal		Local Authorities Development Program	
Sierra Leone	National Commission for Social Action	Institutional Reform and Capacity Building Project	

(continued)

Table 4.4. Strategies of Active Operations in the Africa Region, by Country Context (continued)

Context and country	Community management (B1)	Local government planning and community management (B2)	Local government and community co-management (C1)	Local government management (C2)	Intergovernmental fiscal management (D)
Zambia		ZAMSIF (P)		ZAMSIF (S)	
Consolidating decentralization					
Ethiopia			Pastoral Community Development Program		
Ghana				CBRDP	
Tanzania		TASAF (S)	TASAF (P)		
Uganda		NUSAF	LGMSDP		Local Government Support Project
					LGMS

Source: Authors' compilation.

Note: Dark gray designates a conservative strategy; medium gray designates a matching strategy; and light gray designates a leading strategy. Countries with an operation characterized by a P and an S have two components (a primary and a secondary), resulting in a mixed strategy in which each component employs a distinct strategy. These mixed-strategy operations are often said to employ two financing windows, each with its own eligibility criteria and disbursement or management procedures. Abbreviations are as follows: CAP, Niger's Community Action Fund; CBRDP, Burkina Faso's Community-Based Rural Development Project and Mauritania's Community-Based Rural Development Program; LEEMP, Nigeria's Local Empowerment and Environmental Management Project; LGMSDP, Uganda's Local Government Management and Service Delivery Program; MASAF, Malawi Social Action Fund; NUSAF, Northern Uganda Social Action Fund; TASAF, Tanzania Social Fund; VCSP, Guinea's Village Communities Support Program; ZAMSIF, Zambia Social Investment Fund.

Most active local development projects have strategies that take advantage of the opportunities for institutional development. Of 34 projects, only 8 (24 percent) have followed conservative strategies. The other 26 (76 percent) have followed a matching strategy (18 projects, 52 percent), a leading strategy (2 projects, 6 percent), or a mixed approach that combines two strategies, at least one matching or leading (6 projects, 18 percent).

Dysfunctional Countries: Matching Strategies. Most local and community development projects in dysfunctional countries have followed a matching strategy that relies almost exclusively on communities, minimizing the role of local governments and other public bodies in implementation. In the Central African Republic, Democratic Republic of Congo, Liberia, and Sudan, operations predominantly have followed the classic community management model of CDD. In Liberia and Sudan, preliminary steps have been taken to establish consultative links to local administrative bodies, including introducing district planning to promote integrating fund-supported community investments in broader public investment plans.

Projects in Angola and Chad have employed leading strategies, with program designers judging local performance risks to be acceptably low despite dysfunctional national governance.

Angola's Third Social Action Fund Project (implemented since 2003) combines a large conventional community driven component with a smaller pilot that links the fund agency directly with deconcentrated district authorities (in Angola known as *municipios*). The pilot introduces district-level investment planning to complement community priority setting. After minimum conditions are satisfied, subproject funds are disbursed as grants to district administration (a C1 strategy).

Chad's Local Development Support Program, approved in 2004, uses an adaptable program loan (APL) to define the criteria for a national transition from classic community development (B1) in phase one to mixed community–local government co-management (C1) in phase two and, ultimately, to a community driven, local government–managed approach (C2 or D) in phase three.

Deconcentrated Systems: Various Strategies. In national contexts that lack statutory local governments or where local governments only exist in urban centers, various LCDD strategies have been employed. In these countries, the minimum goal is to improve the responsiveness and account-ability of deconcentrated administrative bodies to local people (B2). Niger's Community Action Program (CAP) follows a matching strategy, but other projects have tried to do more or do less with regard to institutional devel-opment, reflecting contrasting assessments of in-country performance and policy risk.

Mauritania's Community-Based Rural Development Program (CBRDP) adopted a conservative strategy. In Mauritania's high-risk environment, national decentralization policy was not advancing, and communes were weak decision makers and resource managers. CBRDP's funding mecha-nism, approved in 2004, employs classic community driven methods for its field investment operations and supports the central government in decentralization and local capacity building. Expectations for the govern-ment's political and administrative empowerment of communes are mod-est, so the project focuses on empowering community-based institutions in the subproject cycle and gradually introducing strategic area-based devel-opment planning at the commune level. CBRDP thus uses relatively static community management (strategy B1).

Niger's CAP adopted a matching strategy. The legal, political, and institutional bases for the developmental responsibility of communes (local governance entities) are substantially stronger in Niger than in Mauritania. So CAP, approved in 2003, employs a sequential strategy formalized through an APL. During the first phase, CAP provides field support for classic CDD: an empowerment and small investment pro-gram in several communes. Meanwhile, capacity-building investments prepare local officials to lead in participatory community development, in area-based planning, and in managing local investment resources.

CAP also supports the central government's decentralization effort. Sub-sequent phases anticipate expanding CDD, strengthening the capacity of communes, and gradually empowering more committed and capable com-mune authorities to lead community driven local development. The APL defines triggers for both local performance and national policy, including commune elections, as a precondition for continued funding. CAP's lead-ing strategy aims to move the country from stagnant deconcentration to incipient decentralization. After local elections took place in 2004, CAP strongly supported capacity building of the local governments.

Mozambique's District Planning and Finance Program adopted a lead-ing strategy. Because local government is constitutionally limited to urban areas, the rural-focused program aims to promote participatory and accountable local governance and more community-responsive development (strategy C2), in the context of institutionalized deconcentration. Even without local elections and statutory autonomy for districts, the project introduces elements typically characteristic of devolved local government, such as representative councils, participatory area development planning linked to local investment budgeting, and accountable financial management linked to subproject implementation. The limited mandate of district administration and limited budgets for education, health, and water have limited local plans, but the gradual institutionalization of consultative community councils to the management of program discretionary funds has boosted responsiveness and accountability. Even so, no opportunities are apparent for policy change that favors establishing statutory local governments outside urban towns.

Incipient Decentralization: Hybrid Strategies. Incipient decentralization is the most common country context for local and community development projects in Sub-Saharan Africa. Since 1990, many countries have established local government systems and created at least some local governments. In most, however, territorial coverage is incomplete, functional mandates are limited, access to discretionary resources is constrained, and capacities are low. Where decentralization is incipient, the minimum ambition for institutional development is to empower weak local governments by transferring resources through them and building their capacities for responsive, responsible, and accountable behavior (C1 or C2 strategies).

The 15 countries in a context of incipient decentralization that have active local and community development projects follow a variety of strategies. Benin, Burkina Faso, Burundi, The Gambia, Guinea, Mali, Rwanda, and Senegal follow a *hybrid matching strategy*, allocating funding and management responsibilities in part or in full to local governments (C1 strategies). Cameroon, Madagascar, Malawi, and Zambia follow a *mixed approach* that includes conservative and matching strategies combining direct financing to communities (either B1 or B2 type) and financing to local governments (C1 or C2 type) through parallel financing windows. Kenya and Sierra Leone have two *concurrent operations*, one with a conservative and the other with a matching strategy. Nigeria follows a *conservative strategy*.

Funding Stream as a Key Indicator of Strategy Type: Hybrid and Mixed Strategies

In *hybrid strategies*, all funding flows through local governments, with some or all of the funds assigned by the local governments to lower councils or community organizations for implementation. In *mixed strategies*, by contrast, projects allocate only part of the funding to local governments (to those that qualify as capable of managing funds), with a significant portion still going directly to community organizations. These strategies also differ in their engagement with decentralization policy reform, their scaling-up approach, and the organizational structure under the central government.

The following are some of the key features of hybrid strategies:

- *Importance of decentralization policy reform.* Projects with a hybrid strategy have tried to support community driven decentralization. Their aim is to build local governments from the ground up and to support decentralization reform. These operations tend to include reforming or implementing the legal and policy framework for fiscal, administrative, and political decentralization.
- *Sequential scaling up.* The typical approach is to test and initiate CDD in many rural local governments—a minimum of a third of local governments in the country—and then expand it to the whole country.
- *Organizational structure.* At the central government level, these programs create project implementation units in the ministry responsible for decentralization. If a social fund agency already exists, it is closed and mainstreamed into the ministry's unit. This has happened in Benin and Burundi. In Malawi, the unit was mainstreamed in the Ministry of Finance.

Projects pursuing a mixed strategy are more cautious in their alignment with decentralization policy. They try to manage the risks of decentralization by keeping two financing windows (one for financing local government and one for funding the community, corresponding to C2 and B2 strategies, respectively). Shifting resources from the community window to the local government window is often contingent on the performance of local governments. Allocating responsibilities to both communities and local governments allows program designers to hedge performance risk, while ensuring a reliable flow of targeted benefits through community-based institutions. Doing so combines conservative with matched or leading strategies. The following are some of the key features of mixed strategies:

- *Decentralization policy.* While these funds aim to demonstrate more participatory tools for local government planning and management, the funds do not engage directly with reforming the framework for legal and administrative decentralization.
- *Gradual territorial scaling up.* The programs scale up gradually, either operating within territories of the state or expanding from, for instance, one province or region to more provinces or regions.
- *Organizational structure.* Programs following a mixed strategy are usually implemented through semiautonomous agencies. One risk is that the agency might reduce the incentives to transfer responsibilities to local governments. The upside is that this structure preserves institutional capacity, which might be an asset in unstable institutional environments.

Concurrent Strategies: Sierra Leone. In Sierra Leone, two LCDD programs coexist, pursuing two different strategies. The National Commission for Social Action relies on community-based strategies and was designed as a postconflict response, before the government initiated a process of devolution through the Local Government Act and local elections of 2004. The Institutional Reform and Capacity-Building Project relies on local government strategies and is designed to support implementation of the new decentralization policy. Unlike traditional local government reform programs, this project takes a strong developmental, results-oriented approach to capacity building, emphasizing structures and mechanisms to promote downward accountability through participatory local planning, transparency, and access to information about local government performance.

The National Commission for Social Action began a process of adjustment that included modifying the feeder road component to provide direct financing to local governments and strengthening the capacity of local governments to manage public works projects. While the future role of the agency is still being discussed, the social fund is deepening its engagement along the lines of a fund for social assistance to vulnerable groups (for example, piloting use of a conditional cash transfer for vulnerable groups).

The Bank has also supported an LCDD pilot program called GoBifo (which means Go Forward). This program has been experimenting with village-level participatory decision making, civic engagement in local governance, and local government block grants to villages. Experiments that prove to have value added (through rigorous evaluations) will be mainstreamed through the Institutional Reform and Capacity-Building Project.

Conservative Strategies: Nigeria. Although local governments are elected in Nigeria, local and community development programs still transfer all of their resources through the community management approach—a conservative strategy (B1 or B2). The strategic decision to *underdesign* reflects a more cautious approach to supporting decentralization.

In Nigeria, the overall governance environment and decentralization framework were so problematic—that is, policy and performance risks were high—that the project teams decided that a local government management strategy was too risky.[5] Even with the election of local governments and some fiscal transfers, corruption in government was high, and the decentralization framework was deficient. Both the Community Poverty Reduction Project and the Local Empowerment and Environmental Management Project (LEEMP) opted for community management, but their strategies differed. The former completely bypassed local governments (B1), while the latter created a local council with participants from the local government, community-based organizations, and deconcentrated sectors. That council had authority for approving projects and for local planning (B2). The programs avoided overlapping on the ground by operating in different areas.

But the two approaches to CDD proved confusing and inefficient for the government and for Bank management. In response, the Bank gradually merged the approaches. The first step was to harmonize the operations manuals as much as possible (unifying the co-financing percentages across projects, for example). The next step was to design the follow-up project in an integrated manner, building on the lessons from the first set of projects. LEEMP is proposing to make access to its funds conditional on local governments' adoption of a participatory and transparent planning mechanism. This would move indirectly toward a co-management strategy (C1), even if the follow-up project continues to use community management.

Consolidating Decentralization: Varied Strategies

Where decentralization is consolidating, the key potential contribution of an LCDD program is to promote improvements and innovations on the demand side of local governance. Public sector reform programs usually focus on strengthening local governments' functional mandate and resource base. The emphasis is on systems for planning, budgeting, financial management, and accounting—the supply side. Two other capacities are needed for accountable local development:

- Local government's capacity to engage with local civil society
- Local civil society's capacity to co-produce services and to hold the local government to account.

These demand-side innovations need to be introduced carefully to avoid coordination problems or conflicts with supply-side reform and capacity building. Because demand-side efforts require engaging beneficiaries, community organizations, and other civil society actors, they require a different approach. South Africa has undertaken several programs that have employed grants to build demand and promote accountability grants (not financed by the Bank).[6]

Out of the four countries with active LCDD, Ethiopia, Ghana, and Uganda have followed matching strategies, Uganda has followed a concurrent approach, and Tanzania has followed a combined concurrent, mixed strategy.

Matching Strategy: Uganda. In Uganda a matching strategy institutionalizes a community-managed grant within the intergovernmental transfer system. In more mature systems, the intergovernmental transfer and capacity-building system might be adapted to absorb CDD at the lowest level of local government, without the need to create a separate fund. Uganda's Local Government Management and Service Delivery Program takes this approach with its recently approved operation, which earmarks a percentage of transfers to local governments for financing community-managed projects.

Concurrent Approach: Uganda. Projects in northern Uganda follow a conservative strategy in view of high performance risks. Even where decentralization is consolidating, a fund-based strategy might be warranted to deal with exceptional circumstances, such as regional conflict or a geographically or ethnically defined target group marginalized socially or economically. This is the case for the conflict-motivated social fund in northern Uganda (Northern Uganda Social Action Fund) and for the Pastoral Community Development Program in Ethiopia, both of which are now in a second phase and still use the same approach, but with more linkages to local government being established.

Combined Strategy: Tanzania. In Tanzania, a local and community development fund complements an operation that seeks to strengthen decentralization and local government. While the first phase of the Tanzania Social Fund (TASAF, 1999–2004) adopted a conservative strategy, the second phase (starting in 2004) deepens and complements efforts to consolidate decentralization. There is a clear division of labor between TASAF and the Local Government Support Project. TASAF supports interactions at the subdistrict level (villages) and bottom-up relations with the district. Meanwhile, the Local Government Reform Program supports the central government's relations with districts. In countries with multiple-level local governments and many village-level governments, local and community development funds can strengthen capacities at that lowest level, while public sector reforms focus on higher levels.

Implementation Strategies and Local Governance Outcomes

The previous section shows that most active LCDD projects are designed to strengthen the institutional basis for good local governance. This section looks at implementation—the institutional outcomes. A comprehensive and systematic assessment, however, is outside the scope of this review. The idea is to provide illustrative evidence, to highlight challenges facing the projects, and to examine possible solutions.

Field experience indicates that good local governance requires empowered local governments and empowered citizens and communities.[7] Such empowerment requires interventions in the following three areas:

- A legal and policy framework that defines the responsibilities and resources of local governments, along with the mechanisms for accountability
- Systems and capacities for responsive, transparent, and accountable local public expenditure management—including public sector systems for planning, budgeting, financial management, accounting, and monitoring and evaluation—and for citizen and community empowerment to influence decision making (see World Bank 2004f)
- A strong but lean central government unit that monitors the quality of local governance and supports proactive, adaptive local institutional reform and capacity building.

How LCDD Projects Influence the National Policy and Legal Framework. The legal and policy framework for decentralization influences whether local governments and communities will be able to harvest the promised service delivery and governance benefits of decentralized development. Whether and how much LCDD projects can and should engage in decentralization policy reforms is a matter for debate. Some believe that these should be left to pure public sector reform or local government strengthening.

The experience of various LCDD projects shows that some operations can be structured to support various aspects of decentralization policy under different types of country contexts (the case of Burkina Faso, Ghana, and Guinea). The case of Zambia illustrates both the risk of neglecting policy reform (2000–05) as well as the risk of trying to address policy reform (2006–07).

In a *deconcentrated context*, Burkina Faso's Community-Based Rural Development Project (CBRDP) has been instrumental in the emergence of elected local governments. When the project began in 2000, Burkina Faso had a deconcentrated state in rural areas and devolution in urban areas. This APL supports the government's National Program for Decentralized Rural Development (2001–15), which seeks to devolve power to rural areas. The first phase (2001–07) supported the formulation and implementation of the country's decentralization policy. The result was a revised Local Government Code, the establishment of 302 new rural municipalities, and the holding of the first rural municipal elections in April 2006. Political decentralization was one trigger for the second phase.

CBRDP spurred political decentralization from below, showing the capacity of village committees (*commissions villageoises de gestion des terroirs*) to act as village governments by planning and managing public funds through participatory local governance. The Local Government Code, acknowledging the importance of village government, replaced the village committees with elected village councils for development (*conseil villageois de développement*) and mandated that they contribute to municipal development plans, promote local development in the village, develop annual investment programs, and receive transfers from the commune councils.

In a context of *incipient decentralization*, Guinea's Village Communities Support Program (VCSP) supports fiscal decentralization, legal reform, and capacity building. When the program started in 1999, Guinea was in incipient decentralization, but stagnant.[8] The first phase (1999–2007) initiated a learning process for implementing decentralized rural development by demonstrating that committees for rural development could plan and manage local investments in close collaboration with communities (strategy C1) and by supporting institutional reforms. A recent study on decentralization in Guinea showcases VCSP as moving the country's

decentralization forward (World Bank 2007b). On fiscal decentralization, the study recommends scaling up the local investment fund piloted
by VCSP,[9] which had been designed to evolve into the government's main
instrument for making fiscal transfers to committees for rural development. On institutional reforms and capacity development, the VCSP is
critical on four dimensions:

- Streamlining the legal and regulatory framework for decentralization,
  resulting in a substantially better decentralization framework being
  approved in 2006[10]
- Reforming the finance law regulating the local development tax, bringing dramatic improvements in tax collection—in some case as much as
  50 percent—partly in response to communities' close involvement in
  decision making
- Building the capacity of rural development committees to develop and
  manage participatory local development plans
- Strengthening the capacity of the Ministry of Territorial Administration and Decentralization.

All triggers for going from phase one to phase two were achieved.[11]

In the context of *consolidating decentralization*, Ghana's Community-
Based Rural Development Program (CBRDP) introduced a new fiscal transfer mechanism. It became a transitional system, moving to
performance-based block grants under the emerging district development
fund and the functional and organizational assessment tool arrangements.
The block transfer system applies a formula similar to that of the district
assemblies' common fund, though modified to emphasize rural districts.
It relies on government-mandated planning and procurement systems but
requires project-specific reporting and auditing procedures.

After almost 10 years of classic community-based development, in 2000
Zambia's third Social Investment Fund (ZAMSIF) introduced a strategy to
move gradually toward the intergovernmental model (strategy D). While
Zambia had elected local governments and a sound decentralization law,
the erratic and limited transfers were absorbed by weak and debt-ridden
local administrations. ZAMSIF proposed a three-phase, 10-year APL aimed
at building local government capacities for participatory local development
while shifting control of the investment funds from communities to local
governments. The first phase had two financing windows, a community
investment fund that transferred funds to community-managed investments identified through a local investment plan (strategy B2) and a district

investment fund that transferred funds to district governments to manage investments (strategy C2). It devolved greater management responsibilities as districts acquired capacity and met performance milestones.

ZAMSIF's decision to rely on separate public sector reform to address the other bottlenecks in the intergovernmental administrative framework backfired. Those operations never materialized. Bloated local governments saddled with debt fostered high turnover among local officials, rendering ZAMSIF's training and capacity-building ineffective. They also limited efforts to strengthen absorptive capacity among district governments. The district investment fund component did not move forward, and the overall graduation strategy was stuck. ZAMSIF's community window allowed quick restructuring, scaling down the district window and scaling up the community window.

As the restructured ZAMSIF III came to a close, Zambia's decentralization gathered new momentum with approval of the Decentralization Implementation Plan. Learning from past experience, the Bank decided that, rather than design a fourth ZAMSIF phase with a greater focus on engaging local government, it would support a new decentralization operation linked to the ministries of local government and finance. This new operation—driven by the national decentralization policy and focusing principally on intergovernmental fiscal systems and local authority for development planning, personnel management, and service delivery— would preserve and incorporate the best community driven elements introduced into the new local government framework by the social fund.

But the people defending decentralization in the cabinet came under political pressure from those concerned about the distribution of resources among localities with varying political affiliations. The resulting tensions paralyzed the reform, which precluded reaching consensus on the terms of a new support program among the government and its development partners, including the Bank. As a result, Zambia lost the continuing benefits of a highly productive social fund *and* the prospective benefits of a support operation for community driven, local development–oriented decentralization.

How LCDD Programs Build Capacities to Implement National Policies for Local Governance

The comparative advantage of local and community development programs has been on the demand side of local governance. The programs have been particularly effective in demonstrating the viability of more participatory and accountable local planning systems; transparent practices in procurement, financial management, and accounting; and greater citizen oversight and feedback loops for service providers.

The trend away from community management and toward local government management has expanded the investment allocated through participatory local development plans led by local governments. In the best cases, these plans both allocate program resources and leverage local governments' own resources and those of other government programs to meet community demand for services. In Zambia, the Ministry of Finance integrated ZAMSIF's participatory district planning methodology into guidelines for district planning and budgeting. In Guinea, the Guinea Education for All Project recently agreed to build more than 100 elementary schools through fund-supported local plans in the context of the VCSP. In addition, all development projects in rural Guinea agreed to use the local development planning process pioneered by the VCSP as the sole vehicle for implementing local development (World Bank 2007b: 7). In Burkina Faso, CBRDP I ended with 100 percent of villages having completed their local development plans and 88 percent having developed an annual investment plan between 2002 and 2006. Some villages have obtained funding for their subprojects from donors other than the World Bank.

Despite the almost universal introduction of participatory local planning, learning and cross-fertilization about methods, good practices, and common challenges remain limited. LCDD programs should tap into the obvious overlaps between their participatory planning and the vast experience with participatory budgeting in Latin America.

Accountability and Performance-Based Approaches to Building Local Capacity. LCDD projects have experimented with a variety of social accountability tools to mitigate the risks of corruption and misuse of resources and to build citizens' capacities to oversee service providers.[12] The Malawi Social Action Fund (MASAF) III has expanded and deepened the accountability regime by introducing a social accountability framework. One mechanism, the comprehensive community scorecard, was piloted in more than 500 communities between October 2005 and March 2006. In Ghana, CBRD used integrated citizen report cards and community scorecards as part of its beneficiary assessment and piloted a diagnostic tool for measuring empowerment during decentralization (see Yaron 2008). In The Gambia, the Community Driven Development Project created a Good Governance Facility, financed with about 5 percent of the Community

Development Facility (about $500,000). It will finance community-service organizations' proposals to strengthen accountability and transparency related to the project, with an annual call for proposals.

Piloting performance-based grants tied to improvements in local government capacity is an opportunity that most African LCDD programs have yet to tap. The programs in Sierra Leone, Tanzania, and Uganda are leading this process. They are on the trajectory of local government reform, which introduces a system of performance incentives for accessing grants that is contingent on demonstrating good practices in local public expenditure management and includes transparent procurement and financial management procedures.

Zambia's ZAMSIF was one of the few LCDD programs on the community-based trajectory. It developed a district performance assessment tool that gauged the development of capacity of rural district governments, and it achieved the incentives of greater access to funds and responsibilities. The follow-on to ZAMSIF tried institutionalizing it, but, as mentioned, the project stalled during preparation. One of the key challenges is to embed demand-based indicators in the performance incentive system, as the CBRDP empowerment pilot is trying to do in Ghana (Yaron 2008).

Lessons Learned: The Importance of LCDD Fit to Country Context

First, *adjusting to the country context is different from seeking to change it*. Development programs must be highly adaptable to institutional conditions in an environment of weak governing capacity at the national, state, and local levels, unstable and unpredictable policy making, and limited democratic culture and civic capacity. LCDD programs, with their highly flexible design based on a few core principles and a handful of proven methodologies, fulfill this requirement.

Program designers must make strategic choices between improving access to services, developing local institutions, and allocating responsibilities among the central program agency, local governments, communities, and the private sector. Because the methodological options for LCDD programs are well known and rapidly disseminated, these decisions can be based on local experience and regional or international good practice. To build on existing capacities and experiences, the final configuration can be adapted based on the context and trajectory of preexisting programs.

The criticism that LCDD programs use a cookie-cutter approach has some validity, but it is exaggerated. These programs are not designed the same way. They share some basic principles, but they rely on a variety of institutional strategies and management instruments. Program strategic design today reflects a contingency approach, with program elements combined based on the country-specific policy priorities, institutional contexts, and experience. Even so, learning and adaptation are required. This reflects the challenges of implementing complex programs in low-capacity African countries and the path dependence of each country's reform and institutional development. Each stage of capacity building must be grounded in prior stages.

Sometimes changes in strategy reflect adjustment to changing country contexts, but sometimes leading strategies change country contexts. Less risk-averse program designers employing leading strategies in Burkina Faso, Mozambique, and Rwanda have encouraged central governments to adopt policies more friendly to decentralization and community empowerment.

Second, *managing the transition from community management to local government management strategies remains a challenge.* Successful LCDD programs that rely on community management face significant challenges when they expand the roles and responsibilities of local authorities. As local governments gradually assume greater roles, risks must be carefully managed—both fiduciary risks and risks associated with empowering public intermediaries as well as direct beneficiary representatives. Accommodating the shift requires strengthening the accountability of local officials to community members—a significant new challenge for most programs, which are more accustomed to working directly with community institutions. As decentralization advances, the adoption and sequencing of mixed or hybrid approaches depend both on the country's readiness to vest authority in local governments and on the prudence of maintaining an institutional safeguard given the nature of community–local government relations.

The third lesson sounds a cautionary note: *central government institutions can undermine local accountability.* Some African governments have started to promote a different approach to local development: constituency development funds. In essence, the governments allocate discretionary resources to members of parliament as the preferred means of achieving decentralized financing. The amounts are usually small, but not always, and members of parliament have full discretion regarding their use. This can lead to opaque and personalistic local spending. Officially, members are held accountable by parliament, their constituents, and the press. Constituents may have a strong sense that the money is theirs, held in trust, and demand local accountability, even putting reelection in play. Coordination between funding for discretionary spending and sectoral plans and funding for local government and community plans has often been very difficult.

Notes

1. These "structural factors" reflect relatively static characteristics and policies of national regimes, factors that do not vary significantly in the short term or that depend on local conditions. Other characteristics that are related to the specific capacities and behaviors of local actors are discussed in relation to the dynamic analysis of the risks associated with fund reliance on local governments as decision makers and resource managers.

2. In some countries, such as Mozambique, statutory local governments exist in urban areas but are by statute or even by constitutional provision not authorized in rural districts, where a majority of the population resides.

3. While the primary bias is toward local governments, a secondary bias is toward local public sector institutions, even if they are not statutory local authorities but rather delegated or deconcentrated state bodies responsible for local governance and service delivery. In other words, private (for example, NGO-managed) or parallel direct-to-community fund modalities are assumed to be the least desirable options, except in circumstances where poor national or local governance justifies bypassing the local public sector.

4. For instance, some cases of incipient decentralization are dynamic and forward moving, even though they are at early stages of installing a local government framework (low policy risk). In other cases, political and institutional support for ongoing change processes is weak, and thus decentralization and local government development stagnate (high policy risk).

5. Nigeria had two active community driven operations that financed local infrastructure: the Community Poverty Reduction Project and the Local Empowerment and Environmental Management Program. A third operation, FADAMA, focused on productive projects supporting small farmers' organizations. As of 2009, there are only two LCDD operations: the Community Social Development Program and FADAMA III. Efforts are being made at the local government level to harmonize the two teams.

6. The experience of the U.S. Community Partnerships Grants, which spread to South Africa and other countries, is relevant. These programs provide small grants to citizens to help them to cover the costs of citizen-initiated neighborhood projects. The central element is that small groups of citizens are the prime movers in initiating proposals, organizing work plans, competing for

grants, and carrying out projects that improve daily life in their communities (Adams, Bell, and Brown 2002, 2003).

7. For a framework that identifies the supply- and demand-side elements required to empower local governments and communities as part of a devolutionary policy, see World Bank (2007e).

8. The Decentralization Law, passed in the mid-1980s, was incomplete and inadequate to guide policy implementation, leaving the elected local governments (*Communautés Rurales de Développement*) without the resources or technical skills needed to promote local development and assert themselves vis-à-vis central government.

9. The local investment fund ($20 million) allocated matching grants to 70 of the 303 rural development communities based on a formula drawing on population and poverty data and requiring a 20 percent contribution from rural development and other communities.

10. The Local Government Code harmonizes, for the first time, all previous texts regulating the functioning of local governments and spells out decentralization arrangements in a single, comprehensive text.

11. The second phase, approved in 2007, aims to expand coverage of the program to all 303 rural development communities and puts greater emphasis on initiating and leading a harmonization effort, expecting that, by the end of this phase, all financing for local development planning and implementation will be channeled through a single mechanism, following procedures outlined in the new framework.

12. For a review of mechanisms to build social accountability around local government performance, see Serrano (2006).

Scaling Up, Step by Step: Analysis, Policy Reform, Pilot Phase, and Implementation

Hans P. Binswanger-Mkhize, Tuu-Van Nguyen, Jacomina P. de Regt, Willem Heemskerk, and Gerard Baltissen

Well-functioning small-scale local and community driven development (LCDD) successes are a prerequisite for scaling up, but they rarely can be scaled up directly. We sometimes refer to these small-scale successes as "boutiques," as they may be nice, expensive, and not replicable. Consequently, a diagnostic phase is often necessary to establish the preconditions for a scaled-up LCDD program. This should be followed by a pilot phase in which the processes, logistics, and tools for scaling up to national levels are first developed and fully tested. Such scaling-up pilots should cover all communities and subdistricts in at least one district of a country. The scaling-up pilot leads to proven procedures, logistics, and tools that can be summarized in an operational manual that subsequently can be translated into local languages, rolled out, and further adapted in the remaining districts of a country, province, or state. Only then can a truly scaled-up LCDD program be put in place that can cover an entire country. Box 5.1 presents the series of steps involved in the scaling-up process.

In addition to achieving small-scale LCDD success, a second prerequisite to scaling up is obtaining national policy and institutional support. Unlike a discrete LCDD project, which can succeed independent of national interest or benign neglect, scaling up is a national initiative that requires national policy and institutional support. The diagnostic phase will determine and ensure the minimum conditions and effective local-level participation.

The *minimum conditions* consist of laying the national groundwork: assessing country context for scaling up LCDD, achieving buy-in among

---

BOX 5.1

Steps to Scaling Up

- Diagnostic phase to ensure minimum conditions
- Preprogram development at the national level
- Preprogram development at the local level
- Pilot phase of scaling up
- Resource flows and accountability´
- Scaling up
- Consolidation

---

government and sector leadership, reviewing the policy environment and synchronizing policy and partnerships among the national government, development institutions, and donors, and defining the exact components of a national LCDD program. This consensus building is necessary so that the scaling-up program is clearly defined and effectively supported, financed, and advanced. The LCDD toolkit has been developed to facilitate the diagnosis and consensus building at this stage.

Effective local-level preparation begins with the selection of one or several pilot districts or small provinces within which the LCDD program can be scaled up to all local government areas and communities. These pilots are critical to developing the mechanisms, logistics, manuals, and tools that can then be applied in subsequent scaling up to regional or national levels. This process includes defining the actors, functions, and responsibilities; undertaking training, facilitation, and participatory planning; and clarifying resource flows, resource allocation, and accountability mechanisms, following through with the diverse elements of LCDD at the scale of an entire local government area. When the pilot design is proven to work, it is possible to follow through on a larger scale, keeping in mind that constant learning will shape each subsequent level of scaling up.

The chapter presents a step-by-step approach to ensure a comprehensive analysis leading to at least the minimum conditions of government support, followed by designing and planning the scale-up of multisectoral LCDD initiatives.[1] This chapter is not a straightjacket approach. Given the varying governance structures, capacities, and social, economic, political, and historical specifics of each country, scaling up and program design must be tailor-made. Therefore, whenever possible, the chapter presents several options from which to select or adapt those most appropriate for the specific country context. Each section of the chapter presents key guidelines or a menu of options, tools, and design elements to address a specific goal.

Later, during the pilot phase, all of the tools and logistics for scaling up should first be developed and tested in one district or small province, as in the Borgou pilot in Benin, or in a few districts or provinces, as in Mexico's decentralized regional development (DRD) projects or Indonesia's Kecamatan Development Program (KDP). Such field-testing will quickly identify bottlenecks, which may, for example, prevent rapid disbursement or require legal or regulatory changes. It will result in a full set of logistics, operational and training manuals, materials, and tools that can then be translated into other national languages and adapted to local conditions in a rollout process that ultimately covers all districts or provinces. Furthermore, the program development phase can provide additional cues as to how the national policy or institutional environment should be reformed to support the process.

For LCDD to be scaled up from a boutique project to a national program, it is necessary for national leadership to support the approach fully, for central institutions and sectors to be aligned, for administrative and fiscal decentralization to be making progress, and for governments' own fiscal resources, both national and local, eventually to become the main support for LCDD programs. Ensuring that these conditions exist begins with a diagnostic phase.

Diagnostics and Alignment

Ideally, as part of the preparation of a poverty reduction strategy[2] or some similar long-range strategic planning vision, interdisciplinary teams would carry out a diagnostic of the current situation and policies and formulate a national strategy on LCDD before any national or scaled-up program is designed (see box 5.2). This can be an indirect way of finding or nurturing interest at key levels of government.

The discussion of scaling up LCDD can take form with key actors at the national level who, together, determine the pace and scope of such a scaled-up effort. However, key actors (such as officials at ministries of finance and planning, key sectoral ministries, and donor agencies) may not have the

---

BOX 5.2

Steps to Scaling Up: Diagnostic Phase to Ensure Minimum Conditions

- Assess the LCDD underpinnings in the national context
- Align with the national government, donors, and other partners
- Synchronize and transform policies, regulations, and laws with LCDD
- Have national leadership and coordination.

---

full picture of what is already occurring in the country or of the role that national policies play in fostering or hindering the scaling up of project-level experiences to a national program. For instance, many national procurement laws do not cover procurement by local governments, communities, or informal associations in communities. While such national laws may be overruled or ignored in the spirit of a pilot program, policies and regulations need to be aligned if a national, scaled-up program is to succeed.

Such a review was carried out in both Benin and Burkina Faso, bringing together all of the actors. In Benin, the government issued a community driven development (CDD) policy that guides the LCDD program, which is now at national scale. Although this program is not funded as a sector-wide approach (SWAp), all actors meet regularly to discuss further harmonization.

The LCDD national stocktaking and review toolkit,[3] developed by the Royal Tropical Institute (KIT) on behalf of the World Bank, is designed to enable interdisciplinary teams[4] to analyze a country's readiness to scale up LCDD and identify what is required to create the political, economic, and legal foundation for scaling up to succeed (Heemskerk and Baltissen 2005). It is not a toolkit to guide precise quantitative analysis; rather, it is a toolkit to facilitate a process that, in the course of inventory and analysis of national progress, helps to (a) stimulate exchange and learning between actors, (b) build consensus about LCDD, and (c) foster national ownership of LCDD implementation.

The toolkit will help an LCDD strategy team to (a) provide, to national government officials and donors, a description and analysis of the "state of affairs" with respect to LCDD implementation; (b) contribute to strategic planning for further implementation; and (c) identify issues for further study and more detailed analysis.

The expected results include the following:

- A useful description of the state of affairs with respect to LCDD
- Analysis of the state of affairs
- Elements identified for strategic planning and future LCDD implementation
- Elements identified for further study and analysis
- A visual presentation (colored matrix) of a shared appreciation and understanding of the LCDD state of affairs.

Examples of Questions to Be Pursued in the Diagnostic Phase

The diagnostic toolkit is designed to answer systematically a large number of questions. The answers to many of these questions may be found in previous studies, such as poverty assessments, social and gender assessments, public sector capacity assessments, and financial systems and procurement assessments. Table 5.1 provides examples of the questions to be answered, but it is not meant to be exhaustive. All potential questions can be found in Heemskerk and Baltissen (2005). A key task, therefore, is to bring together the documents that contain these analyses and to complement them with more information, as necessary.[5]

Visual Representation of an LCDD Readiness Matrix

Table 5.2 presents an example of such a shared appreciation of the state of affairs in a country regarding decentralization and community development. This is the state of affairs at that point in time as agreed by the actors who participated in the process. The toolkit should not be used to compare countries, as each country is unique. It might be used in one country to compare the state of affairs over time (if the actors in the multidisciplinary teams are similar). It is interesting to see how similar groups in different states in Nigeria assessed the situation in their state prior to the 2006 elections. Even with the same national or federal policy toward decentralization and local governments and the lack of a federal community development policy, states differed in their approaches, and these differences showed in the collective perceptions of the assessors.

National Commitment and Preconditions

While a sector-specific LCDD program can succeed in a country that does not meet minimum conditions, a multisectoral LCDD program must have

Table 5.1. Examples of Key Questions to Be Pursued during the Diagnostics Phase

Topic	Questions	Key analytical tools and reports
The role of the center and the capacity of local governments	Is central government already playing a coordination rather than an implementation role? To what extent are elected local governments accountable to the public and to community-based organizations? How credible are local governments regarding service delivery? Is central government transferring an adequate share of financial resources to local governments? Is central government transferring sectoral staff to local governments? Assuming that local governments have the power to levy taxes, how willing are they to tax their constituencies?	*Institutional analysis reports* examine the capacity and deficiencies of the various groups that will be involved in the co-production of the program (communities, local governments, sectoral agencies, NGOs), identify the institutions (formal and social) on which to build at the community and local levels, and map out the relationships between these institutions.
The capacity of communities and civil society	Do the communities have a culture of self-mobilization and self-help? If yes, in what form? How strong is civil society?	*Participatory social assessment reports* examine village needs and priorities as well as the sociocultural, historical, and political context of the program. They include tools such as the stakeholder analysis and the analysis known as Strengths, Weaknesses, Opportunities, and Challenges.
The structure of the sectors	Are sector policies delegating service delivery to local governments?	*Analyses of existing planning and budgeting systems* examine the planning and budgeting systems within and between governmental structures and agencies and provide information on organizational and decision-making dynamics within government.

Other or past programs	Have past programs tried similar approaches? If yes, what can be learned from them? Are any other CDD-type programs operating in the country to which the program could be grafted or with which it could collaborate?	*Inventories of past or ongoing CDD-related programs* indicate where capitalization on, or harmonization with, other programs may be possible, desirable, or required. Relevant programs may include single-sector CDD programs, social funds, local government development programs or funds, or broader decentralization or poverty reduction efforts. The research tool developed in Uganda could be used to assess perceptions of stakeholders regarding different LCDD programs.
Poverty levels	Where are the major pockets of poverty that the program should initially target or to which it should devote more resources?	*Poverty assessment reports* identify the major pockets of poverty and analyze its major causes at both the national and local levels. This information can provide guidance on areas that the program should initially target.
Accountability systems	How is the accountability structure set up?	*Fiduciary system assessment reports* map out the intergovernmental financial allocation and transfer systems. They also examine the procurement systems and accountability measures of the various governmental agencies.

Source: Binswanger and Ngyuen 2005.

Table 5.2. A Shared Appreciation-Readiness Matrix (Level of Progress)

	Community strengthening	Local government strengthening	Realigning the center	Accountability	Capacity development
Vision	Very strong	Strong	Average	Weak	Average
Enabling environment	Average	Average	Very weak	Weak	Weak
Tangible results	Weak	Weak	Very weak	Very weak	Weak

Source: Heemskerk and Baltissen 2005.
Note: Assessments made by multidisciplinary team in a given country.

a national commitment if it is to scale up successfully. A country must meet certain preconditions, including the following:

- Strong political commitment to local empowerment and decentralization
- A well-designed decentralization program geared toward local empowerment
- An effort to build on existing efforts, such as one or several successful, cost-effective community and local government projects
- Government and donor willingness to work toward unified disbursement mechanisms.

The extent to which these minimum conditions are met varies enormously among countries, and where they are not met, there are no simple cookie-cutter approaches to achieving them. It is extremely important to have a clear diagnosis on where each country is at the start of the process (see box 5.3). Given that donors increasingly provide budget support for reforms such as decentralization and local empowerment, the donors are also piloting the development of tools with which to assess the political economy of such reforms[6] in order to determine the likelihood that such reforms will succeed.

Where the preconditions are not met, the diagnostic toolkit is an aid to initiate a process that ensures that the minimum conditions are put in place as part of, or in parallel to, the scaling up of LCDD. This process facilitates intensive discussions among stakeholders and puts them in the position of problem solvers. If stakeholders are strategically chosen, this process helps to transform and align national policies and strategies with the programs being scaled up.

Strong Political Commitment

Strong political commitment to local empowerment and to decentralization is vital to scaling up. In many countries, however, the political and

BOX 5.3

Mexico DRD I: Building on Lessons Learned

In Mexico, the success of the first program of decentralized regional development (DRD I) was in large part due to the fact that its design was based on the lessons learned from the previous integrated rural development programs. DRD I grafted itself onto Solidaridad, a large, ongoing national poverty reduction initiative, and took full advantage of the ongoing decentralization process.

social institutions are not conducive to shifting power to the grassroots and are often directly opposed to it. Central governments are often reluctant to let go of their traditional roles on the basis that they have a comparative advantage in the supply of public works and services, that local empowerment may threaten the current political balance, and that communities or even local governments will never be able to learn to manage their own projects and resources.

Where the political commitment is still missing, the LCDD team can start shifting political opinion in favor of local empowerment in two ways. First, it can showcase the successes of local and community development. In most countries, well-documented successful LCDD approaches can convince even tough skeptics that empowered communities and local governments can effectively plan, contract, construct, operate, and maintain their own projects and services and manage their own budgets. Where successful approaches do not exist, tours by key decision makers to successful programs outside the country, and additional pilots in the country, can fill the gap. Indeed, a major indicator of success in Brazil's Northeast Rural Development Program and India's Kerala Water Supply Program was the political success of local and regional leaders who had endorsed the approach. Showcase programs also give rise to local and regional LCDD champions who can become instrumental in shifting the political tide.

Second, the team can conduct information campaigns to raise the consciousness of both the general public and the government. Disseminating the successes of various local empowerment programs through free broadcast media (television and radio) or community radio can generate public demand and pressure, while holding stakeholder forums can confront authorities with the demands and concerns of their beneficiaries. Open communication and regular dialogue can help to build confidence, trust, and a common vision between a government and its public.

Decentralization of Financial and Governing Structures

A central premise of LCDD is that decentralization is the key to both scaling up and the sustainable fostering of participation and resource transfers to communities. While scaling up can begin without waiting for a fully decentralized structure, it is preferable for political, fiscal, and administrative decentralization[7] to be under way at program launch and, if possible, supported by a capacity development program with the following features:

- *Willingness to reform the intergovernmental fiscal system, including transfers and local revenue generation.* Such reforms can ensure that local governments ultimately receive resources commensurate with their increased responsibilities. In Indonesia, for instance, in light of the tremendous progress of the first two phases of KDP and the growing management needs of their districts, the government decided to issue new decentralization laws that gave the districts control over 40 percent of public spending and required them to regulate village government to promote village autonomy and empowerment.
- *An existing local government structure or fairly well-defined plans for a future local government structure.* This can provide the basis for local governance planning. In the LCDD programs in Burkina Faso, Madagascar, Mali, and South Africa's new municipalities, the local government structures allow funds and technical assistance to be routed to communities directly through local governments.
- *Sectors that are working on their decentralization visions and plans.* A multisector LCDD program involves many, if not most, sectors of government and the economy. Ensuring technical excellence in each of the sectors, while at the same time responding to local needs, will require a coordinated effort between local governments and sector-specific management and supervision processes. This can only be achieved if sectoral staff, resources, and responsibilities are assigned directly to local government offices. In the meantime, deconcentration can be a useful first step to provide some administrative resources to the grassroots level. However, individual deconcentrated sectoral offices will, in the long run, impose a burden on coordination and management processes and thus should only be seen as a temporary

expedient. In many countries, the deconcentrated sectors become one of the main obstacles to full decentralization, as deconcentrated staff, for career reasons, resist being switched from employment with the parent ministry to employment with a local government.

Building on Earlier Community or Local Government Empowerment Efforts

Earlier successful, cost-effective community and local government programs or pilots that aimed to support local development or decentralization, such as social funds or local development funds of the United Nations Capital Development Fund (UNCDF) can act as a springboard for the emerging program. Such programs provide ready-made structures and processes and a wealth of experience, which can be built on or coordinated with and can be used as demonstration programs.

Government and Donor Willingness to Use Unified Disbursement Mechanisms

Unified disbursement mechanisms, in which communities and local governments satisfy the same requirements and follow the same procedures no matter who ultimately finances their expenditures, would significantly simplify resource flows and dramatically reduce learning and transaction costs and co-production difficulties. Unified disbursement mechanisms should become a single national system for transferring resources to communities and local governments and ideally should include all of their own government and donor funds. The mechanisms should allow for the coexistence of fungible development funds at the local government and community levels for the bulk of resource transfers, with small windows earmarked for exceptional needs and circumstances. Building these unified disbursement and accountability mechanisms should be viewed as a component of the reform of government's own disbursement and accountability systems and be embedded in the intergovernmental fiscal transfer system. Once donor funding is pooled and disbursed through government's own intergovernmental fiscal transfer system, a major hurdle in developing SWAps has been met.

When Decentralization Systems Are Poorly Developed

The level of decentralization varies from country to country. Given different initial conditions, LCDD programs can build incrementally from the country's specific starting point. At this point, however, a design team is likely to encounter difficulties when faced with the uncertain direction of the decentralization process. The best option is to work with stakeholders in the decentralization process to clarify the likely future institutional setup, as was done in both Burkina Faso and Mexico in the preparation of large programs. Based on the findings, the team can then design program mechanisms so that they fit into the emerging institutional structure and can later be transferred to them.

The fact that a country is considering scaling up an LCDD program is a significant beginning, implying the willingness to create the national preconditions for scaling up. Once that process is under way, the *local* program development phase can begin.

Following through on Reforms

It is imperative that the reform effort and other commitments by government, sector players, and development partners are genuine. Ideally, the buy-in process will bind government leaders, country moral leaders, and international donor institutions into the kind of partnership that allows the scaling-up implementation team to keep the momentum going for decentralization, policy reforms, and supportive regulations. And, as a backup, an agreed-to mechanism to enforce cooperation will be in place as well. Reforms may be implemented incrementally rather than as a precondition to scaled-up LCDD programs, but still would require all actors to stay the course over long periods of time.

Local Preprogram Development: Defining a Common Vision, Objectives, and Design Features

Following the diagnostic phase, an LCDD design team should be appointed to carry forward the process. It should start by hosting a national stakeholder workshop to get government and other stakeholders (including external partners) to agree on what is to be scaled up and how it should proceed (see box 5.4). The following issues need to be discussed:

- Major findings from the diagnostic phase
- The vision of the proposed program
- Objectives to be achieved, key components, and key design elements of program
- Broad roles of different actors and levels (the details will be developed as part of the development phase itself)

BOX 5.4

Steps to Scaling Up: Preprogram Development

Preprogram development at the national level

• Define the program
• Select pilot districts
• Appoint scaling-up team.

Preprogram development at the local level

• Select districts
• Assess the LCDD underpinnings in the local context
• Achieve local buy-in
• Set up communications.

• Institutional homes and lead agencies, at central and local levels
• Expected outputs of the development phase such as detailed institutional arrangements, operational and training manuals, scaling-up logistics, and monitoring and evaluation (M&E) reports
• Principles and major mechanisms of a transparency and accountability system
• Objectives and accountability of an M&E system
• Agreement on a detailed development phase
• Key questions to be answered in the development phase
• Expected outputs
• Expected cost, financing sources, and financing arrangements for the development phase
• Structure and composition of the development team from the lead agency or agencies and required specialists
• Record of the outline of the program and agreements reached.

Initiating the Pilot Phase for Scaling Up

Starting from small-scale, successful LCDD or CDD projects that have covered select communities or subdistricts, the task now is to develop the systems, logistics, and tools that can cover all communities and all subdistricts within at least one district (see table 3.1 on the magnitude of scaling up). The experience will be recorded in an operational manual that can subsequently be used for national scaling up. This is the pilot phase for scaling up (see box 5.5).

Selecting One or Several Pilot Districts

There is always pressure to cover more than one district, but the capacity to follow closely what is happening in more than one district is often lacking at the central level. Developing the program simultaneously in more than one district is therefore dependent on adequate capacity. It could be done, for example, in a federation where separate development teams for one district each can be fielded in each state.

Selection Criteria: Matching Program Complexity with Local Capacity. A district can be selected based on its capacity and on the complexity of the program being designed. In Burkina Faso, for instance, the low-capacity Poni Province was selected to pilot a relatively simple HIV/AIDS (human immunodeficiency virus/acquired immune deficiency syndrome) prevention program. The program successfully disbursed small matching grants to newly formed HIV/AIDS committees in 500 villages and urban neighborhoods. Within the span of several months, the program had trained more than 2,000 program participants and trainers on how to prepare simple village projects, monitor their outputs, manage financial resources, and deal with the basics of the disease and its prevention. However, this was only possible because of the relative straightforward nature of the project. The approach relied entirely on existing or latent administrative and training capacities and on existing infrastructure within the province.

BOX 5.5

Steps to Scaling Up: Pilot Phase

- Define players and roles
- Provide adequate training and intensive facilitation
- Undertake participatory planning
- Provide technical support.

If one or more components of a program are particularly complex, the better match is a district where local participants—communities, nongovernmental organizations (NGOs), and local governments—have substantial experience with individual components or tasks that are to be scaled up. In contrast to Poni, the Sanmatenga Province in Burkina Faso was recently selected as the pilot district for scaling up a multisectoral CDD approach to HIV/AIDS care and support. The district has relatively high capacity and was able to master the complex design issues involved in the program. In urban areas, service delivery by NGOs and specialized community-based organizations was already partially developed.

In rural areas, ample capacity existed in the structure of HIV/AIDS committees at the provincial, departmental, and community levels and among the provincial and departmental training teams. Other community driven projects provided skilled participatory diagnosis and planning at the community level, and there was strong political leadership. Finally, when selecting several districts, it is always best to select districts that have different capacities and characteristics. Lessons learned from each district may be useful when the time comes to scale up nationally.

Once one or several districts have completed the pilot phase of scaling up, the focus of the LCDD design team moves from the national to the local level.

Local Buy-in for the Development Phase

Crucial to the success of the development phase is local buy-in. At the onset of the process, together with the lead agency and development team members, a participatory stakeholder workshop should be held in the local area to expose all participants to the proposed program and the development phase. The workshop will be attended by the program management committee, community leaders, the greater community, and, in particular, the top leader(s) of local government and local representatives of central government who will drive the process.

The workshop will offer a chance to discuss possible local implementation arrangements and mechanisms as well as the initial list of possible local co-producers. Local stakeholders and the development team will conduct field visits to subdistricts and communities to familiarize all stakeholders with the local institutional setup, capacities, and existing local experience and programs on which to build. The program outline will be revised, refined, recorded, and distributed back to central stakeholders.

Local-Level Diagnostics

The stakeholder workshop will already have reviewed the results from the national review process, including the summaries of existing studies and analyses of local conditions and how they vary across the country. The local diagnostics should not redo the national review, but instead should build on it with complementary local fact finding. The local stakeholder workshop should identify the specific gaps in local knowledge that have to be filled.

Simple fact-finding visits, rather than complicated additional analysis, should be used at this stage to fill the gaps in knowledge, looking at capacity in the community and local government, existing financial structures and relationships with the center or donor institutions, and other topics linked to the LCDD plan. That knowledge will help to guide program designers in the next phase.

Information, Education, and Communication

A good communications program is central to promoting transparency and accountability, but it needs to be designed in scale with the rest of the program and not overwhelm it.[8] Information, education, and communication (IEC) activities are essential to creating awareness and learning and to enabling process monitoring. Simple but effective IEC programs should keep the communities informed and could aim to empower communities with the ability to self-reflect; identify their own needs, challenges, and resources; give the poor a voice in public dialogue; facilitate education and learning about sectoral and multisectoral topics for behavior change toward sustainable development, empowerment, and other LCDD values; and facilitate community access to market information. Above all, the actors who are in contact with a community should be required to inform, educate, disclose, and ask for feedback, so that IEC programs do not become a separate entity.

Any mode of national media can be used for this purpose. The Malawi Social Action Fund (MASAF), for instance, has designed a strategy that communicates messages to all stakeholders throughout the community-project cycle by using radio plays and television dramas. Messages are also broadcast explaining the importance of principles such as accountability and transparency and offering instruction on specific technical issues such as procurement and contracting. Where media are restricted, a highly effective alternative way of disseminating information is local radio, which gives daily information on the ongoing program and does not pose the literacy-related problems of newsletters.

To meet process monitoring needs, an effective communication plan will also focus on creating two-way channels of communication, monitoring, evaluation, and feedback between co-producing agencies. Bottom-up and interagency linkages can be created to channel to all stakeholders any relevant information on program processes, inputs, outputs, and outcomes. Only then can deficiencies be corrected, designs adapted, and efficiency and equity enhanced. Moreover, the information generated and disseminated by these systems is central to enhancing all forms of accountability.

Pilot Phase: Defining the Actors, Functions, and Responsibilities

LCDD is the co-production of outputs by a joint venture of communities, local governments, and the central government, with support from the private sector and civil society. The previous section explains how to foster a common vision among stakeholders. This section explores the important tasks of consolidating program content, designing the local implementation arrangements, assigning program functions unambiguously to different participants at each level, and fully describing them (box 5.6; see also appendix B).

In order to ensure that local actors can scale up a program, ideally they should design the implementation arrangements. They usually cannot do this by themselves, but instead require the guidance and facilitation of the LCDD program design team.

BOX 5.6

What to Do Where Local Governments Are Nonexistent or Nonfunctional

Countries can start by setting up local development committees at the district level under the leadership of the local representative of the central government. These should mimic what will eventually emerge when local governments are formally constituted. Once a local government is elected and in place, the development committee will be assimilated into the new local government structure and will include elected councilors. UNCDF often assists in setting up such committees, in building capacity, and in developing systems: for instance, in Mozambique, Niger, and Timor-Leste.

Defining the local actors, functions, and responsibilities is therefore best done in a highly participatory manner at the local level. This process should involve all of the stakeholders, since only they have the detailed knowledge of the actors, systems, processes, and relationships on which the program will need to build. Such a participatory approach will uncover many latent capacities that exist in a district or even in many or all districts. These latent capacities come in the form of institutions, such as the development committees discussed below, and in the form of existing administrative or coordination capacities, local public, private, or civil society organizations, and individuals who either already perform certain functions or could be mobilized to do so. Building on these latent capacities, and assigning formal roles and functions to them, is the most promising approach to ensure program sustainability and economy. It also avoids reinventing the wheel or duplicating effort through parallel structures and processes.

The process of discovering all of the latent capacities and assigning responsibilities and functions will usually involve the following steps:

- Holding one or several broad stakeholder workshops
- Appointing subcommittees to conduct subcommittee sessions
- Reporting the results to the workshop plenary sessions
- Recording the results so that they can be integrated into the operational manual.

Such a process need not take more than a week except when specific social or institutional analyses are needed to clarify who can, and should, do what, where, and how. It is critical that the design team communicate the objectives for the LCDD program that have been defined nationally, explain options to be considered, and facilitate the work of local stakeholders, rather than impose its own ideas.

In any LCDD program, coordination, approval, and communication functions are assigned to the formal institutions of local government. Depending on the context, an LCDD design team may encounter a range of institutional options depending on existing governance systems. Despite variations, however, certain basic structures, as shown in figure 5.1, will be needed to meet the management and coordination needs of the emerging program.

The Community Development Committee

The community development committee provides the core of community representation in LCDD. Although similar in structure, manner,

Figure 5.1. Basic Institutional Requirements for an LCDD Program

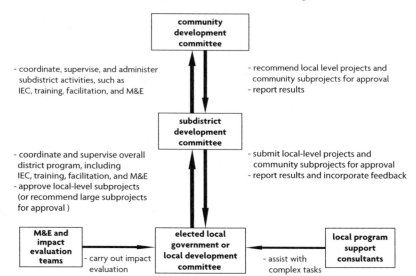

Source: Authors.

and functions to the district development committee (DDC), the community development committee maintains the implementation functions for the community development program and community projects. Ideally, the committee is the following:

- A legal entity
- Elected by the community and includes, but is not limited to, a chairperson, vice chairperson, treasurer, financial manager, and secretary
- Able to ensure accountability by reporting on physical and financial progress to the community in a regular and public manner
- Set up with specific mechanisms to ensure that membership in the project management committee is representative of women and other marginalized groups. Such social safeguards are important for guarding against elite capture and social exclusion.

The role of the community development committee is to manage all processes at the community level from participatory appraisal to program implementation, including money management, resource mobilization, contracting, financial control, M&E, auditing and reporting, upward and downward accountability, and delegation of execution responsibility for specific community projects to subcommittees.

The District Development Committee

In most countries, district governments already have DDCs (see box 5.6). These DDCs should have broad representation among all the stakeholder groups, including local politicians, subdistricts, communities, NGOs, relevant private sector actors, local managers, and technicians of deconcentrated sector agencies. These committees usually have subcommittees such as for planning, project approval, monitoring and evaluation, financial control, education, health, water, agriculture, and HIV/AIDS, which are constituted in a manner similar to the main committees.

Therefore, the local development committee could take several forms:

- A subcommittee of the local elected council within local government, with added members from civil society, the communities, subdistricts, and technical agencies
- Where there is not yet a local elected council, a committee created by a central government agent such as the prefect or high commissioner or by a law or decree of the ministry of local government.

The role of the DDC is to coordinate the LCDD program, including the following:

- The initial and subsequent information campaign and IEC component of the scaled-up LCDD program
- Coordination and supervision of the training, facilitation, and community and local planning process
- Coordination and integration of the development plans of subdistricts
- Approval of subdistrict and district-level projects *and* recommendation for approval at a higher level of large district projects
- Final no-objection or approval of community projects and projects of NGOs or local sector offices
- Recommendation of measures for local resource mobilization (from local revenues, cost recoveries, and other sources), including commitments for operations and maintenance (O&M) if such funds normally come from the sector ministry budgets
- Monitoring and evaluation of the local development program and the performance of implementers
- Reporting to the local and central authorities and the population at-large.

Delegation of Specific Functions by the DDC

Different activities and initiatives may need to be delegated to different subcommittees or other actors. Examples include the following.

The Final Approval of Plans. Final approval of plans at the local and community levels and of projects or sets of projects can be a function of one of several entities, including the development committee itself, an elected council, or—for large local projects—a higher-level authority such as the ministry of local development, a social fund, or other program or project unit. Disbursement orders are then given by the respective chief financial officer or treasurer, with checks signed by the person or persons designated in the operational manual or financial regulations.

If there are many communities in a district, the DDC should delegate evaluation and approval of the community annual programs or community projects to the subdistrict development committee. Another option is for the subdistrict committee to vet and improve the proposals and submit them as a package for final approval or nonobjection to an approval committee of the DDC. Still another option is for small projects to be approved at the subdistrict level and for larger ones to be approved at the district level.

Monitoring and Evaluation. The DDC is responsible for M&E at the district level and for reporting upward to central government, downward to communities and local governments, and horizontally to other districts. To fulfill these functions, the DDC may need to create an M&E subcommittee. In addition, M&E should be made the responsibility of the communities and the subdistrict committees, preferably via participatory M&E. These delegations of responsibilities can significantly reduce the progress monitoring tasks of the DDC and should therefore be made an integral part of the district M&E system. Regular reports in easily understandable form and expressed in local languages are needed to disseminate information on program progress and financial information. The district can integrate these reports into its IEC strategy.

Technical Subcommittees for the Different Sectors. Such subcommittees would deal with the technical design and supervision of sector-specific subprojects financed under an LCDD program. Many existing DDCs will already have such subcommittees when the design team arrives.

IEC Plan and Activities. The DDC is also responsible for designing and carrying out the district-level IEC plan. Community radio can be used to communicate key messages to all stakeholders, convene meetings in an area where mail and telephones are weak, and serve as a conduit for two-way information. For instance, Sri Lanka's community radio has a panel of resource persons who answer questions from listeners on a wide range of issues and problems. Where they do not exist, community radio systems can be set up at low cost with community contributions and district sponsorship. Other IEC options include the dissemination of information by community theater groups or during customary community gatherings.

Stakeholders and communities can stay informed and connected through emerging Internet technologies. A wide array of cost-effective Web-based conferencing tools, such as Skype or video-over-Internet protocol, could be supported by donors in the technology sector.

The Subdistrict Development Committee

A local DDC cannot be expected to coordinate and supervise the LCDD programs in districts, which may have 300 to 500 communities, or more, and, in some cases, a corresponding number of local governments. Further decentralization to a subdistrict development committee is almost always needed to manage initiatives, and such committees often already exist. Their functions and composition are similar to those of the DDC, but the precise division of responsibility between the two levels should be part of the detailed definition of roles and functions.

Local Program Development Support Team

As discussed, the detailed design of the LCDD program and its scaling up should be done by the local stakeholders who have to implement it in the future and, most important, by the program's DDC, subdistrict development committees, and community development committees as well as participating public servants and co-producers from the private sector and civil society. Proper facilitation by the national LCDD design team is essential.

The national team members will include high-level civil servants and consultants who are unlikely to be able to move to the pilot district(s). In addition, they will not have the time or capacity to document fully all of the steps, processes, tools, logistics, and training materials that will be developed and then summarized in comprehensive operational and training manuals. Nor can councilors and other local stakeholders be expected to fulfill these tasks. It will usually be necessary to hire a team of consultants to provide support for and document the pilot phase of scaling up and to produce all of the outputs that are expected from it.

Such a team (or teams, if several districts are involved) can help to solve problems at the level of the district, the subdistricts, and the communities and to assist the stakeholders in making the many decisions that have to be made during the pilot phase of scaling up. The local team will report progress and decisions to the national LCDD team and pass issues to the national level for resolution. A major responsibility of the local team is to document all decisions and prepare the outputs, reports, tools, and operational manuals. Team responsibilities include the following:

- Monitoring and documenting the progress of the pilot phase and lessons learned
- Assisting local stakeholders in working out the logistics of the program training and implementation processes in a cost-effective manner
- Assembling all of the decisions, tools, and logistics into an operational manual and revising the operational manuals and tools continuously so that they remain up to date
- Developing the corresponding training manuals and tools and keeping them up to date
- Translating operational and training manuals into local languages and producing them in sufficient quantities.

The local program development support team will usually consist of consultants with the required facilitation, program design, training, documentation, and writing skills. They need to support the leadership of local stakeholders in program design, to translate what is going on in the field and in the councils into tools, operational manuals, and training manuals, and to translate, produce, and distribute them. Consultants will need to be residents of the district for the duration of the pilot phase.

Clear terms of reference can define the role and limits of such a team. They should be approved by the DDC. The following are particularly important functions that should be included:

- Assembling operational procedures, manuals, and tools from existing programs and approaches, integrating them into a single set of operational and training manuals and tools, and developing those components that do not already exist
- Revising these materials continuously in light of experience
- Assisting the district in the development of its IEC strategy and tools
- Assisting the secretary and staff of the development committee to prepare the committee's sessions and reports
- Reporting on the progress of the development program at regular intervals
- Assisting in the design and implementation of the M&E program, processes, tools, and reports.

Specialists for M&E and for Impact Evaluation

A sound M&E system has four broad components: participatory M&E by communities, local governments, and users for implementation monitoring; financial and accounting systems for financial monitoring; a management information system for progress monitoring; and independent monitoring.[9]

The M&E system should be simple and capitalize on existing systems. Pushing for standardization can also help to consolidate information at the local, national, and donor levels. Implementing these improvements in M&E will require a small task force that would provide support to ministries and agencies and help to strengthen national capacity. In order to be close to operations, this task force should consist of a network of monitoring and evaluation specialists spread out horizontally in the various sectors and vertically across the administrative levels and out to the communities.

At the local level, M&E is the responsibility of the DDC, the subdistrict development committee, and the community development committee. Programs frequently assign a special subcommittee for M&E. During the pilot phase, these committees are supported by an M&E specialist whose role is to ensure that the system is properly designed, functions from the beginning, and is capable of producing regular outputs for consideration by the DDC, the local development support team, and the central design team.

Aside from all of the structures mentioned above, one should keep in mind that monitoring is done for the sake of knowing in time what is happening with the processes and the results, so adjustments can be made quickly. Managers at all levels need to know, starting with the community development committee. Therefore, simple metrics, understood by all in the community, are to be chosen, preferably by the community itself as part of participatory M&E with at least one measurable indicator, one metric, that points to outcomes in a meaningful way (see box 5.7). An example comes from Uganda: the number of families eating beer bananas—a clear leading indicator of food shortage—can be counted even by children because the discarded peels are visible.[10]

Evaluating impact of the pilot phase is highly desirable in order to justify subsequent expansion of the program to national levels. It is a task separate from the regular M&E process and not an integral part of program implementation (see box 5.8). Evaluation requires a good baseline of communities and households as well as subsequent surveys.

BOX 5.7

Metrics

The question of what is monitored and evaluated involves metrics: the term for benchmarks of performance that help to measure whether goals are being achieved. How those metrics are chosen and defined is an important and delicate task, preferably coming through a facilitated process including stakeholders and participants.

BOX 5.8

Making Provisions for Fully Independent Monitoring

The KDP hired independent NGOs in each province to independently monitor the program. It also provided an association of journalists with travel costs and a per diem to periodically visit the program areas and communities and report on what they found in the press.

The impact of the program is evaluated by comparing the changes that occurred with the communities and households who participate in the program and a set of comparator communities and individuals who do not. The evaluation is best done on a subsample of communities or subdistricts, which need to be chosen at random. Control groups with no program interventions (without-treatment communities) are ideally located within the same district, but this is often politically difficult, because the communities or subdistricts that are left out will protest. In such cases, the without-treatment communities need to be located in neighboring districts, with some matching of the selected villages to observed characteristics of the with-treatment villages.

Conducting impact evaluation is a research task. The impact evaluation should cover the impact of the LCDD program as a whole on the welfare of communities in the district. It may also evaluate the impact of particular ways of implementing the program, such as performance-based allocation of resources, or the relative impact of training and facilitation versus additional financial resources. To ensure objectivity, a separate group of *impact evaluation specialists* should be hired to conduct the impact evaluation. These researchers need to be coordinated closely with the design of the pilot and with its monitoring and evaluation system. Responsibility for coordination rests with the DDC assisted by the program development consultants.

Training, Facilitation, Participatory Planning, and Technical Support

Developing the ability of communities to plan and map out their own development is the heart of an LCDD program and requires that adequate training and intensive facilitation be provided throughout the planning process. This component sets the tone, highlights the shared values, and introduces the key skills that will make scaling up possible. The magnitude of this undertaking is significant. In a district-level program seeking to reach 300 to 500 communities and their local governments, these activities are likely to be very costly. The following subsections provide ways to minimize the costs of the large training and facilitation component that is necessary and then explore the main issues involved in participatory planning at the community, subdistrict, and district levels. Cost-effectiveness is not just a question of low budgets and low bids; more important, it is about careful planning, contracting, and logistics.

Training and Facilitation Requirements at the Community Level

LCDD requires training in various skills:

- Participatory assessment and planning
- Setting up or strengthening of the community development committee and its subcommittees (as well local government committees, where relevant)
- Procurement and financial management
- Planning and community project preparation
- Auditing
- Participatory monitoring and evaluation
- Additional technical skills for all but the simplest infrastructure community projects.

Training Communities and All Program Entities. Within each community, training will have to include between 4 and 8 people to ensure that members of different genders and ages, minority groups, and technical specialists receive training. If 4 members are to be trained in each community, and the district, for example, covers 400 communities in 10 subdistricts, the mandatory training effort will exceed 2,000 people (4,000 people if 8 are trained per community).

Training also has to be provided to all other program participants who are engaged in any of the co-production tasks of the program, including development committee members and administrators at the local government, subdistrict, and district levels, staff and volunteers from participating NGOs and sector agencies, and facilitators and service providers from the private sector. These bureaucrats and technicians, above all, will need training aimed at changing attitudes and skills; they will need to learn to listen to the community and to support it.[11]

Training such large numbers separately within each community, and hiring professional trainers and facilitators for these activities, is likely to be prohibitively expensive, irrespective of whether the trainers and facilitators come from the private sector, NGOs, or government agencies (see box 5.9).

Cost-Minimizing Logistics for Training and Facilitation. The HIV/AIDS Prevention Program in Burkina Faso shows how cost-effective training can be organized in training camps at the district and subdistrict levels (see figure 5.2). The villagers (one male and one female adult; one male

---

BOX 5.9

Train the Facilitators First

Facilitation plays a critical role in the early stages of scaling up because it is the process for building agreement of terms, goals, and methods as well as for establishing teamwork and familiarity among the actors.

Participatory planning (and monitoring) processes at all levels must be properly facilitated by outside trainers and facilitators. Facilitation will typically also be needed during the formation or election of village committees, community project preparation, and initial participatory evaluation to ensure social inclusion and adequate participation. Unlike training, the facilitation has to be done separately in each community or subdistrict and district development committee.

Figure 5.2. Visualizing Training Logistics between the Subdistrict Center and the Villages

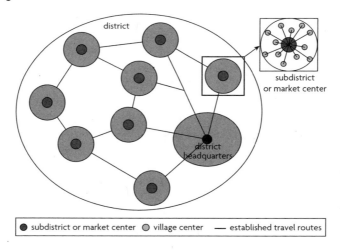

Source: Binswanger and Ngyuen 2005.

and one female youth) are assembled at the subdistrict level for two week-long training workshops in which the elements of the project cycle and financial management are covered along with basic knowledge of HIV/AIDS and its prevention.

A district team of trainers is formed from residents of the district headquarters and operated from there. The district training team selects the subdistrict training teams. These are ideally recruited from among the subdistrict residents, among whom the capacities to train can often be found (former teachers, extension agents, or motivated educated adults or youth). They then travel along established routes to the district headquarters for a training camp, thereby minimizing transport costs. Upon their return, they provide training to surrounding communities from the subdistrict or local market town. The Burkina Faso HIV/AIDS Prevention Program also adopted the principle that no program participant should travel on a route other than the usual one to the market or the local subdistrict center, thus sharply reducing the logistics and costs of transport.

The Subdistrict Training Teams. Once established and trained, training teams can mobilize local specialists for specialized training (nurses, doctors, agricultural extension agents). During the pilot phase, teams use their training experience to revise and improve the curricula, sessions, materials, and the original training manuals. Suggestions are integrated, by the local design support team, into the next version of the training manual. They are paid only for the days they work or receive training. Subsequent to the training, they are sent to villagers to facilitate program and community project development, either on a supply-driven basis or at the request of communities. They can be reactivated whenever a new training or facilitation need arises.

Cost-effectiveness is enhanced by mobilizing latent local capacities, that is, by recruiting qualified local volunteers, such as retired people, educated spouses, educated youth, and village elders, who may previously have been teachers, health practitioners, or agricultural extension workers, among others. Thus composed, four to six trainers can manage a subdistrict training program of workshops, to be attended by four to six people per village. Community-based workers often are the ideal candidates for this kind of training (AICDD 2007).

The Community-to-Community Extension Approach. An alternative or complementary approach is to organize specialized training and facilitation via a community-to-community extension approach, which relies on and strengthens latent community capacities and therefore produces additional cost savings. The process begins with a training program or a participatory planning exercise facilitated by professional facilitators (hired from NGOs, government, or the private sector) in a preselected *lead community*. Three to five representatives from neighboring communities are invited to participate, with a view to building a corps of locally based trainer-facilitators. In addition to their participation in the exercise, representatives can build further skills through extra formal training in specialized subject matter or facilitation. The newly trained trainer-facilitators then return to their villages, occasionally accompanied by members of the lead community, to facilitate the participatory planning process and to train the population there.

Capacities to facilitate community processes can be significantly expanded at a very low cost by training some of the subdistrict training committee members to become community facilitators. The training can be incorporated into the district training-of-trainers modules described above. These locally resident community facilitators can then provide mandatory facilitation—or facilitation requested by the communities—and be paid a per diem for the days worked (see box 5.10).

Facilitating the Participatory Approach to Planning and Budgets

The core outcome of the community planning process is the annual plan and budget, which are part of an outline of a longer-term three- to five-year development program for the community. As with the simplified financial reports covered in chapter 2, guidelines for simplified annual plans and budgets should be part of the preparation for scaling up (see box 5.11).

Intensive facilitation is needed throughout the participatory planning process, in particular to ensure that all community members, including

---

BOX 5.10

Standard per Diem for Volunteers

To avoid protracted negotiations about per diems with volunteer trainers and facilitators, per diems should be uniform, irrespective of the qualifications of the trainer or facilitator. They should cover the costs of the facilitators and a bit of pocket money; they should not be important sources of income for volunteers. Typically, per diems allow trainers to feed themselves in little eateries or to buy groceries for cooking.

BOX 5.11

An Irony of Elaborate Plans and Reports

Requiring carefully written development plans at the community level in English or French instead of a regional or national language enables external consultants to dominate the planning process because they inevitably will be hired to produce the reports. In the Burkina Faso CDD program, consultants consumed more than $2 million of the funds of the second phase of the program. Yet these documents were rarely used at the community level and generated few added investments beyond the program.

---

women and minorities, are given a fair chance to participate, thereby avoiding elite capture. A facilitator should spend at least half of the time devoted to participatory planning in the village, either continuously or in repeated visits.

Technical Training and Support

In addition to broad-based mandatory training and facilitation, communities that undertake projects in specific sectors will need specialized training and facilitation for specific subsector community projects and other technical support.[12] Such training and support should be primarily demand driven and based on the development plans of the communities. Training and support should be recognized as a legitimate cost of LCDD, and communities should be able to spend part of the money they receive to finance or co-finance these services. The precise source and logistics of providing these services need to be worked out locally by the respective sectors, in coordination with the DDC. Some district-level projects can be used to finance some of the basic training costs for NGOs, private firms, or local sector offices of the government.

Technical support should also include access to standard designs and intensive technical support specific to each project. Technical designs for typical projects need to be vetted and approved to reduce a common tendency to overdesign projects. The approved designs can then be assembled into a sourcebook or catalogue.

Technical support can be provided in a number of ways. The most important is to allow communities to use part of the project resources to purchase technical support services from any provider they can identify (see box 5.12). These providers would include the private sector (individual engineers, consultants, and firms), specialized NGOs, producer organizations, and local offices of the public sector (in the latter two cases, probably on a partial cost-recovery basis or by paying for transport and other costs of providing the service). Competition among these service providers helps to improve the quality of their support.

In addition, within an LCDD program, private firms, NGOs, and local branches of sector agencies can also be invited to submit proposals to the DDC to provide technical support services to communities. In order to submit such providers to a market test, it would be best to provide only partial funding for their services directly from the DDC, with the balance coming from the communities requesting the services.

Participatory Planning at the Community, Subdistrict, and District Levels

Development plans should be prepared in a participatory way, starting from the community plans. These plans are then coordinated across communities at the subdistrict and district levels to ensure that larger investments, such as roads and schools, can serve several communities.

User-Friendly Annual Plan Templates. Templates for an annual plan should be provided to the community, subdistricts, and districts as one of the scaling-up tools. For communities, the templates should be set up so the plans can be filled in, mainly via lists and tables, without the need for extensive writing. Like all tools, these templates need to be developed and tested in the field. Several copies are needed, as the plan has to be submitted to the local government, subdistrict, or district, and copies should also remain in the village or community.

BOX 5.12

Finding Locally Available Specialists

Some programs, such as the KDP in Indonesia, have hired engineers as consultants and posted them at the kecamatan level to provide technical support to communities. An alternative approach and part of the local focus, the LCDD program could compile a list of local, prequalified vendors and specialists and include them in a resource guide.

The resulting three- to five-year plan for the community should describe the findings of the community about its strengths and key resources, its links to and from the outside world, the support structures that are available to it, its weaknesses and challenges, and a vision of what the community wants to achieve over the period. All, of course, should be in the local language, in a form that is accessible to all and likely to survive in the harsh conditions of the community. The plan should discuss the governance structure that the community has set up or amended to pursue these objectives. It should include a list of priority projects, along with who will be responsible for pursuing them and key partners who will be approached. The plan should clearly indicate which challenges it can meet itself from internal resources and for which it will require outside resources.

The nature of the annual plan depends on the structure of the LCDD program. It will include the projects and services that the community can provide for itself out of its own labor and cash resources, with timetables and allocation of resources in cash and in kind. If the community is given a budget to allocate to its particular project, the annual plan will allocate the annual budget to the top priorities, along with own co-financing in cash or in kind. This budget is complemented with timetables, advisory or facilitation inputs, and precise allocation of responsibilities. If the community has to submit projects for funding to the local government, subdistrict, district, or other funders, the annual plan will be based on the expected or approved resources that are made available and contain the same management elements for each project.

The annual plan should also include provisions for the following:

- How the plan is monitored
- How progress is reported back to the community
- How funds are accounted for
- The annual district development budget.

The most important output of planning at the district level is the annual district development budget and subdistrict budgets, if subdistricts have their own budget (rather than executing projects under the supervision and financial control of the district). The annual budget needs to be embedded in a clear understanding of the district priorities or plan (and subdistrict priorities) for the next three to five years. International experience on planning at the district level is also clear. In the Mozambique Decentralized Finance and Planning Program, which builds on a pilot program of UNCDF in Mampula Province, the district development plans required the active participation of subdistrict administrative staff and communities. In fact, the government developed a set of guidelines on participation in district planning that promote the establishment of *local consultative councils*, where community representatives and local administrators debate and approve priorities for the district development plan and its consequent annual investment plans (districts in Mozambique are equivalent to local governments in other countries).

In many instances, however, too much effort and cost are required to prepare a three- to five-year plan for each subdistrict and then to integrate them into a district plan. Attempts are often made to integrate the multi-year district plans into regional, provincial, or national three- to five-year plans. Such attempts for bottom-up, medium-term regional or national planning processes have systematically failed all over the world. Requiring carefully documented and well-written three- to five-year plans mainly produces documents that will rarely be used for future decision making, because they do not synchronize with the annual budget cycle; it also leads to planning processes dominated by consultants, who inevitably influence the annual budget decisions.

Moreover, such attempts tend to delay or block the final approval of the plans, and they also delay the preparation and approval of the much needed and far simpler annual budgets for the district and all the lower levels. Yet a vision of what should be done over the next three to five years is important to anchor the annual budgets and reduce conflicts over priorities. This can often be done in simple terms, as agreed-upon lists of priority projects.

The key lesson is simplicity. Report writing should focus primarily on core outputs, both in the form of simple documents in the local language and wall charts that can be easily understood and made widely available to the district and subdistrict stakeholders (Bonfiglioli 2002).

Resource Flows, Resource Allocation, and Accountability Mechanisms

Central to the success of the program is for fiduciary arrangements to channel funds directly into the hands of communities (de Silva 2002; see box 5.13). (A local development program should also include funding at the local government level for projects going beyond the community level.) The funds should preferably be untied and provide an open menu of options, except for a negative list of what the money may not be used for (see box 5.14). Earmarking should only be used in exceptional

---

BOX 5.13

Steps to Scaling Up: Resource Flows and Accountability

- Provide direct financing to communities
- Devise options for allocating funds
- Devise options for managing and disbursing financial resources.

BOX 5.14

Priority List Menus

In an *open menu*, the community representatives can suggest any item or service (except those on a negative list). A *negative list* includes items for which LCDD program funds cannot be used, such as weapons, religious items, or entertainment services.

---

circumstances, where gaps in knowledge or stigma prevent the allocation of resources to important national priorities, such as climate change adaptations or HIV/AIDS. The menu and negative list should be designed in close consultation with stakeholders and experts.

Funding is typically accompanied by a set of rules and training that ensure wide local participation, promote transparency and accountability, prevent fraud and misuse, avoid elite capture and social exclusion, and ensure that, through local resource generation mechanisms, the community can manage and maintain the asset after completion of the community project.

Disbursements can be in tranches based on statements of progress of the project or on statements of expenditures. The community finance committee and the treasurer are responsible for preparing and submitting these documents to the local government, subdistrict, or district. The subdistrict or district will rarely be able to verify directly the accuracy of the statements of expenditures in the community; therefore, we advocate working on statements of progress in implementation (see box 2.12, point 2). Therefore, verification of the proper use of the money is the primary responsibility of a community's own finance and audit committees and of the general assembly of community members that meets periodically. In addition, community accounts should be subject to the threat of audit by the subdistrict or district level. Auditing hundreds or thousands of small community accounts is not cost-effective; it should be part of the M&E plan and be carried out on a random sample basis. Audits should include the financial records, the decision-making processes, and the quality of the output produced.

For fiduciary and disbursement purposes, a community project can be part of an annual community budget comprising either several community subprojects or individual community subprojects. A community project consisting of several community subprojects, combined with disbursement against the budget in two or, maximum, three tranches, is the most empowering, because it allows the community full freedom to allocate money across subprojects. Individual community subprojects, which are financed from earmarked resources, mean that much more power rests with the funder and that savings from one project cannot be allocated to another project.

In certain cases, the laws or regulations of national governments may not allow direct disbursement to communities. Often, these laws state that money can only be transferred to legalized entities. This is a case where national policy may need to recognize LCDD disbursement issues. Generally, however, it is possible to work around such restrictions. For instance, legalization of the community group can be a simple procedure that only involves registering the committee with the relevant government authority (see box 5.15).

Simple mechanisms can be found to assist this process, and, during pilot phases, exceptions can often be put in place to test whether community organizations use funds properly if and when they meet certain simple requirements.[13] In the long term, to go beyond specific donor-funded programs, the legal barriers to direct funding will need to be dismantled and adapted.

BOX 5.15

Ethiopian Method for Gaining Legal Status

In Ethiopia, a law was passed so that the minutes of a meeting reporting the formation of a community development committee are sufficient to gain legal status and become eligible to receive public funds.

Community Co-financing

Most LCDD programs require community co-financing. This reduces the fiscal costs of the program and improves ownership and accountability at the community level (see box 5.16). Communities should be asked to contribute a predetermined minimum share of the cost of each of their projects. Whether in cash, labor (including management time), or materials, such community contributions may constitute between 10 and 40 percent of the total cost of a community project. In very poor areas, the contribution may be entirely in labor and materials. In relatively more affluent areas, communities may prefer the cash option. Flexibility in this mix should be built into each matching grant. The *minimum co-financing* requirement can also be used to incorporate national priorities into the program, although these may conflict with local priorities (or even global priorities such as climate change and environmental protection, which is why there is a Community Development Carbon Fund).

Options for Allocating Funds across the Program

There are two basic options for allocating resources to communities, local governments, subdistricts, and districts. Allocations could be based on proposals submitted from each of these levels to higher levels, as in the KDP in Indonesia, or they could be based on norms, that is, be an entitlement of each level, as in the Burkina Faso LCDD program, which sets a community's allocation at $3 per capita.

BOX 5.16

Finding a Co-financing Balance

In Mexico, many municipalities started to build basketball courts, an eligible expense, but not high on the national set of priorities. The co-financing requirement for these community projects was increased significantly, and most municipalities shifted resources to other projects. Eventually, a co-financing matrix set different co-financing requirements for different types of projects and adjusted them to the marginality of the municipality. These are ways to reflect national priorities without prohibiting certain projects or earmarking funds, leaving greater autonomy and empowerment to the local decision-making processes.

In a large-scale program where there will eventually be thousands of community projects, there are several disadvantages to proposal-driven allocations. Communities and subdistricts will be tempted to submit proposals, the aggregate of which vastly exceeds available resources. The proposals then will have to be sent back and cut down, inevitably leading to disappointment and disillusionment. Moreover, without a clear initial envelope, planning at each of these levels is much more complicated and may take on the characteristics of producing wish lists.

The clear allocation of a norm forces choices to be made quickly at each of the levels. Norms can be based simply on the number of people, as in the case of Burkina Faso, or they can be based on more complex formulas, taking into account the degree of marginality of the community or district and other factors. For instance, Bolivia's Rural Communities Development Program allocated funding to 100 municipalities selected on the basis of poverty, development potential, and institutional capacity. Resources for productive investments were made available nationwide and allocated on the basis of proposals received.

Norms can also be used to allocate the small management budgets for subdistrict development committees and training committees. These committees need small amounts of money to function, and if funds are not provided, the program quickly slows down, and key people turn away.

Increases in annual budgets or norms of communities, subdistricts, and districts can be based on performance of each of these units and compared to agreed-upon benchmarks of performance. Lack of performance should lead to a constant or declining budget, and fraud should lead to exclusion of the community from the program for one or several years. Uganda's performance-based grant system for local governments is a standard for this kind of system (see box 5.17).

Of course, there are projects at the subdistrict or district level, such as service provision by specialized entities or facilitation, that cannot be based on simple population or membership norms and in which a proposal-driven allocation process is inevitable.

Options for Managing and Disbursing the Financial Resources at All Local Levels

As discussed in chapter 4, there are various widely used options for managing and disbursing funds.

BOX 5.17

Zambia and Uganda: Linking Performance, Accountability, and Incentives

Zambia's social fund created a graduation scheme setting positive and negative incentives in line with a set of predetermined benchmarks for performance. Under the scheme, to encourage learning-by-doing, no district council was penalized for a wrong choice of projects.

The experience in Uganda with performance-based grants to districts (that is, local governments) has been positive, and Uganda serves as an example for many other countries in the world (Steffensen 2006). The system was tested with assistance from UNCDF beginning in 1997 and gradually rolled out countrywide; it is supported by several development partners through budget support (a World Bank development policy loan through the Local Government Management and Service Delivery Program). Districts have to have in place minimum conditions in order to obtain access to a development grant, and the amount of the grant is determined by performance on more than 100 indicators, showing performance both in management and institutional functioning of the district as well as in delivery of services. In addition, Uganda provides districts with sector-specific grants; for instance, to improve school facilities, districts receive additional funds if they have good ratios of input to output.

The results in Uganda include the following:

- Significant improvement on performance in areas such as planning and financial management
- Improved legal compliance
- Identification of weaknesses and areas in need of capacity building (which can be addressed through use of a capacity-building grant available to all districts)
- Publication of results, which has created healthy competition and stimulated discussions on ways and means to improve performance
- Enhancement of dialogue between central government and local governments and between local governments and citizens
- Use of Local Government Development Program (LGDP) funds for service delivery through nonsectoral grants and more local government autonomy if the incentives are right
- Reinforcement of decentralization objectives and help orienting local governments toward efficient service delivery and better accountability.

A Single District Budget and Development Fund. This model has been widely developed by UNCDF pilot projects in many countries. In the Mozambique Decentralized Finance and Planning Program, based on a pilot financed by UNCDF, the government is establishing institutions and mechanisms to support districts in developing plans that are multisectoral and require alignment with the various sector directorates at subnational levels. This ensures that recurrent costs and sector standards are accommodated. The plans are the basis for allocating money to the district development fund and for mobilizing additional funds through the government's budgeting process as well as from other possible partners, including donors, NGOs, and communities themselves (World Bank 2004a).

Projects in the district development plan are executed by the district administration itself or are delegated to subdistricts, NGOs, the private sector, and communities. The district budget then determines how much each community or subdistrict benefits from the fund.

A District Development Fund with a Special Window for Communities or Separate District and Community Development Funds. The advantage of having separate community or subdistrict funds or windows is that this division better advances empowerment and learning-by-doing at these lower levels than a process that maintains all of the allocation power at the district level. The disadvantage is that sequencing and economy of scale are more difficult to accommodate than in a single, fully fungible budget at the district levels.

In Rwanda, for instance, the government adopted an antipoverty strategy to empower local government to provide economic and social services to local communities, while at the same time empowering communities to demand such services from their local governments. Thus Rwanda's Decentralization and Community Development Program supports direct funding of community projects following a bottom-up planning process that involves communities throughout the project cycle. However, financial management and funding for larger district-level projects are done separately by the district administrations, with considerable institutional and capacity building at local levels (World Bank 2004a).

Allocation to the communities from the community window or fund could be based on proposals from these levels, or they could be based on ex ante allocation to each community or subdistrict based on a formula. Other rules can also be devised to ensure an equitable allocation of resources. Mexico's DRD projects adopted the principle that at least half of the resources had to be used for rural communities within a municipality, rather than the central municipal town, and the program should preferably target the poorest communities.

Local governments can be encouraged to contribute to the community window or the separate community fund and thereby help to co-finance community projects. As a result, funding for community projects would comprise the joint contributions of central government, local government, the community, and donors, with a progressively decreasing reliance on donor funding to achieve long-run fiscal sustainability of the program. There can also be separate local government windows, which would allow local governments to finance infrastructure that benefits more than one community, as in Madagascar and Zambia.

Channeling Financial Resources for Communities through a Special Fiduciary Agency, such as a Social Fund. The social funds of the early 1990s widely used these options; at the same time, they maintained the functions of identifying beneficiary communities, providing facilitation and technical support, and managing project approval, disbursement, supervision, and monitoring and evaluation. Increasingly, social funds have transferred the coordination, identification, approval, supervision, and some of the M&E functions to DDCs, as in the case of the social funds in Malawi and Tanzania.

More and more, as shown in chapter 4, these social funds concentrate on program development and supervision. They assure the financial flows and other fiduciary functions such as monitoring, evaluating, and reporting to government, donors, and other stakeholders. In many cases, however, the funds still write the checks to the communities, after being given disbursement orders from the DDCs. So the power to approve and initiate disbursements is transferred to the local level, while the actual check writing and reporting functions are centralized, *thus separating decision making about resources from the actual resource flows.* This is an appropriate division of labor in environments where financial management capacities at the local government are limited and corruption at that level is rampant. Given economies of scale in these financial transfer and other fiduciary functions, this may also be an appropriate long-term division of labor; social funds, or similar specialized fiduciary agents, could become permanent features of the intergovernmental fiscal system.

Channeling Money through NGOs. This approach was popular in the early 1990s, when it offered an alternative to large donor or government bureaucracies. NGOs helped to put in place many useful pilots, but this approach has been shown to have severe limitations for scaling up. First, it tended to be very costly, increasing transaction costs (such as management fees or other charges) and therefore the pass-through rate of financial resources allocated to the program and significantly reducing the amount of funds that actually reached communities. Second, it tended to disempower communities. Usually the NGOs exercised too tight control over the resources. Third, NGOs rarely had the capacity to scale programs up to district or national coverage. Finally, it eliminated the coordination functions of local government.

From Development Phase to National Scaling Up

This can be considered the countdown, with each number a step toward fully scaling up (see box 5.18).

Reviewing the Elements That Are in Place

With the elements to scaling up in place and the pilot phase of the LCDD program running properly in one or a few districts, the various documents

---

BOX 5.18

Steps to Scaling Up

- Ensure that the elements are in place
- Plan finances
- Manage bureaucratic hurdles
- Design a management system
- Focus on costs and logistics
- Devise a communications strategy
- Set up an M&E system
- Take special conditions into account
- Undertake prelaunch activities.

and tools used by the program need to be properly reviewed, updated, integrated, and presented. These include the operational manual, training materials, costs, M&E reports, initial impact evaluation results, and other relevant instruments.

The materials are an essential input into planning the national scale-up. They can be reviewed, improved, and presented for final revisions at a national stakeholder workshop and then aggregated into a comprehensive operational manual and translated into the major national languages.

Planning the Budgets and Financing

The planning process involves the preparation of detailed budgets and a financing plan involving all possible sources of funds: national government, local government, communities, and external donors. Financing norms and the pace of scaling up may have to be adjusted to fit the available financing to which the partners are willing to commit. Budgeting and financing options include the following:

- Fold similar ongoing programs into the new program. Similar programs may be financed nationally or by donors. Candidate programs should already have been included in the participatory reviews that were part of the program development phase.
- Allocate additional tax bases to local governments and communities that are to be used for co-financing the program.
- Allocate existing national revenues and donor funds to the program via the intergovernmental fiscal system.
- Raise additional taxes or donor resources for funding any likely shortfalls.

Identifying and Overcoming Remaining Bureaucratic Hurdles

It is also important for all participating stakeholders to identify gaps in the national and local institutional framework and remaining bureaucratic hurdles and to define time-bound plans to overcome them. Issues to be discussed may include the development of functioning local and subdistrict governments, further alignment of sectors with the national decentralization framework and community empowerment, strengthening of the central institutions in charge of decentralization and local governments, further simplification of procedures seen as causing delays or bottlenecks, and efforts to address weaknesses in national statistical systems and Poverty Reduction Strategy monitoring.

Designing the Program Management System

Based on experience in the planning phase, the national system for managing the program also has to be designed in detail with a focus on the central program office and its subsidiary branches, their capacities, terms of reference, and staffing. Planners will also need to consider phasing. There may have to be two or three phases to reach national coverage, depending on the number of districts in the country and the number of districts covered in each phase. There are two options for phasing:

• Beginning with the larger districts that have better capacity, allow a program to quickly expand the population reached. For instance, in Burkina Faso, the HIV/AIDS Prevention Program's 13 lead provinces (out of a total of 45 provinces) covered more than half of the population.
• Select a range of districts with different sizes and capacity levels, allowing fine-tuning of operational approaches and manuals to different situations.

Focusing on Program Management Costs and Efficient Logistics

As in the case of individual districts, scaling up across districts, states, or provinces also requires detailed planning that pays attention to the costs of managing the program. Cost elements during the planning phase need to be carefully reviewed along with further opportunities to reduce them. Cost-minimizing approaches involve the same principles of minimizing travel costs. Mobilizing existing structures to manage the program is better than developing new ones or hiring special staff and consultants to do the job.

Options for managing the large-scale training needs of district program managers include holding workshops at the national level, setting up lead districts and allowing neighboring districts to participate in the program rollout in a learning-by-doing mode, using the district-to-district extension approach, or using a combination of these approaches.

Implementing the Communications Strategy

At this time implementation of the national communication strategy becomes critical. The participants and communities that were part of the program development phase should be used intensively in the communication effort, because they will be the most knowledgeable, skilled, and committed to it.

Putting in Place the National M&E System

The national M&E system and the impact evaluation program need to be put in place to ensure regular and speedy feedback during the scaling-up phase. Similarly, a national IEC strategy will be needed to ensure national access to program information. Learning-by-doing never stops; therefore, operational manuals and training materials should not be regarded as static, but rather as subject at least to annual revisions to build in the lessons from the scaling-up phase.

Assessing Special Conditions or Circumstances

Depending on the results of further social analyses, it may be necessary to adapt program design to special district conditions. Considerations that may arise are the inclusion of marginalized or stigmatized communities (ethnic minorities, people living with HIV/AIDS) that may require special facilitation or subdistricts or communities with particularly pronounced social stratification or even conflict that may require special assistance from the central design team.

Holding a Prelaunch Workshop

The final step is to hold a program launch workshop with representatives from all of the key co-producers and from the next batch of lead districts.

Consolidation (Post–Scale Up)

Consolidation is not as hard as getting a program started and scaled up, but it does require careful attention (see box 5.19). The systems in place may require minor or major adjustments to manage the enormous complexity of scaled-up LCDD. Consolidation includes the following steps:

- Pulling together M&E data and evaluation reports to improve program design, management systems, and operating procedures

---

BOX 5.19

Steps to Scaling Up: Consolidation

- Achieve self-sustainability.

- Reviewing and adjusting cost-sharing rules, training, facilitation, and technical support systems
- Gradually shifting the program from basic infrastructure and services to economic development and social protection, depending on context and community demand
- Making the program fiscally sustainable by developing the fiscal base of local governments and communities and negotiating with higher-level governments on cost sharing.

With the basic structure in place, emphasis and resources can move toward deepening accountability mechanisms, improving technical and organizational capability, and expanding targeted programs to tackle issues that communities may have neglected. Furthermore, while the initial focus of LCDD may typically have been on rural areas, urban areas may be added in the consolidation stage, if not earlier.

Finally, as these elements are progressively being put in place, the program should work toward reducing its dependence on donors and the ultimate exit of foreign donors. This can be achieved by increasing the reliance at local and community levels on locally raised resources, while remembering the limitations of the poorest and most needy areas; by developing or strengthening the use of poverty formulas in the allocation of central government and donor funds; by developing the borrowing capacities of larger local governments; by fully integrating nonlocal funding into the intergovernmental system; and by refocusing donor finance on other programs or phasing it out altogether.

The ultimate success of LCDD is when a scaled-up program is, essentially, self-sustaining, and each participating community, district, and state has established its capacity to manage and execute its projects, improve its governance, and expand its economic options. Appendix B provides a matrix of scaling-up design elements and tools, including tables that present aspects of every design element, why it is used, and what its impact is for the LCDD program.

Notes

1. These are multisectoral LCDD programs for the production of public or semi-public infrastructure services, which are produced by communities with the help of local governments, nongovernmental organizations, and private sector actors.

2. World Bank (1996) offers a guide to assist countries in the development and strengthening of poverty reduction strategies; chapter 9 deals specifically with the cross-cutting issue of LCDD.

3. See http://www.kit.nl/smartsite.shtml?id=SINGLEPUBLICATION&ItemID =1829.

4. The teams can be collectively defined as LCDD strategy teams.

5. The CDD toolkit includes a wide variety of diagnostic exercises. It can be downloaded at http://www.kit.nl/smartsite.shtml?id=SINGLEPUBLICATION &ch=FAB&ItemID=1829. To learn more about KIT, see http://www.kit.nl/ smartsite.shtml?ch=FAB&id=4358. Further guidance on how to structure the diagnostic work can be found in Bonfiglioli (2002) and World Bank (2004c).

6. http://web.worldbank.org/external/default/main?menuPK=4062481&pagePK =224802&piPK=224813&q=political%20economy&theSitePK=244363; http://connect.worldbank.org/units/prem/PD.GIEA/pdgpe/default.aspx; World Bank (2007g); Rurdra and Sardesai (2009).

7. *Political decentralization*: local governments are characterized by (a) democratic political representation of local constituencies and (b) a mandate to respond to local needs within devolved or assigned powers. *Fiscal decentralization*: local governments are (a) being granted a reliable, adequate share of central revenue and (b) given the authority to levy, keep, and manage taxes. *Administrative decentralization*: (a) administrative responsibilities are being delegated to local governments, and (b) central government sectoral functionaries are being transferred to local governments.

8. For a detailed guide on how to design an IEC campaign, see Mozammel and Schechter (2004).

9. For complete and thorough guidance on how to design a national M&E system, see Adams (2006); Van Domelen (2007); Wong (2003).

10. Personal communication from Keith Rennie.

11. This is in line with the original participatory rural appraisal "behavior reversal" paradigm.

12. Communities will have to become familiar with the community project cycle. For a complete discussion of the community project cycle, see the highly recommended publication by de Silva (2002). A village participation manual has been designed to compress the process into one or two weeks. See World Bank (2002c).

13. In World Bank–funded programs, the legal agreement can state that any community organization created for the purpose of the project is considered legal. However, this does not automatically mean that all the country's institutions will comply.

Operational Functions and Manuals, by Level

Operational function and manuals	Community	Local	District	National
Exclusive national functions				
Mobilization and coordination of aid				X
Decentralization policy and management				X
Intergovernmental fiscal system				X
Sector program design and management				X
Management and coordination manuals or chapters				
Governance and decision making	X	X	X	X
Diagnostics and priority setting	X	X	X	X
Management training	X	X	X	X
Monitoring and evaluation				
Resource mobilization and management manuals or chapters				
Resource mobilization	X	X	X	X
Beneficiary selection and targeting	X	X	X	X
Financial management and accountability	X	X	X	X
Procurement, contract, and materials management	X	X	X	X
Technical manuals				
Technical design and management	X	X	X	X
Specialist training and retraining	X	X	X	X
Logistics manuals or chapters				
Rollout logistics	Not needed	X	X	X
Logistics training	Not needed	X	X	X

Source: Authors' compilation.

Design Elements and Tools for Large-Scale LCDD Programs

The national policy toolkit (Heemskerk and Baltissen 2005) contains diverse tables to guide the diagnostic process. The following tables present the design elements and tools from the step-by-step guide (Binswanger and Nguyen 2005).

Table B.1. Phasing and Sequencing

Design element	Main reason for use	Impact on cost-effectiveness and efficiency
Proper study of earlier experience	Inform overall design and planning	Multiple gains in every area
Diagnostics of issues and capacities	For details, see table B.3	Multiple gains in every area
Field-test the scaling up in one or several districts	Test the logistics and design of the proposed program and improve overall design by making room for troubleshooting at an early stage	Improved x-efficiency; lower transaction costs; avoidance of costly delays in scaling-up phase
Grafting to a larger program or development process	Ensure political commitment; capitalize on existing macro-governance and management systems; develop common information base, values, and approaches; improve information and decision making; enhance incentive compatibility	Reduced management costs; multiple gains in transaction and management costs; reduced losses from moral hazard, opportunity cost of program delays, and failures; greater x-efficiency and allocative efficiency; lower central fiscal cost

(continued)

Table B.1. Phasing and Sequencing (*continued*)

Design element	Main reason for use	Impact on cost-effectiveness and efficiency
Explosion	Immediately achieve scale	Rapid economic gains; risk of costs of failure and delays; little room to correct faulty design in the short run
Field-tested operational manuals for all primary functions at all levels	Serve as a basis for program performance and timely implementation	Reduced management costs; lower opportunity cost of delays, inadequate coverage, mistakes in decisions, and mismatch of resources
Regular revision of operational manuals	Provide room for troubleshooting or fine-tuning	Multiple gains on all levels
Replication after adjustments from feedback	Improve design and planning	Multiple gains in every area

Source: Binswanger and Nguyen 2005.

Table B.2. Decentralization and Local Government Empowerment

Design element	Main reason for use	Impact on cost-effectiveness and efficiency
Gradual handover of responsibilities to local government	Build ownership and common values and vision; improve information and decision making; achieve incentive compatibility and greater accountability; mobilize latent capacities and local resources	Reduced transaction, communication, and travel costs; greater x-efficiency; allocative efficiency
Assured flow of funds to local governments, mostly fungible and some earmarked for specific programs	Allow local governments to allocate resources and effectively carry out their functions; provide incentives for resource mobilization, cost savings, accountability to constituencies	Long-term fiscal sustainability; greater allocative efficiency and x-efficiency
Local government power to levy taxes and some user fees	Same as above	Same as above
Formula-driven allocation of funds to local governments	Achieve fiscal equity; allow for poverty targeting	Improved transparency and lower transaction costs
Capacity development for local governments (for example, participatory planning, financial management, accountability, monitoring and evaluation)	Mobilize latent capacities; reduce logistics problems, help to build common values	Lower transport, communications, and transaction costs

Source: Binswanger and Nguyen 2005.

Table B.3. Participation and Social Inclusion

Design element	Main reason for use	Impact on cost-effectiveness and efficiency
Review of poverty assessments and use of poverty maps	Identify key pockets of poverty both geographic and by social groups	Lower targeting costs; lower losses from mistargeting
Social analysis (for example, stakeholder analysis, social stratification, civil society organizations and capacities)	Determine the operation's primary stakeholders; identify their interests in and influence over the program; identify and assess institutions at local, regional, and national levels and processes on which to build; provide a foundation and strategy for participation	Avoidance of faulty design and inefficient implementation
Participation of women in all aspects of the program, especially skills development	Develop a culture of social inclusion; mobilize latent capacities; build ownership	Greater x-efficiency; wide spread of program benefits within communities
Participation of marginalized groups, especially skills development	Reduce risk of elite capture; develop a culture of social inclusion; mobilize latent capacities; build ownership	Greater x-efficiency; wide spread of program benefits within communities
Clear social inclusion rules for the formation of village development committees	Develop a culture of social inclusion; mobilize latent capacities; build ownership	Greater x-efficiency; wide spread of program benefits within communities

Source: Binswanger and Nguyen 2005.

Table B.4. Community Setup

Design element	Main reason for use	Impact on cost-effectiveness and efficiency
Improvement or creation of community development committees and subcommittees to manage community program and projects	Make program into a legitimate village activity; build ownership and common values; provide the basis for inclusion of all local stakeholders; put in place the basic management and accountability structure; mobilize latent capacities	Lower transaction costs; higher allocative and x-efficiency
Periodic village elections for development committee positions	Build beneficiary ownership; enhance downward accountability; mobilize latent capacities; reduce risk of elite capture and corruption	Higher allocative and x-efficiency
Giving of legal status to village development committees	Satisfy requirements of national legal and procedural systems	Lower transaction costs, logistical problems, and opportunity costs of delays

(continued)

Table B.4. Community Setup (*continued*)

Design element	Main reason for use	Impact on cost-effectiveness and efficiency
Participatory appraisal and planning approaches resulting in a community development plan and list of immediate priorities	Develop common information base, values, and approaches of community and local stakeholders; improve community development institutions; put in place committees to manage community projects and audit and control committees	More welfare-enhancing community choice for all; short- and long-term gains via use of local knowledge, skills, and commitment for planning, implementing, monitoring or maintaining, and evaluation
Community contracting of technical services	Achieve empowerment, accountability, quality, timeliness, and reductions in logistics problem of advisory services	Lower technical assistance costs, quality losses, and opportunity cost of delays; expanded local market for the provision of goods and services
Channel for complaints and dispute resolution	Enhance downward accountability; provide information feedback to other co-producers	Lower costs and fewer delays associated with unresolved disputes
Promotion of intervillage cooperation	Undertake projects that transcend village boundaries and deal with spillover effects; share knowledge and advice among communities	Need for fewer extension workers in private, public, or nongovernmental organization (NGO) sectors

Source: Binswanger and Nguyen 2005.

Table B.5. Funding Arrangements for the Community

Design element	Main reason for use	Impact on cost-effectiveness and efficiency
Fungible funds: unconditional grants for an open menu of projects, accompanied by a negative list (earmarked grants in exceptional circumstances)	Strengthen empowerment; improve the ability to allocate money to priority projects; enhance transparency and accountability	Greater allocative efficiency: economic gains from better alignment of choices with community preferences; greater mobilization of community co-financing, latent capacities, volunteer efforts, and labor
Assured flow of funds to communities (that is, money in the hands of the community)	Strengthen empowerment; provide incentives for resource mobilization, cost savings, and accountability to members	Average 40 percent reduction in project costs

(*continued*)

Table B.5. Funding Arrangements for the Community (*continued*)

Design element	Main reason for use	Impact on cost-effectiveness and efficiency
Matching grants and community co-financing (in cash or in kind)	Strengthen ownership and accountability; build common values	Improved x-efficiency; significant reduction in fiscal costs
Simple, rapid, and transparent funding procedures and elimination of financial intermediaries	Strengthen empowerment and accountability to primary stakeholders; simplify logistics	Lower transaction costs and program overhead
Progressive integration of direct disbursement procedures into standard government disbursement processes	Build ownership and capacity; simplify logistics; improve accountability	Lower transaction costs and program overhead; higher allocative efficiency
Formula-driven fund allocation within local areas	Improve equity, transparency, and accountability by simplifying the process of preparing and approving community projects within known budget envelopes	Lower transaction costs for all; lower management costs

Source: Binswanger and Nguyen 2005.

Table B.6. Institutional Setup and Program Management

Design element	Main reason for use	Impact on cost-effectiveness and efficiency
Mainstream of LCDD into existing local governance systems	Achieve transparency and accountability at the local level; mobilize latent capacities for management; reduce coordination and logistics problems	Reduced management and transaction costs; increased allocative efficiency and x-efficiency
Principle of subsidiarity to allocate functions to communities, local, and central levels	Improve information and decision making; achieve incentive compatibility; reduce moral hazard; strengthen empowerment and accountability; mobilize latent capacities and local resources; help to build a common vision	Same as above
Clear definition of roles for all primary functions at all levels	Reduce co-producer and logistics problems and minimize coordination costs; help to build a common vision	Same as above

(*continued*)

Table B.6. Institutional Setup and Program Management (*continued*)

Design element	Main reason for use	Impact on cost-effectiveness and efficiency
Learning-by-doing by all participants	Develop latent capacities; put formal training to immediate use; build common values	Increased x-efficiency; reduced training costs
Simplification of bureaucratic processes	Self-explanatory	Reduced transaction and management costs; reduced losses from moral hazard and opportunity cost of program delays; greater x-efficiency and allocative efficiency; lower central fiscal cost
Transfer of community project identification, appraisal, approval, supervision, and participatory monitoring and evaluation (M&E) activities to local development committees	Use latent local capacities and local knowledge; manage tens of thousands of community projects	Reduced transaction, communication, and travel costs; greater x-efficiency and allocative efficiency

Source: Binswanger and Nguyen 2005.

Table B.7. Training

Design element	Main reason for use	Impact on cost-effectiveness and efficiency
Local recruitment of trainers and "trainers of trainers" at district and subdistrict levels	Mobilize latent capacities (knowledge of the area, language, and culture; ability to adapt and translate training materials); create a resident cadre of trainers who can be mobilized for later program phases; reduce logistics problems; help to build common values	Lower per diems, transport, communications, and transaction costs; no need for permanent employees
Careful logistics design of cascade training	Minimize transaction costs and delays	Reduced costs of training and delays
Systematic use of training manuals	Reduce program delays, frustrations, and slippage in coverage	Saved opportunity cost of program delays and slippages
Training of local facilitators in facilitation and participatory planning	Mobilize latent capacities; create a resident cadre of facilitators; reduce logistics problems; help to build common values	Same as above

(*continued*)

Table B.7. Training (continued)

Design element	Main reason for use	Impact on cost-effectiveness and efficiency
Use of national and local NGOs, universities, and private sector actors to support the training program rather than implement it	Mobilize latent capacities; use on-the-ground infrastructure and expertise; build local capacity; help to build common vision and values	Improved training quality and x-efficiency
Training for village development committees in necessary skills (such as participatory planning, financial management, procurement, accountability, participatory monitoring and evaluation, and specific program content)	Mobilize latent management and technical capacities; build ownership and common values and approaches in the community; promote empowerment of previously excluded groups	Reduced costs and improved effectiveness and efficiency of the operation by narrowing the gap between delivery of goods and services and decision making and corrective action; maximize volunteer labor and skills

Source: Binswanger and Nguyen 2005.

Table B.8. Facilitation

Design element	Main reason for use	Impact on cost-effectiveness and efficiency
Make facilitation available during all phases of the program	Assist communities in managing their participatory planning and programming, M&E, accountability processes, and technical design and execution	Greater allocative and x-efficiency; reduced cost of failure; reduced risk of elite capture
A carefully designed, mandatory facilitation program on core capacities and program components	Bring communities to the minimum level of capacity	Same as above
Facilitation and technical assistance made available on demand at the local level and provision of resources to communities to pay for these services or contribute to their costs	Allow communities to deepen and broaden their capacities as prioritized by them	Greater allocative and x-efficiency; reduced cost of failure
Use of trained village members as facilitators	Expand capacity to facilitate the program in all villages; allow communities to recruit their own part-time local facilitators and technicians	Reduced costs of facilitation and technical support and reduced opportunity costs of delays; improved quality

(continued)

Table B.8. Facilitation (*continued*)

Design element	Main reason for use	Impact on cost-effectiveness and efficiency
Use of local government and sector staff as facilitators and technical advisers	Mobilize latent capacities for management; reduce logistics problems; help to build common values	Reduced management and coordination costs
Use of specialized actors (NGOs, private sector, universities) to support facilitators and technical specialists	Mobilize latent capacities, use on-the-ground infrastructure and expertise; build local capacity; help to build a common vision and values	Improved program quality

Source: Binswanger and Nguyen 2005.

Table B.9. Information, Education, and Communication

Design element	Main reason for use	Impact on cost-effectiveness and efficiency
Comprehensive communication strategy	Enhance empowerment; provide rapid access to information and knowledge about the program and its progress, achievements, and problems	Enhanced x-efficiency, reduced opportunity cost of misunderstandings, delays, and political interference
Sensitization campaigns conducted in each community and via the radio and the press	Spread knowledge about the program as a precondition for starting the program	Beginning of the process of program preparation in the villages
Regular and systematic public information to all communities and co-producers using radio, the press, facilitators, and direct channels to communities	Support the smooth functioning of the program; enhance transparency and accountability; reduce crises and political problems	Improved x-efficiency and reduced delays
Ensure the flow of information within communities via regular meetings and postings of critical information such as funds received and spent	Same as above	Same as above
Use of flyers and newsletters to inform all co-producers	Same as above	Same as above

Source: Binswanger and Nguyen 2005.

Table B.10. Monitoring and Evaluation

Design element	Main reason for use	Impact on cost-effectiveness and efficiency
Monitoring and evaluation plan	Basic program management tool	Control of costs; improved efficiency
Participatory monitoring and evaluation carried out at different levels	Provide immediate feedback; enhance quality; strengthen common values and empowerment; control costs	Reduced risk of mismanagement; lower economic and fiscal costs due to errors and omissions in design or implementation by providing immediate feedback; maximized synergies among various operational components
Monitoring of the process, implementation, and sustainability at all levels	Provide feedback to technical agencies; make technical improvements in the program	Greater x-efficiency as a result of improved quality
Impact evaluation, starting with a baseline study (usually done by universities or specialized consulting firms with research capacities)	Improve the impact of the program and justify its continued funding	Improved allocative, targeting, and x-efficiency
Community monitoring of their own projects, including via community finance and audit committees	Enhance empowerment, downward accountability, and ownership; help to build sustainable partnerships among communities, service providers, and public and civil society stakeholder groups	Reduced fiscal costs
Use of NGOs, civil society, and journalists as monitoring agents	Use where local governments are not up to the task	Reduced elite capture and corruption; increased legitimacy of the program

Source: Binswanger and Nguyen 2005.

Table B.11. Community and Local Government Projects

Design element	Main reason for use	Impact on cost-effectiveness and efficiency
Community and local government project funds paid in tranches based on statement of expenditures	Enhance accountability; facilitate auditing	Reduced quality losses and lower risk of misuse of funds
Annual budget allocations for communities and local governments based on performance benchmarks	Provide incentives for performance	Same as above
Contracting by communities and local governments of private sector goods and services	Strengthen empowerment; mobilize latent capacities; strengthen willingness to co-finance	Increased x-efficiency; reduced fiscal costs
Community responsibility for operation and maintenance of community projects	Build ownership	Reduced fiscal costs
Contract between local government and village development committees on their development plan or projects	Provide a transparency and accountability mechanism; improve information between levels of decision making; encourage ownership and co-financing by local government	Greater x-efficiency

Source: Binswanger and Nguyen 2005.

Table B.12. Government, NGO, and Donor Harmonization

Design element	Main reason for use	Impact on cost-effectiveness and efficiency
Involvement of interested donors and civil society partners in initial consultations, program design, and supervision	Promote exchange of innovations and good practices; build a network among stakeholders; encourage harmonization of approaches and co-financing; develop the basic trust and understanding for development of a unified fiduciary and accountability system	Improved allocative and x-efficiency; reduced fiscal cost; reduced transaction costs
Dissemination and exchange of newsletters between donors and high-level civil society partners	Same as above	Same as above
A common fiduciary and accountability system for all government and donor funds	Radically reduce transaction costs of all co-producers	Improved allocative and x-efficiency; reduced fiscal costs; reduced transaction costs

Source: Binswanger and Nguyen 2005.

The Four Core Expected Outcomes of LCDD

This appendix discusses the four core expected outcomes of local and community driven development (LCCD) that form part of the vision for community driven development (CDD) articulated by the Africa Region of the World Bank. These outcomes are real participation (which takes up the bulk of this section), improved accountability, technical soundness, and sustainability.

Real Participation

The importance of real participation has been demonstrated in theory and practice. Real participation aims to reach all key stakeholders at the very outset by conducting a stakeholder analysis using institutional diagnostics and toolkits. This conceptual framework adopts the World Bank operational definition of stakeholders as "those affected by the outcome—negatively or positively—or those who can affect the outcome of a proposed intervention." Key stakeholders are those whose real participation is essential for the initiative's success.

Real participation means involving citizens at every stage and level. This includes the micro or community level, the meso or intermediate level (local governments, nongovernmental organizations [NGOs]), and the macro or national policy level (central government, World Bank staff). Real participation implies that development choices are taken under conditions of full information, full representation of all interests, and a hard budget constraint. These conditions can be met in substantial measure, if not fully, by good program design. Under these conditions, elites will be driven toward proposals that benefit all stakeholders, including poor and marginalized groups. Some caveats are in order. If poor and marginalized groups are prevented from participating effectively, elite capture will follow. Similarly, if community members dependent on natural resources and other environmental interest groups are inadequately represented, environmental degradation may result.

Empowerment means real control by communities over resources, project or program design and selection, implementation, and monitoring and evaluation (M&E). A good test of whether a pilot program will foster empowerment is whether the community or local government has full control over the financial resources to be used in the program—that is, whether the money is in the hands of the community—and whether these resources are part of a single untied development budget rather than earmarked for specific purposes.

Shifting power from the top to the bottom requires strong political commitment. Good design is all-important: without it, power may simply move from ineffective central governments to ineffective local ones. So empowerment requires both political commitment and good design. These, in turn, should be used to ensure six critical factors:

1. Devolution of authority and resources
2. Real participation of primary stakeholders
3. A communication program that provides a two-way flow of information
4. Co-financing by communities to promote local ownership
5. Availability of technical assistance and facilitation from the private sector or higher administrative levels
6. Pro-poor market development, including facilitation of producer or user groups that can federate upward to tap national and global markets (Narayan 2002).

Devolution of Authority and Resources

Shifts in power relations are fundamental in LCCD (Narayan 2002). Communities and local governments can be truly empowered only by having an assured flow of funds from the central government as well as the authority to levy local taxes and user charges. Only then can they participate fully in development bargaining. Untied funds enable communities and local governments to choose their own priorities and create skills through learning-by-doing. It allows them to evaluate propositions against a single budget constraint, one of the preconditions of welfare-improving social choice (World Bank 2000a). Earmarking of resources is justified only where community decision making cannot take place under our proposed bargaining conditions. For example, resources for HIV/AIDS (human immunodeficiency virus/acquired immune deficiency syndrome) may have to be earmarked as long as the disease leads to stigma and cannot even be talked about. Earmarking may also be needed for measures such as biodiversity and soil conservation, since communities may ignore benefits to outsiders (World Bank 2000a). Working toward a unified budget constraint implies that decentralization should give local governments a predictable, transparent share of revenue (including foreign aid), preferably by a legally mandated formula. This will empower them with financial viability. Short-lived donor programs and ad hoc central grants cannot lead to empowerment (World Bank 2000a).

Decentralization should be based on the principle of subsidiarity (World Bank 2000a). Responsibility for all tasks should be devolved to the lowest level that can effectively manage them. The subsidiarity principle improves efficiency and reduces fiscal costs by assigning tasks on the basis of comparative advantage. It is a powerful design element to harness latent capacities, thus reducing program costs. Fiscal rewards and penalties can spur competition between local governments and between communities. They can accelerate the development of skills by providing incentives for improved performance. This reduces fiscal costs. Zambia has pioneered the grant of additional authority and funds to local governments that meet specified benchmarks. Other African countries are considering similar incentive schemes.

Even after decentralization and participation are in place, central programs will be needed for issues and sectors that local governments may neglect or be unsuitable to handle. This includes trunk roads and canals cutting through several jurisdictions and projects with environmental or social externalities.

Real Stakeholder Participation

Real stakeholder participation is required in appraisal and planning, implementation, and M&E.

Participatory appraisal and planning by all stakeholders helps to strengthen decision making at the community level. It requires skilled external facilitators and has been successfully used in urban and rural programs. It is the starting point for citizens to acquire information about options, resources, constraints, latent capabilities, and the likely consequences of each subproject for each stakeholder (World Bank 2002c). It helps to bring about the conditions for optimal social choice discussed above.

Based on an initial stakeholder analysis, ideally complemented by social and institutional analysis, key stakeholders are divided into relevant groups to analyze their constraints, aspirations, and options. Participatory workshops may then bring together all levels of stakeholder groups into a single event or may be sequentially phased. These processes also strengthen or create a community development committee and relevant subcommittees and identify group leaders and appropriate institutional arrangements. Through bargaining, key stakeholders approve a list of agreed projects. Subcommittees are then empowered to pursue the approved projects. Elite capture and social exclusion are ever-present dangers, and careful design of the participatory process is needed to check them.

The next step is participatory implementation and operations and maintenance (O&M). Communities and local governments need to be involved in the design, execution, maintenance, and operation of projects. This improves ownership and, in many instances, has reduced the costs of small infrastructure by 20–40 percent. In the past, infrastructure has suffered from poor O&M, for want of sufficient funding and motivation from central agencies. Local governments and communities have historically not been empowered to operate systems, levy user charges, or undertake maintenance. Recent experience shows that communities are willing to bear the entire O&M costs for rural water supply plus part of the capital costs.

Process monitoring provides feedback to project authorities while implementation is in progress. This is accomplished through continuous observation, interpretation, and institutional learning involving participant observation and assessment. All stakeholder groups in a project see and judge it. Dynamics within and between stakeholders are usually not "visible," so process monitoring helps to reveal these. It looks at both internal and external processes and helps to analyze the interaction within and across groups and levels.

Participatory M&E recognizes that communities may be well placed to identify the most relevant and easily trackable indicators and may be better motivated than government surveyors to be thorough. In Guinea, for example, the Village Communities Support Program (VCSP) has established an

M&E unit that coordinates process monitoring and helps communities to establish their own monitoring. Evaluation is carried out mostly by independent organizations such as universities and NGOs.

Keep it simple. To enable village communities to participate fully, simple, transparent rules and procedures are needed that can be replicated easily across large areas. However, creating simple but appropriate rules and procedures is not simple at all, yet it is essential to ensure real participation.

Communications

Scaling up requires a well-designed communications program. Information, education, and communication activities have to meet the need for awareness and learning in addition to process monitoring. Equal access to information by all participants is critical for welfare-enhancing social choice. Decentralization, community empowerment, and capacity building can be aided by a multidimensional communication program that will also contribute independently to information, voice, and organizational capacity.

In Poni Province, Burkina Faso, a local radio station (Radio Gaoua) gives information daily on an ongoing AIDS Prevention Program and has greatly improved awareness of this health issue. It is used to convene meetings in an area where mail and telephones are weak. Community radio can be a two-way source of information. Sri Lanka's community radio has a panel of resource persons, and listeners can phone in to request a wide range of information and solutions to problems. To take off, community radio requires a favorable regulatory environment and possibly promotional financing.

The success of Grameen Village Phones in Bangladesh proves the value of telecommunications even in poor, remote areas. Here again, regulations need to facilitate rural mobile telecommunications, and spending on promotion may be necessary initially. The Gyandoot Project in Madhya Pradesh, India, shows that rural Internet kiosks can greatly facilitate e-governance and e-commerce, improving the voice and incomes of poor villagers. The Internet can also be used to provide training and build capacity. It is used in Andhra Pradesh, India, to train rural midwives, thus reducing maternal mortality.

A communication strategy should include the following elements:

1. *Communication rationale.* Empowerment and voice for the poor, capacity building, community mobilization and education, cross-stakeholder partnerships, accountability and transparency, and political incentives

2. *Target audience.* Subsegments within major stakeholder groups, including central, state, and municipal governments, community organizations and groups, private sector institutions, and other geographic, gender, economic, social, and political divisions
3. *Types of message.* Benefits and tradeoffs, incentives, awareness, actions required, education and learning needs, and avenues for complaints and suggestions
4. *Strategic scope and delivery style.* National or regional, mass communication or specialized, targeted means, and interpersonal or popular (that is, radio, Internet, grassroots media, computerized management information systems)
5. *Creators of communication capacity.* NGOs, public relations firms, consultants, radio-Internet operators.

Co-financing by Communities

To inculcate a sense of local ownership, communities should contribute to both capital costs and maintenance costs of projects meant for their benefit. Contributions can be in cash or in kind (labor, materials). Where communities have no sense of ownership, assets may atrophy for want of motivation in O&M. In many countries, new rules and laws are required to devolve authority to levy local taxes and user charges.

Local contributions mobilize additional resources, reduce the fiscal costs per community member, and ease the fiscal strain on central governments. Global experience warns us that devolving excessive funds to municipalities may induce the latter to reduce local taxes. So scaling up should be based at least partly on matching grants, rewarding those municipalities and communities that make the most effort to raise their own resources.

Technical Assistance and Facilitation from Local and Higher Levels

To assist with participatory appraisal, planning, and implementation, communities need external facilitators and technical specialists. The facilitators need to guide the gathering and processing of information and provide fuller knowledge about the benefits and costs of various development projects, their technological options, and the consequences for the various stakeholders. The facilitators need to ensure real participation and empowerment.

Communities and local governments have latent capabilities, and empowerment harnesses these skills and enhances them through learning-by-doing supplemented by relevant capacity building. Technical designs and assistance should be available on demand from formally trained specialists at local and higher levels. As communities take on increased responsibilities, the complexity of their technical needs will increase. So they need resources to upgrade the skills of community specialists, such as community health workers, and to purchase facilitation and technical inputs from different sources. In northeastern Brazil, communities proved that they could cut costs by procuring technical services in innovative ways. Sectors, in collaboration with the private sector and NGOs, need to strengthen or develop a continuous system of training and retraining their sector specialists and to acquire the ability to respond to requests from communities. The training and visit approach to agricultural extension has many elements of such a system.

Pro-poor Market Development

Higher income is an essential form of empowerment and requires pro-market policies that enhance the capacity of poor people to benefit from participation in provincial, national, and global markets. Preconditions for these policies are good macroeconomic and sectoral policies and good governance and enforcement of property rights that encourage entrepreneurship. The sourcebook on empowerment and poverty reduction classifies pro-poor market development into three categories: access to information, inclusion or participation, and local organizational capacity (Narayan 2002).

Examples of pro-poor market development through better access to information include (a) global connectivity for villagers through Grameen Village Phones, Bangladesh; (b) e-commerce vehicles such as Drishtee .com, Novica.com, and PeopLink.org; (c) credit ratings for self-help groups (Andhra Pradesh, India) that facilitate credit with minimal transaction costs; and (d) smart cards that microfinance groups use to cut delays and transaction costs in India and Swaziland.

Examples of market development through inclusion and participation are (a) one-stop shops in Bali, Indonesia, for facilitating government clearances for hawkers and other low-income entrepreneurs; (b) the Urban Property Rights Project in Peru, which confers formal title on previously unregistered dwellings, increasing property values dramatically and enabling property owners to obtain credit using their newly registered property as collateral; and (c) microfinance institutions catering to those outside the formal credit system.

Examples of market development through improved organizational capacity include the Self-Employed Women's Association in India, the

Rice Millers' Association in Cambodia, the Metalworkers' Network in Honduras, and the Hammock Makers' Network in Nicaragua.

Improving Accountability

Traditionally, almost all accountability has been upward, to central governments and donors. This violates the first condition for optimal public choice, namely full and equal information to all stakeholders, including reports and data that establish accountability. LCDD aims to correct this fatal flaw by shifting the emphasis to horizontal and downward accountability to community members, users, and local peers and by empowering them to take corrective actions against errant co-producers. This means, for example, that communities should be able to hire, pay, and discipline staff delivering frontline services such as primary education and health. This approach can be initiated in pilots and ultimately scaled up nationally.

Formal reporting and audit mechanisms have failed to achieve high standards of accountability in poor countries. Yet successful social funds show that accountability can be harnessed through social capital in communities. Scaling up community empowerment can therefore scale up accountability. Greater participation in projects, transparency in local decision making, and a strong communication strategy can all help to improve accountability. Greater political accountability through local government elections can be even more important.

Fiscal rewards and penalties for good or unacceptable performance can induce greater accountability from local governments and communities. Zambia is a good example of this (chapter 4). Community leaders in high-performance communities not only get bigger budgets but also build reputations and advance their political careers.

In Bangalore, India, an NGO asks people to rate the local services they receive and presents the findings as a report card on public services. Similar report cards on five other Indian cities have since been published, and this approach has been tried as well in Ukraine, the Philippines, and Washington, DC. This rating helps to improve accountability.

Upward accountability also needs to be overhauled. Traditional disbursement and audit mechanisms are unsuitable for disbursement to and oversight of tens of thousands of small community accounts. For this reason, the World Bank has gradually developed and now summarized community-based disbursement and procurement methods and guidelines.

These guidelines give communities simple methods to account for funds to their members and higher authorities and to procure goods and services for their projects. Greater reliance can be placed on peer pressure within communities, fiscal rewards and penalties, and random audits.

Participatory M&E mechanisms integrating micro, meso, and macro levels of an initiative can improve not only downward but also upward accountability through timely tracking that quickly reveals technical or financial flaws.

Accountability to donors is often balkanized into different channels for each donor, even within the same sector and district. Accounts and reports often have to be prepared in the language of the donor, and this facilitates capture by elites, who alone know nonlocal languages. This requirement makes a joke of alphabetization programs, which are usually in the local language and often financed by the same donor. A woman who has acquired reading and writing skills will still not be able to check the community accounts! While scaling up, donors need to harmonize assistance and procedures to produce a single line of accountability, with all local-level documents in the local language. Translation from the local language to that of donors can be done by locally recruited staff.

Technical Soundness

Technical soundness implies using economically viable and locally tested technologies. Islands of success have produced a wide choice of simple technical solutions. To ensure wide replicability, these solutions should be field-tested in several environmental and social regions. Technical soundness is more about program design than about technology. The following are some key elements:

- Designing LCDD in phases taking into account the special history and characteristics of each country
- Ensuring real participation and guarding against elite capture and social exclusion
- Making sure that political decentralization is accompanied by administrative and fiscal decentralization
- Adapting country decentralization plans to make use of local institutions and all latent skills and capacities

- Preparing field-tested manuals and tools for every actor, sector, and level of government, so that all know precisely what they should do in LCDD and how
- Ensuring the availability of replicable, adaptable technical designs
- Ensuring the availability of technical advisory services on which communities, local service providers, facilitators, and local governments can draw.

Sustainability

Sustainability has many elements: institutional, fiscal, asset, environmental, and social.

Regarding *institutional sustainability*, social funds financed by donors have initiated CDD in some countries, but the process cannot rely forever on donor programs. It must be embedded in a permanent institutional framework. This framework can take the form of local governments or federations of producer groups, user groups, and self-help groups. CDD is driven not by community members but by community institutions, which need to be created and empowered with authority and rights (for example, parent-teacher associations should be able to influence schools). Groups without rights or resources are unlikely to function sustainably.

Regarding *fiscal sustainability*, matching grants for communities from donors can kick-start CDD, but thereafter LCDD should be financed by intergovernmental transfers mandated by a revenue-sharing formula, giving communities and local governments an assured shared of central revenue. In addition, powers to levy taxes and user charges need to devolve to local governments and communities. Fiscal sustainability can be improved by harnessing the resources of communities, local governments, and other co-producers. The revenue-sharing formula can help to equalize fiscal capacities across advanced and backward regions. Funding for communities should become a fiscal right, not largesse from donors or the central government.

Regarding *asset sustainability*, experience shows that assets such as roads and canals can erode or collapse for want of maintenance. Communities and local stakeholders should be given the responsibility for maintaining most assets and the authority to levy user fees and local taxes to finance maintenance.

Regarding *environmental sustainability*, the management of land, water, forests, pastures, groundwater, and other environmental resources must aim to use sustainable practices. Giving ownership or permanent usufruct rights and management responsibility to communities helps to solve open-access problems and provides powerful incentives for sustainable management.

Regarding *social sustainability*, LCDD must be socially inclusive, build on existing local-level institutions, and include conflict resolution mechanisms. Participation and real empowerment are the bedrock on which all forms of sustainability must rest. Only through these processes can real fiscal, asset, environmental, and social sustainability be ensured. Seldom do participatory processes achieve perfection and even less so at the outset. The constant improvement of participation and stakeholder empowerment is therefore a major objective of scaling up.

The key principles that lead to welfare-enhancing social decisions also enhance sustainability. In a setting in which all stakeholders are well informed about the financial, social, and environmental consequences of the development options discussed and make their decision in the context of a unified budget constraint, the choices will also lead to sustainability. Real participation thus enhances not only efficiency but also sustainability. Environmental and social safeguards are needed when these ideal conditions for social choice are not met, for example, when information is lacking or poorly distributed or when key stakeholders are excluded from the decision-making process.

Adams, Charles F., Michael E. Bell, and Trevor Brown. 2002. "Building Civic Infrastructure: Implementing Community Partnership Grant Programs in South Africa." *Public Administration and Development* 22 (4): 293–302.

———. 2003. "Strengthening Civic Society in South Africa: The Community Partnership Grant Program." Proceedings of the 95th Annual Conference of the National Tax Association, Orlando, FL.

Adams, Sarah. 2006. "Evaluating Social Fund Impact: A Toolkit for Task Teams and Social Fund Managers." Social Protection Paper 0611, World Bank, Washington, DC.

AICDD (African Institute for Community-Driven Development). 2007. "Community-Based Worker Systems, Guidelines for Practitioners, Khanya." AICDD, South Africa (September). http://www.khanya-aicdd.org/search?SearchableText=community+based+workers.

Aiyar, Swaminathan, ed. 1995a. "Decentralization: A New Strategy for Rural Development." AGR Dissemination Note 1 (August), World Bank, Washington, DC.

———. 1995b. "Decentralization Can Work: Experience from Colombia." AGR Dissemination Note 3 (August), World Bank, Washington, DC.

———. 1995c . "How Well Has Decentralization Worked for Rural Development?" AGR Dissemination Note 2 (August), World Bank, Washington, DC.

———. 1996. "Has Decentralization Aided Biodiversity Conservation?" AGR Dissemination Note 11 (September), World Bank, Washington, DC.

———. 2003. "What Jalanidhi Tells Us about Community-Driven Development: A Case Study of Kerala's Rural Drinking Water and Sanitation Project." World Bank, Washington, DC. http://info.worldbank.org/etools/library/latestversion.asp?209158.

———. 2004. "Institutional Frameworks at the Ecosystem Level: Lessons for Africa from Other Continents." Prepared for the Global Environment Facility, World Bank, Washington, DC.

Aiyar, Swaminathan, Keith McLean, and Suzanne Piriou-Sall, eds. 1996. "The Political Economy of Democratic Decentralization." AGR Dissemination Note 9 (September), World Bank, Washington, DC.

Aiyar, Swaminathan, and Suzanne Piriou-Sall, eds. 1996. "How Rules and Incentives Can Improve the Working of Demand-Driven Rural Investment Funds." AGR Dissemination Note 10 (September), World Bank, Washington, DC.

Amazonas, Fatima, Túlio Barbosa, Hans Binswanger, Alberto Costa, Naércio Menezes, Elaine Pazello, and Claudia Romano. 2006. "Avaliação do Projeto de Combate à Pobreza Rural-PCPR, 1993–2005." Draft report (June), World Bank, Washington, DC.

Arcand, Jean-Louis, and Leandre Bassole. 2007. "Does Community-Driven Development Work? Evidence from Senegal." World Bank, Washington, DC (June).

Banglapedia. 2005. "The Comilla Model." Dhaka.

Binswanger, Hans, and Swaminathan Aiyar. 2004. "Scaling Up Community-Driven Development: Theoretical Underpinnings and Program Design Implications." Working Paper 3039, World Bank, Washington, DC.

———. 2006. *Historical Roots of Community-Driven Development: Evolution of Development Theory and Practice at the World Bank.* Washington, DC: World Bank.

Binswanger, Hans P., and Tuu-Van Nguyen. 2005. *Scaling Up Local and Community-Driven Development: A Step-by-Step Guide.* Washington, DC: World Bank.

Bonfiglioli, Angelo, ed. 2002. *Local Governance and Poverty: The UNCDF Approach.* New York: UNCDF. http://www.uncdf.org/english/local_development/documents_and_reports/thematic_papers/lg_and_poverty_01.php.

Cernea, Michael. 1983. "A Social Methodology for Community Participation in Local Investments: The Experience of Mexico's PIDER Program." Working Paper 598, World Bank, Washington, DC.

———, ed. 1985. *Putting People First: Sociological Variables in Rural Development.* Washington, DC: World Bank.

Chambers, Robert. 1983. *Rural Development: Putting the Last First.* London: Longman.

———. 1993. *Challenging the Professions: Frontiers for Rural Development.* London: Intermediate Technology Development Group.

CIMA (Community Informatics Multimedia Archive), Community Radio Working Group. 2007. "Community Radio: Its Impact and Challenges to Its Development." CIMA, Washington, DC (October).

Coirolo, Luis, and Jill Lamert, eds. 2009. *Rural Poverty Reduction in Northeast Brazil: Achieving Results through Community Driven Development.* Vol. 1. Fátima Amazonas, Túlio Barbosa, Hans Binswanger, Alberto Costa, Naércio Menezes, Elaine Pazello, and Claudia Romano, eds. 2009. *Rural Poverty Reduction in Northeast Brazil: An Evaluation of Community Driven Development.* Vol. 2. Washington, DC: World Bank.

Crook, Richard C., and James Manor. 1995. "Democratic Decentralization and Institutional Performance: Four Asian and African Experiences Compared." *Journal of Commonwealth and Comparative Studies* 33 (3): 309–40.

———. 1998. *Democracy and Decentralisation in South Asia and West Africa: Participation, Accountability, and Performance.* Cambridge, U.K.: Cambridge University Press.

Davis, Deborah. 2003. "The Second Kecamatan Development Project: Evaluation of Scaling-Up Issues." World Bank, Washington, DC. http://info.worldbank.org/etools/library/latestversion.asp?209161.

———. 2004. "Scaling Up Action Research Program Phase One: Lessons from Six Case Studies." World Bank, Washington DC. http://info.worldbank.org/etools/library/latestversion.asp?209145.

Davis, Gloria. 2004. *A History of the Social Development Network in the World Bank, 1973–2002.* Social Development Paper 56 (March), World Bank, Washington, DC.

de Silva, Samantha. 2002. *Communities Taking the Lead: A Handbook on Direct Financing of Community Subprojects.* Washington, DC: World Bank. http://siteresources.worldbank.org/INTSF/Resources/395669-1124228448379/1563169-1133371159393/DeSilva_CommTakingLead.pdf.

de Silva, Samantha, and June-Wei Sum. 2008. "Social Funds as an Instrument of Social Protection: Analysis of Lending Trends." HNPSP Paper, World Bank, Washington, DC.

Dongier, Philippe, Julie Van Domelen, Elinor Ostrom, Andrea Ryan, Wendy Wakeman, Anthony Bebbington, Sabine Alkire, Talib Esmail, and Margret Polsky. 2003. "Community-Driven Development." In *A Sourcebook for Poverty Reduction Strategies*, ed. Jeni Klugman, ch. 9. Washington, DC: World Bank.

Faguet, Jean-Paul. 1997. "Decentralization and Local Government Performance." FAO (Food and Agriculture Organization), Technical Consultation on Decentralization (December 4).

Fiszbein, Ariel. 1997. "The Emergence of Local Capacity: Lessons from Colombia." *World Development* 25 (7): 1029–43.

Fruman, Cecile. 2008. Presentation at SDN Week on Programmatic CDD-INDH, February.

Garg, Prem. 2006. "Operational Quality of Social Fund/CDD Operations: Some Trends and Issues." Presentation by Quality Assurance Group, World Bank, Washington, DC.

Hancock, Jim. 2003. "Scaling up Issues and Options: Supporting Good Practices and Innovation." AGR Working Paper, World Bank. Washington, DC.

Heemskerk, Willem, and Gerard Baltissen. 2005. *Community-Driven Development: Toolkit for National Stocktaking and Review.* Amsterdam: Royal Tropical Institute (KIT). http://www.kit.nl/smartsite.shtml?id=SINGLEPUBLICATION&ch=FAB&ItemID=1829.

Hegde, Narayan G. 2000. "Community Development in India: An Overview." Proceedings of the seminar Comparative Study on Planning Process of Community Development, Asian Productivity Organization, Ulaanbaatar, Mongolia. August 21–26.

Helling, Louis, Rodrigo Serrano, and David Warren. 2005. "Linking Community Empowerment, Decentralized Governance, and Public Service Provision through a Local Development Framework." Social Protection Discussion Paper 0535, World Bank, Washington, DC. http://siteresources.worldbank.org/INTC DD/544090-1138724740952/20802848/decnetralization05.pdf

JIMAT Consult, ITAD LMT, and O and M Associates. 2008. "MASAF APL 1 Impact Evaluation." Malawi.

Joseph, Sam. 1991. "Participatory Rural Appraisal (PRA): A Brief Note on Action-Aid's Experience." RRA Note 13 (August), World Bank, Washington, DC.

Kendall, Jake, and Nirvikar Singh. 2006. "Internet Kiosks in Rural India: What Influences Success?" Working Paper 06-05 (September), NET Institute.

Kwofie, Kwame M. 2003. "A Case Study of Scaling up Community-Driven Development in Social Investment Fund Programme of Zambia." World Bank, Washington, DC. http://info.worldbank.org/etools/library/latestversion .asp?209160.

Labonne, Julien, and Robert S. Chase. 2007. "Who Is at the Wheel When Communities Drive Development? The Case of KLAHI-CIDDS in the Philippines." Social Development Paper 107 (September), World Bank, Washington, DC.

———. 2008. "Do Community-Driven Development Projects Enhance Social Capital? Evidence from the Philippines." World Bank, Washington, DC.

Manoukian, Violeta. 2003. From Exclusive Boutique to National Culture: Scaling up CDD in Mexico. Washington, DC: World Bank. http://info.worldbank.org/ etools/library/latestversion.asp?209159.

McLaughlin, Karrie, Adam Satu, and Michael Hoppe. 2007. "Indonesia: Kecamatan Development Program: Qualitative Impact Evaluation." World Bank, Indonesia.

McLean, Keith, Graham Kerr, Suzanne Piriou-Sall, and Melissa Williams. 1998. "Decentralization and Rural Development: Characterizing Efforts of 19 Countries." Working Paper 40, World Bank, Washington, DC.

Mozammel, Masud, and Galia Schechter. 2004. "Strategic Communication for Community-Driven Development: A Practical Guide for Project Managers and Communication Practitioners." World Bank, Washington, DC.

Narayan, Deepa. 1995. "The Contribution of People's Participation: Evidence from 121 Rural Water Supply Projects." Occasional Paper 1, World Bank, Environmentally Sustainable Development, Washington, DC.

———, ed. 2002. Empowerment and Poverty Reduction: A Sourcebook. Washington, DC: World Bank.

Onyach-Olaa, Martin, Suleiman Namara, Timothy Lubanga, and Mwalimu Musheshe. 2003. "Scaling Up Community-Driven Development: Case Study from Uganda." World Bank, Washington, DC. http://info.worldbank.org/etools/library/latestversion.asp?209157.

Piriou-Sall, Suzanne. 1996. "Demand-Driven Rural Investment Fund: A New Generation of Social Funds." AGR Dissemination Note 13 (December), World Bank, Washington, DC.

———. 2007. "Decentralization and Rural Development: A Review of Evidence." World Bank, Washington, DC.

Rurdra, Nita, and Shonali Sardesai. 2009. "Political Economy of Decentralization in Bangladesh: Capturing the Stakeholder Perspective." Lunch presentation, World Bank, Washington, DC, April 23.

Salmen, Laurence. 1987. *Listen to the People.* New York: Oxford University Press.

Serrano, Rodrigo. 2006. "Local Governments and Social Accountability." In *Social Accountability Sourcebook.* Washington, DC: World Bank.

Staples, Eugene S. 1992. *Forty Years: A Learning Curve: The Ford Foundation in India, 1952–1992.* New York: Ford Foundation.

Steffensen, Jesper. 2006. "Monitoring and Use of Fiscal Indicators on Local Governance." Paper presented at the Senior Policy Workshop "Local Governance and Pro-Poor Outcomes in Africa," Kigali, Rwanda. October 31–November 2.

Tendler, Judith. 1999. *The Rise of Social Funds: What Are They a Model of?* UNDP Monograph. New York: United Nations Development Program.

UNCDF (United Nations Capital Development Fund). 2005. *Delivering the Goods: Building Local Government Capacity to Achieve the Millennium Development Goals; A Practitioner's Guide from UNCDF Experience in Least Developed Countries.* New York: UNCDF.

Van Domelen, Julie. 2007. "Reaching the Poor and Vulnerable: Targeting Strategies for Social Funds and Other Community-Driven Programs." Social Protection Discussion Paper 0711, World Bank, Washington, DC.

———. 2008. "Global Perspectives on Community-Driven Development." Paper presented at SDN week, World Bank. February.

Voss, John. 2008. "Indonesia: Impact Evaluation of the Second Phase of the KDP in Indonesia." World Bank, Indonesia.

Wennink, Bertus, and Gerard Baltissen. 2003. "Let's Ease Our Pace Because We Are in a Hurry: Scaling Up Community-Driven Development in Benin." Royal Tropical Institute (KIT), Amsterdam. http://info.worldbank.org/etools/library/latestversion.asp?209156.

Wong, Susan. 2003. "Indonesia Kecamatan Development Program: Building a Monitoring and Evaluation System for a Large-Scale Community-Driven Development Program." World Bank, Washington, DC.

World Bank. 1987. "Review of Irrigation Operations." World Bank, Operations Evaluation Department, Washington, DC.

———. 1990. *World Development Report 1990: Poverty.* Washington, DC: World Bank.

———. 1994. *The World Bank and Participation.* Washington, DC: World Bank, Operations Policy Department.

———. 1996. *The World Bank Participation Sourcebook.* Washington, DC: World Bank.

———. 2000a. "The Community-Driven Development Approach in the Africa Region: A Vision of Poverty Reduction through Empowerment." World Bank, Washington, DC.

———. 2000b. *World Development Report: Attacking Poverty.* Washington, DC: World Bank.

———. 2001. *Sourcebook for Community-Driven Development in Africa.* Washington, DC: World Bank.

———. 2002a. *Community-Driven Development: From Vision to Practice; A Technical Sourcebook.* Washington, DC: World Bank.

———. 2002b. *Empowerment and Poverty Reduction: A Sourcebook.* Washington, DC: World Bank.

———. 2002c. "Village-Level Participatory Approaches (VLPA)." World Bank, Washington, DC. http://www.kit.nl/smartsite.shtml?id=SINGLEPUBLICATION&ItemID=1472.

———. 2003a. "Community-Driven Reconstruction as an Instrument in War-to-Peace Transitions." CPR Working Paper 7 (August), Social Development Department (ESSD) Network, World Bank, Washington, DC.

———. 2003b. "Project Appraisal Document on a Proposed Grant to the Republic of Niger for the Community Action Program." World Bank, Washington, DC.

———. 2003c. *World Development Report 2003: Making Services Work for the Poor.* World Bank, Washington, DC.

———. 2003d. *The World Bank Participation Sourcebook: Environmentally Sustainable Development.* Washington, DC: World Bank. http://www-wds.worldbank.org/external/default/main?pagePK=64193027&piPK=64187937&theSitePK=523679&menuPK=64187510&searchMenuPK=64187283&siteName=WDS&entityID=000009265_3961214175537.

———. 2004a. "Community-Driven Development in Local Government Capacity-Building Projects: Emerging Approaches in Africa." Social Development Note 86, Washington, DC: World Bank.

———. 2004b. "Community-Driven Development in Urban Upgrading." Social Development Note 85 (February), World Bank, Washington, DC.

———. 2004c. *Diagnostic Toolkit.* Poverty Reduction Strategy Paper, World Bank, Washington, DC.

————. 2004d. "Local Development." Discussion Paper (June), World Bank, Washington DC.

————. 2004e. "Reducing Poverty-Sustaining Growth: Scaling up Poverty Reduction." Paper presented at a Global Learning Process and Conference, Shanghai, China, May 25–27.

————. 2004f. *World Development Report 2004: Making Services Work for Poor People*. Washington, DC: World Bank.

————. 2005. *The Effectiveness of World Bank Support for Community-Based and -Driven Development*. Washington, DC: Independent Evaluation Group.

————. 2006. "India: District Poverty Initiatives Projects; Joint Interim Assessment. Understanding Differences in Project Design." Policy Note 34719 (March 1), World Bank, Agriculture and Rural Development Unit, South Asia Region, Washington, DC.

————. 2007a. "Community-Driven Development in Latin America and the Caribbean: Review of Experiences of Bank-Financed CDD Operations (1989–2004)." World Bank, Washington, DC (December).

————. 2007b. "Decentralization in Guinea: Strengthening Accountability for Better Service Delivery." World Bank, Washington, DC.

————. 2007c. "Enabling East Asian Communities to Drive Local Development: East Asia Region CDD Flagship Report." World Bank, East Asia Region, Washington, DC (December 1).

————. 2007d. *From Social Funds to Local Governance and Social Inclusion Programs: A Prospective Review from the ECA Region*. 2 vols. ECA Report 39953-ECA (May). Washington, DC: World Bank, Human Development Sector.

————. 2007e. "Local Government Discretion and Accountability: A Local Governance Framework." World Bank, Washington, DC.

————. 2007f. "MENA CDD Stocktaking FY00–2007." Draft report (September 7), World Bank, Washington, DC.

————. 2007g. *Tools for Institutional, Political, and Social Analysis of Policy Reform: A Sourcebook for Development Practitioners*. Washington, DC: World Bank.

————. 2008a. "Community Foundations How-to Series: Getting Started with a Community Foundation." Social Development Note, Community-Driven Development 112 (February), World Bank, Washington, DC.

————. 2008b. "Community Foundations: The Relevance for Social Funds in Urban Areas: The Tanzania Social Action Fund Experience." Social Funds Innovations Note 5, no. 1 (February), World Bank, Washington, DC.

————. 2008c. *Social and Local Development Funds in the Africa Region: Evolution and Options*. Washington, DC: World Bank, Human Development Network, Africa Region.

————. 2008d. *World Development Report 2008: Agriculture for Development.* Washington, DC: World Bank.

————. 2009. *Rural Poverty Alleviation Project (RPAP) Impact Evaluation: 1993–2005.* Washington, DC: World Bank.

World Bank and DFID (Department for International Development). 2005. *Country Partnership Strategy for the Federal Republic of Nigeria (2005–2009).* Report 32412-NG (June 2, 2005). Washington, DC: World Bank.

Yaron, Gil. 2008. "Measuring Empowerment: A Mixed-Method Diagnostic Tool for Measuring Empowerment in the Context of Decentralization in Ghana." World Bank, Washington, DC.

Boxes, figures, maps, notes, and tables are indicated by b, f, m, n, and t, respectively.

A

accountability
  capacity building and, 146–47
  governance agenda of World Bank
    and, 64
  national government, undermining of
    local accountability by, 148–49
  as pillar for success in LCDD, 6b, 79b,
    90, 108, 113
  in step-by-step approach to scaling up,
    184–92, 185–87b, 189b
  upward and downward, 218–19
adaptable program loans (APLs), 113, 115,
    117, 135, 136, 143, 144
adapting to country and local contexts. *See*
    contextual adaptation
administrative decentralization, 197n7
ADPs (area development programs), 2,
    12–13, 12t, 32, 36–37, 41
Afghanistan, xiii
Africa. *See also* West Africa, and specific
    countries
  ADPs and IRDPs in, 36, 37
  AGETIP programs in Francophone
    countries, 45
  analysis of CDD in, 56
  Chinese study visits to, 19
  contextual adaptation in, 18–19,
    121–50. *See also* contextual
    adaptation
  historical development of, 13
  Middle East and North Africa region,
    18–19, 63b, 67, 69, 82m
  scaling up in, 81, 82m, 83t

Agence d'Exécution des Travaux d'Intérêt
    Public (AGETIP or Agency for
    Public Works Management and
    Employment) projects, 43, 45
AIDS. *See* HIV/AIDS
Aiyar, Swaminathan S. Anklesaria, xviii,
    27, 71n5, 73, 119n1
Angola, 123t, 132t, 135
APLs (adaptable program loans), 113, 115,
    117, 135, 136, 143, 144
Arab Republic of Egypt, 33, 47f
Arcand, Jean-Louis, 65
area development programs (ADPs), 2,
    12–13, 12t, 32, 36–37, 41
Asia. *See also* South Asia, and specific
    countries
  East Asia and Pacific, 56, 67–68, 81,
    82m
  Eastern Europe and Central Asia, 67,
    68, 82m
  green revolution in, 12
asset sustainability, 220
Association for Social Advancement,
    Bangladesh, 108

B

Baltissen, Gerard, xviii, 119n1, 151, 155
Bangladesh
  Association for Social Advancement,
    108
  Comilla Rural Development Program,
    11, 27, 31, 32b, 37
  decentralization in, 47f, 92
  emergence of LCDD in, 1, 11, 27–28, 31

Grameen Bank, 34*b*
Grameen Village Phones, 215, 217
    scaling up in, 83*t,* 92, 108
Barboza, Tulio, 65
bargaining models of public choice, 78–81
Bassole, Leandre, 65
Becker, Gary, 80
Beckmann, David, 46
Benin
    Borgou pilot program, 7, 113, 114, 153
    contextual adaptation of existing pro-
        grams in, 132*t,* 137
    decentralization issues in, 97–98, 123*t*
    diagnostic phase of scaling up in, 154*b*
    hybrid strategies in, 138
    scaling up in, 81, 82*m,* 85*t,* 97–98, 99*b,*
        113–14
    step-by-step approach to scaling up,
        153, 154*b*
Binswanger-Mkhize, Hans, xv, xviii, 1, 27,
        70*n*1–2, 70*n*4–5, 73, 119*n*1, 151
Bolivia, 44, 47, 188
Borgou pilot program, Benin, 7, 113,
        114, 153
Bosnia and Herzegovina, xiii
Botswana, 124
boutique projects, 8, 75, 151, 153
Brazil
    CDD programs in, 13, 14, 49–50*f,*
        65–66, 68
    Chinese study visits to, 19
    consolidation stage in, 115
    decentralization issues in, 16, 47*f,* 48
    impact studies, 65–66, 68
    Northeast Rural Development Program,
        82*m,* 85*t,* 159
    political commitment to LCDD in, 88
    scaling up in, 82*m,* 85*t,* 88, 159
    sectoral approach in, 33
    specialized agricultural credit institu-
        tions in, 34*b*
    successful LCDD projects in, 16
    synthesized LCDD approach in, 48,
        49–50*b*
    technical services in, 217
Burkina Faso
    CBRDP (Community-Based Rural
        Development Project), 143, 146
    community empowerment model in, 15
    community radio, use of, 215
    contextual adaptation of existing
        programs in, 19, 132*t,* 137, 148

decentralization issues in, 47*f,* 123*t,* 162
local governance outcomes, 143, 146
National Program for Decentralized
    Rural Development, 143
political commitment to LCDD in, 88
Poni AIDS prevention project, 82*m,*
    83*t,* 108, 164, 177–79, 178*f,*
    194, 215
Sanmatenga Province pilot program,
    165
scaling up in, 82*m,* 83*t,* 88
step-by-step approach to scaling up
    diagnostic phase, 154
    HIV/AIDS program, 177–79, 178*f*
    national policy and institutional sup-
        port, 160, 162
    pilot phase, 164, 165
    program management system,
        designing, 194
    resource flows, allocation, and
        accountability, 187, 188
    training and facilitation, 177–79,
        181*b*
successful LCDD projects in, 16
wholistic agenda in, 17
Burundi, 133*t,* 137, 138

C

Cambodia, 44, 218
Cameroon, 123*t,* 133*t,* 137
CAP (Community Action Plan), Niger,
    132*t,* 134*t,* 136
CAP (Community Action Plan), Uganda,
    82*m,* 86*t,* 110, 111*b*
capacity building
    accountability and performance-based
        approaches to, 146–47
    as pillar for success in LCDD, 6*b,* 79*b,*
        92, 106, 110–13
    pilot phase, selecting district for, 164
    scaling up problems associated with, 94,
        95–96, 96*b*
Caribbean. *See* Latin America and the
    Caribbean
castes, 101, 105, 119*n*4. *See also* social
    inclusion
CBD (community-based development),
    12*t,* 38, 40, 41–42, 55, 56*t*
CBRDP (Community-Based Rural Devel-
    opment Project), Burkina Faso,
    143, 146

CBRDP (Community-Based Rural Development Program), Ghana, 134*t*, 144, 147
CBRDP (Community-Based Rural Development Program), Mauritania, 136
CDD (community-driven development), xvii, 13–15, 40, 42, 48, 51–58, 52*t*, 53*b*, 56*t*, 70*n*1
Central African Republic, 123, 135
Central America. *See* Latin America and the Caribbean
Central Asia, Eastern Europe and, 67, 68, 82*m*. *See also* specific countries
centralization/decentralization. *See* decentralization
CGIAR (Consultative Group on International Agricultural Research), 34
Chad, 123*t*, 132*t*, 135
Chambers, Robert, 38–41
Chase, Robert S., xviii, 65
Cherukupalli, Ravindra, xviii, 121
Chile, 47*f*
China, 19, 25*n*1, 33, 47*f*
co-financing by communities, 187*b*, 216
co-production issues, 75–76, 103–04
Colombia, 47*f*
Comilla Rural Development Program, Bangladesh, 11, 27, 31, 32*b*, 37
communications
    as core expected outcome of LCDD, 215–16
    design elements and tools, 208*t*
    IEC activities, 166–67, 169*f*, 170, 171, 172, 174, 195, 197*n*8, 208*t*
    implementing strategy for, 194
communities
    co-financing by, 187*b*, 216
    commitment to LCDD at level of, 60
    defined, 5*b*
    design elements and tools for large-scale LCDD, 203–5*t*, 210*t*
    empowerment of. *See* empowerment of communities and local governments
    facilitation for. *See* facilitation
    stakeholder participation as core expected outcome of LCDD, 213–15
    step-by-step approach to scaling up, local support for, 152, 162–63, 163*b*
    synthesis of approaches in LCDD and, 2*f*, 3, 48–51, 49–50*b*, 58–59, 58*f*

training and facilitation requirements, 177–80, 178*b*, 178*f*, 180*b*, 206–08*t*
Community Action Plan (CAP), Niger, 132*t*, 134*t*, 136
Community Action Plan (CAP), Uganda, 82*m*, 86*t*, 110, 111*b*
community-based development (CBD), 12*t*, 38, 40, 41–42, 55, 56*t*
community-based procurement and disbursement mechanisms, 52–55, 54*b*
Community-Based Rural Development Program (CBRDP), Ghana, 134*t*, 144, 147
Community-Based Rural Development Program (CBRDP), Mauritania, 136
Community-Based Rural Development Project (CBRDP), Burkina Faso, 143, 146
community consultation model, 12*t*, 14
Community Development Carbon Fund, 24–25, 25*n*3, 187
community development committees, 168–69, 169*f*, 186*b*
community-driven development (CDD), xvii, 13–15, 40, 42, 48, 51–58, 52*t*, 53*b*, 56*t*, 70*n*1
Community Driven Development Project, The Gambia, 146–47
community empowerment model, 12*t*, 14–17
community management as contextual adaptation, 127, 132*t*, 134*t*, 135, 136, 140, 146, 148
community participation model, 12*t*, 14
Community Poverty Reduction Project, Nigeria, 140, 149*n*5
concurrent approach, 141
Congo, Democratic Republic of, 123*t*, 132*t*, 135
Congo, Republic of, 123*t*, 132*t*, 135
conservative or lagging strategies, 125, 129*t*, 136, 140
consolidating decentralization, 124
    analysis of existing programs, 134*t*
    countries classified as, 123*t*
    local governance outcomes of implementation strategies, 144–45

risk assessments and strategies for, 129*t*, 130–31, 140–42
static institutional analysis of strategic fit, 126*t*
consolidation or post-scale up phase, 114–15, 195–96, 195*b*
Consultative Group on International Agricultural Research (CGIAR), 34
contextual adaptation, 10, 16–19, 121–50
assessment of existing programs, 131–37, 132–34*t*
bias toward local governments and local public sector institutions, 149*n*3
capacity building, accountability and performance-based approaches to, 146–47
central government, undermining of local accountability by, 148–49
change versus adaptation, 147–48
characterization/classification of country context, 122–24, 123*t*. *See also* consolidating decentralization; deconcentrated systems; dysfunctional governments; incipient decentralization
community management strategies, 127, 132*t*, 134*t*, 135, 136, 140, 146, 148
concurrent approach, 141
conservative or lagging strategies, 125, 129*t*, 136, 140
contingency approach to, 121–22, 131
design strategies for, 124–28, 126*t*, 128*b*
dynamic risk analysis of strategic fit, 125, 127–28, 128*b*
historical recognition of need for, 61–64
hybrid and mixed strategies, 137–40
leading strategies, 125–27, 129*t*, 136–37
local governance outcomes of implementation strategies, 142–47
local government management strategies, 127, 132*t*, 134*t*, 137, 138–42, 146, 148, 149*n*3
matching strategies, 125, 129*t*, 136
risk analysis, 125, 127–31, 128*b*, 129*t*
scaling up and, 76, 104–08, 106–07*b*, 118
static institutional analysis of strategic fit, 124, 125–27, 126*t*, 128*b*
in step-by-step approach to scaling up, 152–53

transitioning from community to local government management, 148
contingency approach to contextual adaptation, 121–22, 131
core expected outcomes, 5, 6*b*, 78–81, 79*b*, 211–21
corporate use of LCDD principles, 24
costs. *See* financial costs of LCDD
Côte d'Ivoire, 31, 47*f*, 92
Council for Advancement of People's Action and Rural Technology (formerly Freedom from Hunger Campaign), India, 37
country contexts, adapting to. *See* contextual adaptation
Country Partnership Strategy, Nigeria, 61–62
country policy and institutional assessment (CPIA), 122, 123*t*
credit ratings for self-help groups, 217
Crook, Richard C., 48, 92

D

Davis, Deborah, xviii, 73, 119*n*1
DDCs (district development committees), 169*f*, 170–72, 191
de Regt, Jacomina P., xv, xvii, xviii, 1, 27, 70*n*5, 73, 119*n*1, 151
decentralization
administrative decentralization, 197*n*7
characterization/classification of country context by extent of, 122–24, 123*t*. *See also* consolidating decentralization; deconcentrated systems; incipient decentralization
continuing issues with, 14, 16–17
core expected outcome of LCDD, devolution of authority and resources, as, 212–13
design elements and tools for large-scale LCDD, 202*t*
design issues in decentralization plans, 101
fiscal decentralization, 197*n*7
historical trends in, 11–13, 12*t*, 29, 30*b*, 31, 40, 46–51, 47*f*
in hybrid strategies, 138
index, 70*n*3
in initiation stage of LCDD, 113–14
mixed strategies and, 139

pillar for success in LCDD, realignment of center as, 6b, 79b
political decentralization, 197n7
poorly developed decentralization systems, 161–62
scaling up, importance to, 91–94, 93b, 97–98, 101, 109–13, 110–12b
sequencing, role of decentralization in, 109–13, 110–12b
in step-by-step approach to scaling up, 160–62
subsidiarity principle, 48, 101–02, 109, 194, 205t, 213
undermining of local accountability by central government, 148–49
World Bank and, 46–48
Decentralization and Community Development Program, Rwanda, 190
Decentralized Finance and Planning Program, Mozambique, 183–84, 190
Decentralized Regional Development (DRD) Projects, Mexico. See Mexico
deconcentrated systems, 123–24
analysis of existing programs, 132t
countries classified as, 123t
local governance outcomes of implementation strategies, 143
risk assessments and strategies for, 129t, 130, 135–36
static institutional analysis of strategic fit, 126t
Democratic Republic of Congo, 123t, 132t, 135
design
diagnostics, 116–17
elements and tools for large-scale LCDD, 201–10
strategies for contextual adaptation, 124–28, 126t, 128b
technical soundness of, 219–20
Dev, S. K., 27, 30b
development policy loans (DPLs), 62
devolution of authority and resources, as core expected outcome of LCDD, 212–13
diagnostics
conducive conditions for LCDD, 88b
design, preprogram, and maintenance diagnostics, 116–17, 116b

as phase in step-by-step approach, 151, 153–55, 154b, 156–58t
pilot program, local buy-in for, 166
questions to be pursued in, 155, 156–57t
shared appreciation-readiness index, 155, 158t
disbursement mechanisms
community-based, 52–55, 54b
resource flows, allocation, and accountability, 185–86, 188–92
unified, 161
district development committees (DDCs), 169f, 170–72, 191
District Planning and Finance Program, Mozambique, 136–37
districts, defined, 5b
donors
accountability to, 219
commitment to LCDD, importance of, 13–14, 19
design elements and tools for large-scale LCDD, 210t
stakeholder participation as core expected outcome of LCDD, 213–15
unified disbursement mechanisms, willingness to use, 161
DPLs (development policy loans), 62
DRD (Decentralized Regional Development) Projects, Mexico. See Mexico
Drishtee.com, 217
dynamic risk analysis of strategic fit, 125, 127–28, 128b
dysfunctional governments, 123
analysis of existing programs, 132t
countries classified as, 123t
CPIA cluster D values, 122, 123t
matching strategies in, 135
postconflict areas, LCDD in, 20–21, 44, 52, 64
risk assessments and strategies for, 128–30, 129t
static institutional analysis of strategic fit, 126t

E

e-commerce vehicles, 217
earmarking, 184–85, 213

East Asia and Pacific, 56, 67–68, 81, 82*m*.
    See also specific countries
Eastern Europe and Central Asia,
    67, 68, 82*m*. *See also* specific
    countries
economic issues. *See* financial costs of
    LCDD; financial structures
education. *See* training and education
Education for All Project, Guinea, 146
Egypt, Arab Republic of, 33, 47*f*
elected councils, defined, 5*b*
emergencies, LCDD in, 20–21
empowerment of communities and local
        governments
    as aim of LCDD, xiv, 4, 6*b*, 73, 79*b*
    community empowerment model of
        CDD, 12*t*, 14–17
    defined, 73
    design elements and tools for large-scale
        LCDD, 202*t*
    historical failures of, 11–13, 31–33
    as pillar of success for LCDD, 6*b*, 79*b*,
        80, 92, 106, 110–13
    political support for process, 16
    previous efforts, building on, 161
    real participation and, 212
    women and minorities, 101
environmental management, LCDD
        principles used for, 24–25
environmental sustainability of LCDD
        programs, 221
Ethiopia
    consolidated decentralization in, 123*t*,
        124, 134*t*
    contextual adaptation of existing
        programs in, 134*t*
    Learning-by-Doing for At-Scale
        Hygiene and Sanitation
        program, 71*n*9
    legal status for funding in, 186*b*
    matching strategy in, 141
    Pastoral Community Development
        Program, 141
ethnic/racial minorities, 62, 94, 100–01,
        104–05, 119*n*4, 203*t*. *See also*
        social inclusion
Europe, Eastern, and Central Asia,
        67, 68, 82*m*. *See also* specific
        countries
European Union, 68

F

facilitation
    as core expected outcome, 216–17
    design elements and tools, 206–08*t*
    as phase in step-by-step approach,
        176–84, 178*b*, 178*f*, 180–82*b*
    training in, 177, 178*b*, 207*t*
FADAMA, Nigeria, 149*n*5
Faguet, Jean-Paul, 47
field testing. *See* pilot programs and
        field testing
financial costs of LCDD, 75. *See also*
        disbursement mechanisms
    budgeting, step-by-step approach to
        scaling up, 180–81, 193
    community co-financing, 187*b*, 216
    design elements and tools for community
        funding arrangements, 204*t*
    devolution of authority and resources,
        as core expected outcome,
        212–13
    per diems for volunteers, 180*b*
    program management costs, 194
    reducing, 102–03
    resource flows, allocation, and
        accountability, 184–92,
        185–87*b*, 189*b*
    sustainability of programs, 220
    training costs, 102–03, 176, 177–79,
        178*f*, 180*b*
financial structures
    decentralizing, 160–61
    microcredit and MFIs, 33, 34*b*, 217
    pro-poor market development, 217–18
fiscal decentralization, 197*n*7
Fiszbein, Ariel, 47
Ford Foundation, 33, 40
franchising, LCDD compared to, 8,
        77*b*, 118
Freedom from Hunger Campaign
        (later Council for Advancement
        of People's Action and Rural
        Technology), India, 37

G

The Gambia, 123*t*, 133*t*, 137, 146–47
Gandhi, Mahatma, 11, 27, 29
Gandhi, Rajiv, 30*b*
Gandhi, Sonia, 30*b*

Ghana
    CBRDP, 134t, 144, 147
    contextual adaptation of existing
        programs in, 134t
    decentralization issues in, 31, 92,
        123t, 124
    local governance outcomes, 143, 144,
        146, 147
    matching strategy in, 141
GoBifo, Sierra Leone, 139
governance, local, effects of LCDD on,
    xiv, 64, 91, 142–47
governance structures, decentralizing.
    See decentralization
government. See local governments;
    national government level,
    commitment to LCDD at
Grameen Bank, 34b
Grameen Village Phones, 215, 217
green revolution, 12t, 33–35
Guinea
    contextual adaptation of existing
        programs in, 133–34t, 137
    Education for All Project, 146
    head tax, 95b
    incipient decentralization in, 123t,
        133–34t, 137
    local governance outcomes,
        143, 146
    participatory M&E in, 214–15
    scaling up in, 82m, 85t, 95b, 103
    VCSP, 143–44, 146, 214–15
Gyandoot Project, India, 215

H

Haiti, 68
Hammock Makers' Network,
    Nicaragua, 218
head taxes, 95b
Heemskerk, William, xviii, 151, 155
Helling, Louis, xvii, xviii, 27, 58, 121
Hill Community Forestry Project,
    Nepal, 43b
historical development of LCDD, 10–13,
    27–71
    ADPs and IRDPs, 2, 12–13, 12t, 32,
        36–37, 36b, 41
    AGETIP projects, 43, 45
    CBD, 12t, 38, 40, 41–42, 55, 56t

CDD, xvii, 13–15, 40, 42, 48, 51–58,
    52t, 53b, 56t, 70n1
centralization/decentralization trends,
    11–13, 12t, 29, 30b, 31, 40,
    46–51, 47f
design and implementation guidance,
    51–52, 53b
empowerment failures, 11–13, 31–33
evolving development approaches, 12t,
    14–17, 28t
future of, 58–64, 63b
India and Bangladesh, emergence
    of concept in, xvii, 1, 11,
    27–31, 30b
integration of approaches and programs
    into coherent framework, 55–58,
    56t, 60–61
NGOs, role of, 13, 37–38
participatory approaches, 12t, 14,
    38–40, 39b
in post-WWII period, 11, 29
procurement and disbursement
    mechanisms, 52–55, 54b
sectoral approach, 12t, 33, 42–43b
social development programs,
    45–46
social funds, 12t, 13, 24,
    43–45, 44f
synthesized LCDD approach, 48–51,
    49–50b
targeted approaches, 12t, 35–36, 35t
technology-driven approaches, 12t,
    33–35
top-down approaches, shift away
    from, 40–42, 51
HIV/AIDS
    CDD adapted for combating, 52
    earmarking funds for, 185, 213
    in initiation stage of LCDD, 113
    in national scale-up phase, 194, 195
    pilot programs addressing, 164–65, 170
    Poni AIDS prevention project, Burkina
        Faso, 82m, 83t, 108, 164, 177–79,
        178f, 194, 215
    training and facilitation, 177–79, 178f
Honduras, 218
Hoppe, Michael, 66
hybrid and mixed strategies for contextual
    adaptation, 137–40
hygiene and sanitation programs, 71n9

I

IDA (International Development Association), 51, *52t*

IEC (information, education, and communication) activities, 166–67, *169f*, 170, 171, 172, 174, 195, *197n8*, *208t*

IEG (Independent Evaluation Group), 16, 44, 55, 57, 58, *61b*, *71n8*

impact studies, 55–57, *56t*, 65–70

incentives, using, 20, 104, 213

incipient decentralization, 124
analysis of existing programs, *132–34t*
countries classified as, *123t*
dynamism and stasis in, *149n4*
local governance outcomes of implementation strategies, 143–44
risk assessments and strategies for, *129t*, 130, 137
static institutional analysis of strategic fit, *126t*

inclusion. *See* social inclusion

Independent Evaluation Group (IEG), 16, 55, 57, 58, *61b*, *71n8*

India
accountability in, 218
centralization/decentralization trends in, 11–12, 13, *30b*, *47f*, 92
Community Development Program, 11, 12, 27, 33
consolidation stage in, 115
emergence of LCDD in, xvii, 1, 11, 27–29, *30b*, 31
Freedom from Hunger Campaign (later Council for Advancement of People's Action and Rural Technology), 37
Gyandoot Project, 215
impact studies, 69–70
Integrated Child Development Services Program, *43b*
Intensive Agricultural District Program and green revolution in, 33–34
Internet, use of, 215
Jalanidhi Water Supply Project, 16
Kerala Rural Water Supply and Sanitation Project, 105–08, *106–07b*, 159
local government system in, *5b*, *30b*

McDonald's in, *77b*
National Rural Employment Guarantee Program, *30b*
Noonday Meal Program, *43b*
nutrition programs in, *43b*
political commitment to LCDD in, 88
scaling up in, 81, *82m*, 83–84*t*, 88, 92, 101, 105–08, *106–07b*, 114
scheduled castes and tribes, 101, 105, *119n4*
Self-Employed Women's Association, 101, 114, 217
specialized agricultural credit institutions in, *34b*
step-by-step approach to scaling up, 159
successful LCDD projects in, 16
Swajal Rural Water Supply Project, 105, 114
Tamil Nadu Integrated Nutrition Program, *43b*
targeted approaches in, *35t*
tsunami disaster of 2005, xiii
women and minorities in, 101, 114

Indo-German Watershed Development Program, 100

Indonesia
CDD programs in, 13, 14
Chinese study visits to, 19
decentralization in, *47f*, 48
impact studies, 66–67, 68
Kampung Improvement Program, *42b*
KDP, 7, 8, 17, *50b*, 61, 66–67, 68, *85t*, 89–90*b*, 90–91, 115, *116b*, 153, 160, 187
low-income entrepreneurs, one stop shops for, 217
maintenance diagnostics in, *116b*
PNPM, 62, 91, 115
political commitment to LCDD in, 88, 89–90*b*, 89–91
scaling up in, 61, 81, *82m*, *85t*, 88, 89–90*b*, 89–91, 115–16, *116b*, 118
sequencing in, 115–16
step-by-step approach to scaling up, 153, 162
successful LCDD projects in, 16
synthesized LCDD approach in, 48, *50b*
tsunami disaster of 2005, xiii

information, education, and communication (IEC) activities, 166–67, 169*f,* 170, 171, 172, 174, 195, 197*n*8, 208*t*
initiation stage of LCDD, 113
institutional hostility to LCDD, dealing with, 75, 94–101, 95*b,* 96*b,* 99*b*
Institutional Reform and Capacity-Building Project, Sierra Leone, 139, 140
institutional set-up and program management, 194, 205–6*t*
institutional sustainability, 220
Integrated Child Development Services Program, India, 43*b*
Integrated Development Plan of Mangaung, South Africa, 115
integrated rural development programs (IRDPs), 12–13, 12*t,* 32, 36–37, 36*b,* 48
integration of approaches and programs into coherent framework, 55–58, 56*t,* 60–61
Intensive Agricultural District Program, India, 33
International Development Association (IDA), 51, 52*t*
Internet, use of, 215, 217
Iran, Islamic Republic of, 19
ITAD LMT, 66

J

Jalanidhi Water Supply Project, India, 16
Jamaica, 45
JIMAT Consult, 66
Joseph, Sam, 40

K

Kampung Improvement Program, Indonesia, 42*b*
Kapitbisig Laban sa Kahirapan (Linking Arms against Poverty) operation, Philippines, 68
Kecamatan Development Program (KDP), Indonesia, 7, 8, 17, 50*b,* 61, 66–67, 68, 85*t,* 89–90*b,* 90–91, 115, 116*b,* 153, 160, 187. *See also* Indonesia
Kenya, 123*t,* 133*t,* 137

Kerala Rural Water Supply and Sanitation Project, India, 105–08, 106–07*b,* 159
Khan, Akhtar Hamid, 27, 31, 32*b*
KIT (Royal Tropical Institute), 154
Korten, David, 40
Kozel, Valerie, xviii

L

Labonne, Julien, 65
lagging or conservative strategies, 125, 129*t,* 136
Latin America and the Caribbean. *See also* specific countries
analysis of CDD in Central America, 56
community-based procurement and disbursement mechanisms, 52–53
democratization in, 13, 41
historical development of LCDD in, 12, 13
impact studies, 67, 68–69
participatory budgeting in, 146
scaling up in, 81, 82*m*
social capital, leveraging, 24
social funds in, 47
LCDD. *See* local and community driven development
leading strategies, 125–27, 129*t,* 136–37
learning-by-doing
devolution of authority and resources via, 213
historical development of LCDD and, 15, 16, 18, 49*b,* 71*n*5, 71*n*9
institutional set-up and program management, 206*t*
in national scale up phase, 194, 195
as pillar of success for LCDD, 90, 92, 93*b,* 98, 108, 113
resource flow, allocation, and accountability, 189*b,* 190
scaling up and, 19, 81, 90, 92, 93*b,* 97, 98, 101, 105, 108, 110–11*b,* 113
Learning-by-Doing for At-Scale Hygiene and Sanitation program, Ethiopia, 71*n*9
Lebanon, 19
LEEMP (Local Empowerment and Environmental Management Project), Nigeria, 140, 149*n*5

legal status
  of community development committees,
    186*b*, 197*n*13
  of low-income entrepreneurs, 217
LGDP (Local Government Development
    Program), Uganda, 82*m*, 86*t*, 110,
    111*b*, 189*b*
LGMSDP (Local Government Management
    and Service Delivery Program),
    Uganda, 110, 134*t*, 141, 189*b*
Liberia, 123*t*, 132*t*, 135
linkage, concept of, 2*f*, 58–59, 58*f*
Linking Arms against Poverty (Kapitbisig
    Laban sa Kahirapan) operation,
    Philippines, 68
literature review, 10, 64–70
local and community driven development
    (LCDD), xvii–xviii, 1–25
  adapting to country and local contexts,
    importance of, 10, 16–19, 121–50.
    See also contextual adaptation
  commitment of country leaders and
    donors, importance of, 13–14,
    19, 60
  core expected outcomes, 5, 6*b*, 78–81,
    79*b*, 211–21
  defined, xvii, 3–4
  future challenges and opportunities,
    23–25, 58–64, 63*b*
  governance, improving, xiv, 64, 91,
    142–47
  historical development of, 10–13, 27–71.
    See also historical development
    of LCDD
  impact studies, 55–57, 56*t*, 65–70
  lessons from and recommendations for,
    19–21
  literature review, 10, 64–70
  multisectoral versus single sector, 15–16
  origins of term, xvii
  pillars for success, 5, 6*b*, 78–81, 79*b*,
    106–08
  in postconflict and emergency situations,
    20–21, 44, 52, 64
  public resources, efficient use of, xiv
  scaling up, xiii, 73–119. *See also* scaling
    up LCDD; step-by-step approach
    to scaling up
  as synthesis of local government,
    sectoral, and community-driven
    approaches, 2*f*, 3, 48–51, 49–50*b*,
    58–59, 58*f*

  three stages of, 113–15
  transformative nature of, 4
  World Bank support for, xiii–xiv,
    2, 17, 28
local consultative councils, 184
local contexts, adapting to. *See* contextual
    adaptation
Local Development Support Program,
    Chad, 135
Local Empowerment and Environmental
    Management Project (LEEMP),
    Nigeria, 140, 149*n*5
local governance, effects of LCDD on, xiv,
    64, 91, 142–47
Local Government Development Program
    (LGDP), Uganda, 82*m*, 86*t*, 110,
    111*b*, 189*b*
Local Government Management and Ser-
    vice Delivery Program (LGMSDP),
    Uganda, 110, 134*t*, 141, 189*b*
local governments
  commitment to LCDD at level of, 60
  contextual adaptation, local government
    management strategies for, 127,
    132*t*, 134*t*, 137, 138–42, 146,
    148, 149*n*3
  defined, 5*b*
  design elements and tools for large-scale
    LCDD, 202*t*, 210*t*
  empowerment of. *See* empowerment
    of communities and local
    governments
  facilitation for. *See* facilitation
  in India, 5*b*, 30*b*
  national government, undermining of
    local accountability by, 148–49
  nonexistent or nonfunctional, 167*b*
  political support for empowerment
    process, 16
  stakeholder participation as core
    expected outcome of LCDD,
    213–15
  step-by-step approach to scaling up,
    local support for, 152,
    162–63, 163*b*
  synthesis of approaches in LCDD and,
    2*f*, 3, 48–51, 49–50*b*, 58–59, 58*f*
local jurisdictions, names and definitions
    for, 5*b*
local program development support team,
    pilot phase, 172–74
logistical issues, 76–77, 103, 108–09, 194

M

Madagascar, 123*t*, 133*t*, 137, 160, 191
maintenance diagnostics, 116–17, 116*b*
Malawi
  communications strategies, 166
  contextual adaptation of existing
    programs in, 133–34*t*, 137
  DDCs, transfer of functions to, 191
  decentralization issues in, 123*t*
  hybrid strategies in, 138
  impact studies, 66
  local governance outcomes, 146
  pilot programs in, 113
  political commitment to LCDD in, 88
  scaling up in, 88, 113, 117
  social funds in, 45, 191
Malawi Social Action Fund (MASAF), 45,
  66, 117, 133–34*t*, 146, 166
Mali, 123*t*, 133*t*, 137, 160
M&E. *See* monitoring and evaluation
Manor, James, 48, 92
manuals, 7, 9, 16, 18–20, 108–09, 199
market development, pro-poor, 217–18
MASAF (Malawi Social Action Fund), 45,
  66, 117, 133–34*t*, 146, 166
matching strategies, 125, 129*t*, 136
Mauritania, 123*t*, 132*t*, 134*t*, 136
McDonald's franchising, LCDD compared
  to, 8, 77*b*, 118
McLaughlin, Karrie, 66
McNamara, Robert, 32, 36
Mehta, Balwantrai, 30*b*
Metalworkers' Network, Honduras, 218
Mexico
  CDD programs in, 13, 14, 68
  community-based procurement and
    disbursement mechanisms,
    52–53
  consolidation stage in, 115
  decentralization in, 7, 47*f*, 48, 49*f*,
    92–94, 93*b*, 101
  impact studies, 68
  IRDPs in, 36*b*
  National Program for Indigenous
    Peoples, 94
  PIDER projects, 36, 38
  Plan Puebla, 36*b*
  political commitment to LCDD in, 88
  scaling up in, 81, 82*m*, 85*t*, 88, 92–94,
    93*b*, 101
  sectoral approach in, 33

  specialized agricultural credit
    institutions in, 34*b*
  step-by-step approach to scaling up,
    153, 159*b*, 162, 191
  successful LCDD projects in, 16
  synthesized LCDD approach in,
    48, 49*b*
  Zacatecas State Development
    Plan, 38
microcredit and MFIs (microfinance
  institutions), 33, 34*b*, 217
Middle East and North Africa, 18–19,
  63*b*, 67, 69, 82*m*. *See also*
  specific countries
minorities and women, 100–01, 104–05,
  114, 119*n*4. *See also* social
  inclusion
mixed and hybrid strategies for contextual
  adaptation, 137–40
monitoring and evaluation (M&E)
  auditing as part of, 186
  consolidation or post-scale up
    phase, 195
  design elements and tools, 206*t*,
    207*t*, 209*t*
  diagnostic data derived from, 116
  empowerment as control of, 212
  fully independent, 175*b*
  impact evaluation, 176
  local preprogram development, 163
  metrics, 175*b*
  national scaling up phase,
    192*b*, 193
  NUSAF, 112*b*
  participatory, 108, 109, 213,
    214–15, 219
  pilot phase, 169*f*, 171, 174–76, 175*b*
  Ugandan project addressing, 110
Morocco, 34*b*, 62, 69, 88
Mozambique
  contextual adaptation of existing
    programs in, 132*t*, 136–37, 148
  decentralization, encouraging, 19
  Decentralized Finance and Planning
    Program, 183–84, 190
  as deconcentrated system, 123*t*
  District Planning and Finance Program,
    136–37
  local governments in, 149*n*2
  nonexistent or nonfunctional local
    governments, dealing with, 167*b*
Mugwagwa, Norbert, xviii

N

NAAS (National Agricultural Advisory
Services), Uganda, 11*b*, 82*m*, 86*t*,
110, 112*b*
Narayan, Deepa, 42*b*, 70*n*1
National Agricultural Advisory Services
(NAAS), Uganda, 11*b*, 82*m*, 86*t*,
110, 112*b*
National Commission for Social Action,
Sierra Leone, 139
national government level, commitment
to LCDD at. *See also* political
commitment
decentralization, commitment to,
160–62
design elements and tools for large-scale
LCDD, 210*t*
importance of, 13–14, 19, 60, 87–88
local accountability, undermining,
148–49
previous empowerment efforts, building
on, 161
reforms, following through on, 162
stakeholder participation as core
expected outcome, 213–15
step-by-step approach to scaling up,
151–52, 155–62, 159*b*, 163*b*
unified disbursement mechanisms,
willingness to use, 161
National Initiative for Human
Development, Morocco, 62
National Program for Decentralized
Rural Development, Burkina
Faso, 143
National Program for Indigenous Peoples,
Mexico, 94
National Rural Employment Guarantee
Program, India, 30*b*
national scaling up phase, 192–95, 192*b*
natural disasters, LCDD in, 20–21
natural resource management projects,
42–43*b*
Nepal, 42–43*b*
new professionalism, 40
NGOs. *See* nongovernmental organizations
Nguyen, Tuu-Van, xviii, 73, 151
Nicaragua, 44, 218
Niger, 115, 123*t*, 132*t*, 136, 167*b*
Nigeria
assessment of readiness in, 155

Community Poverty Reduction Project,
140, 149*n*5
conservative or lagging strategy in, 140
contextual adaptation of existing
programs in, 133–34*t*, 137, 149*n*5
Country Partnership Strategy, 61–62
decentralization issues in, 47*f*, 123*t*
FADAMA, 149*n*5
LEEMP, 140, 149*n*5
scaling up in, 83*t*
nongovernmental organizations (NGOs)
channeling funds through, 192
design elements and tools for large-scale
LCDD, 210*t*
historical involvement of, 13, 37–38
participatory approach influencing, 40
scaling up issues associated with control
by, 97–98, 99*b*
stakeholder participation as core expected outcome of LCDD, 213–15
target approaches used by, 35
Noonday Meal Program, India, 43*b*
North Africa, Middle East and, 18–19,
63*b*, 67, 69, 82*m*. *See also* specific
countries
Northeast Rural Development Program,
Brazil, 82*m*, 85*t*, 159
Northern Uganda Social Action Fund
(NUSAF), 82*m*, 86*t*, 110, 112*b*,
134*t*, 141
Novica.com, 217
nutrition programs, 43*b*

O

O and M Associates, 66
operations and maintenance (O&M), 63*b*,
102, 105, 119*n*6, 170, 214, 216
Operations Evaluation Department (OED),
World Bank, 37
Owen, Daniel, xviii, 121

P

Pacific Region, East Asia and, 56, 67–68,
81, 82*m*. *See also* specific countries
Pakistan, 34*b*, 47*f*. *See also* Bangladesh
for early LCDD projects in East
Pakistan
Paraguay, 16
participation as core expected outcome of
LCDD, 211–12, 213–15

participatory approaches, 12*t*, 14, 38–40, 39*b*, 203*t*
Participatory Local Development Program, Senegal, 62
participatory M&E, 108, 109, 214–15, 219
participatory planning, 180–81, 181*b*, 182–84
participatory rural appraisals (PRAs), 38, 39*b*, 40
Pastoral Community Development Program, Ethiopia, 141
PeopLink.org, 217
performance-based approaches to capacity building, 146–47
performance-based grants, 189*b*
performance risk, 127–28
Peru, 217
Philippines, 47*f*, 65, 68, 83*t*, 218
PIDER (Programa Integrado de Desarrollo Rural) projects, Mexico, 36, 38
pillars for success, 5, 6*b*, 78–81, 79*b*, 106–08
pilot programs and field testing
  co-production, 16
  for scaling-up manuals, 108
  as stage of LCDD, 113–14
  step-by-step approach to scaling up, 151, 163–76
    basic structures required for, 168, 169*f*
    community development committee, 168–69, 169*f*
    DDCs, 169*f*, 170–72, 174
    defining actors, functions, and responsibilities, 167–76
    geographic boundaries of, 151, 153, 163–64
    initiating, 163–67
    local buy-in, ensuring, 165–67
    local program development support team, 172–74
    M&E, 169*f*, 171, 174–76, 175*b*
    nonexistent or nonfunctional local governments, 167*b*
    selection of district for, 164–65
    steps in, 164*b*
    subdistrict development committee, 169*f*, 172
  in unfavorable political conditions, 98
  usefulness of, 19

Plan Puebla, Mexico, 36*b*
planning, step-by-step approach to scaling up, 180–81, 181*b*, 182–84, 193
PNIR (Programme National d'Infrastructures Rurales), Senegal, 65
PNPM (Program Nasional Pemberdayaan Masyarakat), Indonesia, 62, 91, 115
Poland, 47*f*
Poli, Maria, xviii, 121
policy risk, 127
political commitment
  importance of, 13–14, 19, 60
  scaling up requirements, 87–91, 89–90*b*
  step-by-step approach to scaling up, 158–60
  strategies in absence of, 98–100
political decentralization, 197*n*7
Poni AIDS prevention project, Burkina Faso, 82*m*, 83*t*, 108, 164, 177–79, 178*f*, 194, 215
post-scale up or consolidation phase, 114–15, 195–96, 195*b*
postconflict areas, LCDD in, 20–21, 44, 52, 64. *See also* dysfunctional governments
poverty reduction
  market development, pro-poor, 217–18
  World Bank, as overriding aim of, 48
Poverty Reduction Strategy Papers (PRSPs), 74*b*, 193, 197*n*2
PRAs (participatory rural appraisals), 38, 39*b*, 40
preprogram diagnostics, 116–17
Preston, Lewis T., 46, 48
prioritization, 184–85, 185*b*
pro-poor market development, 217–18
procurement mechanisms, community-based, 52–55, 54*b*
program management design and costs, 194, 205–06*t*
Program Nasional Pemberdayaan Masyarakat (PNPM), Indonesia, 62, 91, 115
Programa Integrado de Desarrollo Rural (PIDER) projects, Mexico, 36, 38
Programme National d'Infrastructures Rurales (PNIR), Senegal, 65
PRSPs (Poverty Reduction Strategy Papers), 74*b*, 193, 197*n*2
public bureaucracies, transforming, 40

public choice theory, 40, 79–80
public resources, efficient use of, xiv

Q

Quality Assurance Group, World Bank,
16, 57

R

racial/ethnic minorities, 94, 100–01,
104–05, 114, 119n4, 203t. *See also*
social inclusion
Ramadan, Bassam, xviii
Ramakrishna, Chief Minister, 31
rapid rural appraisals (RRAs), 38
reforms, following through on, 162
regional impact studies, 67–70
remittances, 25
report cards, 218
Republic of Congo, 123t, 132t, 135
Republic of Yemen, 69, 83t
resource flows, allocation, and account-
ability in step-by-step approach,
184–92, 185–87b, 189b
Rice Millers' Association, Cambodia, 218
risk analysis for contextual adaptation,
125, 127–31, 128b, 129t
River Blindness Eradication Program, West
Africa, 114
Royal Tropical Institute (KIT), 154
RRAs (rapid rural appraisals), 38
Rural Communities Development Program,
Bolivia, 188
Rural Development: Putting the Last First
(Chambers), 38–39
Rwanda
contextual adaptation of existing
programs in, 133t, 137, 148
Decentralization and Community
Development Program, 190
decentralization issues in, 16, 19, 123t
disbursement mechanisms, 190
peace dividends of LCDD in, xiii
replication of Bangladeshi program
in, 83t

S

Sanmatenga Province pilot program,
Burkina Faso, 165
São Tomé and Principe, 123t, 132t

Satu, Adam, 66
scaling up LCDD, xiii, 73–119
bargaining process used in, 78–81
boutique projects, 8, 75, 151, 153
co-production issues, 75–76, 103–04
conducive conditions, diagnosing,
87–94, 88b
contextual adaptation, importance of,
76, 104–08, 106–07b, 118
costs, reducing, 102–03
decentralization important to, 91–94,
93b, 97–98, 101, 109–13,
110–12b
defined, 4, 118
design and testing, importance of,
77–78
diagnostics. *See* diagnostics
difficulties faced in, 75–78, 77b
in hybrid strategies, 138
institutional hostility, dealing with, 75,
94–101, 95b, 96b, 99b
lessons from and recommendations for,
19–20
logistical issues, 76–77, 103,
108–09, 194
magnitude of, 6–8, 7t
manuals for, 108–09
in mixed strategies, 139
NGOs, control of programs by,
97–98, 99b
original designs' failure to consider, 17
of pillars for success and core expected
outcomes, 5, 6b, 78–81, 79b
pilot programs. *See* pilot programs and
field testing
political commitment required for,
87–91, 89–90b
requirements for, 2–3
resources for, 74b
as second stage of LCDD, 114
sequencing, 109–13, 110–12b, 115–16,
136, 201–02t
social conditions unfavorable to,
100–01
step-by-step approach to, 8–10. *See also*
step-by-step approach to scaling up
successful programs, lessons from,
81–87, 82m, 83–86t
Schechter, Galia, xviii
scheduled castes and tribes, 101, 105,
119n4. *See also* social inclusion

sectoral approach
historical trends in, 12t, 33, 42–43b
multisectoral versus single sector LCDD, 15–16
SWAps, 62, 154, 161
synthesized in LCDD with community and local government approaches, 2f, 3, 48–51, 49–50b, 58–59, 58f
Self-Employed Women's Association, India, 101, 114, 217
Senegal
AGETIP programs in, 45
contextual adaptation of existing programs in, 133t, 137
decentralization issues in, 47f, 123t
impact study, 65
Participatory Local Development Program, 62
PNIR, 65
SWaps, 62
sequencing, 109–13, 110–12b, 115–16, 136, 201–02t
Serrano-Berthet, Rodrigo, xvii, xviii, 27, 58, 121
Sey, Haddy, xviii
Sierra, Katherine, xiv
Sierra Leone
concurrent strategies in, 139–40
contextual adaptation of existing programs in, 133t, 137
decentralization issues in, 123t
GoBifo, 139
governance agenda in, 64
local governance outcomes, 147
National Commission for Social Action, 139
social conditions unfavorable to scaling up LCDD, 100–01
social development, 45–46
Social Development Network, 46
social funds, 12t, 13, 24, 43–45, 44f, 191
social inclusion
design elements and tools for large-scale LCDD, 203t
in Eastern European and Central Asian programs, 68
ethnic/racial minorities, 62, 94, 100–01, 104–05, 119n4, 203t
by facilitators, 178b
importance of, 4, 73, 104

National Program for Indigenous Peoples, Mexico, 94
scheduled castes and tribes, 101, 105, 119n4
Support to Ethnic Minority Communities in Remote and Mountainous Areas, Vietnam, 62
women, 100–01, 104–05, 114, 119n4, 203t
social sustainability of LCDD projects, 221
South Africa, 115, 124, 141, 149n6, 160
South America. See Latin America and the Caribbean
South Asia. See also specific countries
analysis of CDD in, 56
historical development of LCDD in, 1, 13
impact studies, 67, 69–70
public bureaucracies, transforming, 40
scaling up in, 81, 82m
sectoral approach in, 33
social capital, leveraging, 24
Soviet Union, collapse of, 40–41
specialized agricultural credit institutions, 34b
Spector, Stephen, xv–xvi, xvii, 1, 27
Sri Lanka, xiii, 172, 215
stakeholder participation as core expected outcome of LCDD, 213–15
stakeholders. See communities; donors; local governments; national government level, commitment to LCDD at; nongovernmental organizations
static institutional analysis of strategic fit, 124, 125–27, 126t, 128b
step-by-step approach to scaling up, 8–10, 151–97
communications
design elements and tools, 208t
IEC activities, 166–67, 169f, 170, 171, 172, 174, 195, 197n8, 208t
implementing strategy for, 194
consolidation or post-scale up phase, 114–15, 195–96, 195b
contextual adaptation of, 152–53
DDCs, 169f, 170–72, 191
decentralization, role of, 160–62
design elements and tools for large-scale LCDD, 201–10

diagnostic phase, 151, 153–55, 154b, 156–58t
local-level support, 152, 162–63, 163b
M&E. *See* monitoring and evaluation
national policy and institutional support, 151–52, 155–62, 159b, 163b
national scaling-up phase, 192–95, 192b
phasing, 9b, 21–22b, 152b, 201–02t
pilot phase. *See under* pilot programs and field testing
planning and budgeting, 180–81, 181b, 182–84, 193
previous empowerment efforts, building on, 161
reforms, following through on, 162
resource flows, allocation, and accountability, 184–92, 185–87b, 189b
training and facilitation, 176–84, 178b, 178f, 180–82b, 206–08t
unified disbursement mechanisms, willingness to use, 161
workshops, prelaunch, 195
strategies for contextual adaptation. *See* contextual adaptation
sub-Saharan Africa. *See* Africa
subdistrict development committee, pilot phase of scaling up, 169f, 172
subdistricts, defined, 5b
subsidiarity principle, 48, 101, 102, 109, 194, 205t, 213
Sudan, 123t, 132t, 135
Suharto, 89b, 91
Support to Ethnic Minority Communities in Remote and Mountainous Areas, Vietnam, 62
sustainability of LCDD programs, 55, 220–21
Swajal Rural Water Supply Project, India, 105, 114
SWAps (sector-wide approaches), 62, 154, 161

T

Tamil Nadu Integrated Nutrition Program, India, 43b
Tanzania
combined concurrent, mixed strategy in, 141, 142
contextual adaptation of existing programs in, 134t
DDCs, transfer of functions to, 191
decentralization issues in, 47f, 123t, 124
head tax, 95b
local governance outcomes, 147
Tanzania Social Fund (TASAF), 134t, 142, 191
targeted approaches, 12t, 35–36, 35t
TASAF (Tanzania Social Fund), 134t, 142, 191
technical soundness of LCDD design, 219–20
technical training and support, 181–82, 182b, 216–17
technology-driven approaches, 12t, 33–35
templates for annual planning, 182–84
Tendler, Judith, 47
Third Social Action Fund Project, Angola, 135
time horizon for sequencing, 115–16
timeline of evolving development approaches, 12t
Timor-Leste, xiii, 17, 167b
toolkits, 10, 17, 18, 60, 108–09, 154, 201–10. *See also* step-by-step approach to scaling up
training and education
community-to-community extension approach, 179–80, 180b
costs, reducing, 102–03, 176, 177–79, 178f, 180b
design elements and tools for large-scale LCDD, 206–07t
for facilitators, 177, 178b, 207t
IEC activities, 166–67, 169f, 170, 171, 172, 174, 195, 197n8, 208t
importance of, 20
Internet, use of, 215
as phase in step-by-step approach, 176–84, 178b, 178f, 180–82b, 206–08t
subdistrict training teams, 179
technical training and support, 181–82, 182b, 216–17
transformative nature of LCDD, 4
transparency
governance agenda of World Bank and, 64
as pillar of success for LCDD, 90, 108, 113

tribes and castes, scheduled, 101, 105,
119*n*4. *See also* social inclusion
tsunami disaster of 2005, xiii
Tunisia, 19, 47*f*
Turkey, 115

U

Uganda
   CAP, 82*m*, 86*t*, 110, 111*b*
   concurrent approach in, 141
   contextual adaptation of existing
      programs in, 134–35*t*
   decentralization issues, 110–12*b*,
      110–13, 123*t*, 124
   LGDP, 82*m*, 86*t*, 110, 111*b*, 189*b*
   LGMSDP, 110, 134*t*, 141, 189*b*
   local governance outcomes, 147
   matching strategy in, 141
   NAAS, 11*b*, 82*m*, 86*t*, 110, 112*b*
   NUSAF, 82*m*, 86*t*, 110, 112*b*,
      134*t*, 141
   scaling up in, 81, 82*m*, 83*t*, 86*t*,
      109–10, 110–12*b*, 113, 114
   step-by-step approach to scaling up,
      157*t*, 175, 188, 189*b*
   successful LCDD projects in, 16
Ukraine, 218
UNCDF (United Nations Capital Development Fund), 39*b*, 161, 167*b*, 183,
   189*b*, 190
unified disbursement mechanisms,
   willingness to use, 161
United Nations Capital Development Fund
   (UNCDF), 39*b*, 161, 167*b*, 183,
   189*b*, 190
urban development projects, 42*b*
urban neighborhoods, defined, 5*b*
Urban Property Rights Project, Peru, 217
U.S. Community Partnerships Grants,
   149–50*n*6

V

van Campen, Wim, xviii
Van Domelen, Julie, xvii, xviii, 27, 61,
   63*b*, 121
Van Wicklin, Warren, xviii, 121
Vietnam, 62
Village Communities Support Program
   (VCSP), Guinea, 143–44, 146,
   214–15

"village republics," 11, 29
villages, defined, 5*b*
Voss, John, 67

W

Warren, David, xvii, 27, 58
Washington, D.C., community report cards
   in, 218
water supply projects, 42*b*
West Africa
   CDD programs in, 13
   River Blindness Eradication
      Program, 114
West Bank and Gaza, 16
Williams, Aubrey, 46
Wolfensohn, James, 48–51, 70*n*4
women, 100–01, 104, 105, 114, 119*n*4,
   203*t*. *See also* social inclusion
workshops, prelaunch, 195
World Bank
   ADPs and IRDPs, 2, 12–13, 12*t*, 32,
      36–37, 36*b*, 41, 48
   APLs, 113, 115, 117, 135, 136, 143, 144
   decentralization, interest in, 46–48, 51
   design and implementation guidance,
      51–52, 53*b*
   DPLs, 62
   impact studies, 55–57, 56*t*, 67–70
   integration of LCDD framework, role
      in, 60–61
   LCDD, support for, xiii–xiv, 2,
      17, 28
   leadership of, 17, 23
   lending data and portfolio, 51,
      52*t*, 62
   national stocktaking and review
      toolkit, 154
   OED, 37, 44
   poverty reduction as main aim of,
      48, 61*b*
   PRSPs, 74*b*, 193, 197*n*2
   Quality Assurance Group, 16, 57
   social development at, 45–46
   toolkits, 60
   top-down approaches, shift away from,
      40–42, 51

Y

Yemen, Republic of, 69, 83*t*
Yunus, Mohammed, 34*b*

Z

Zacatecas State Development Plan, Mexico, 38
Zambia
  accountability in, 218
  capacity building problems in, 94, 95–96, 96*b*
  contextual adaptation of existing programs in, 133–34*t*, 137
  decentralization issues in, 47*f*, 123*t*
  incentives, use of, 213

local governance outcomes, 143–47
resource flows, allocation, and accountability, 189*b*, 191
scaling up in, 81, 82*m*, 86*t*, 94–97, 96*b*, 98
social funds in, 45, 189*b*
Zambia Social Investment Fund (ZAMSIF), 82*m*, 86*t*, 94–97, 96*b*, 134*t*, 144–47
Zampaglione, Giuseppe, xviii
Zimbabwe, 82*m*, 84*t*, 123*t*